MAKING MUSIC AT THE PIANO

MAKING MUSIC AT THE PIANO

Learning Strategies for Adult Students

BARBARA ENGLISH MARIS

UNIVERSITY PRESS

2000

OXFORD

UNIVERSITY PRESS

Oxford   New York

Athens   Auckland   Bangkok   Bogotá   Buenos Aires   Calcutta
Cape Town   Chennai   Dar es Salaam   Delhi   Florence   Hong Kong   Istanbul
Karachi   Kuala Lumpur   Madrid   Melbourne   Mexico City   Mumbai
Nairobi   Paris   São Paulo   Shanghai   Singapore   Taipei   Tokyo   Toronto   Warsaw

and associated companies in
Berlin   Ibadan

Copyright © 2000 by Oxford University Press

Published by Oxford University Press, Inc.
198 Madison Avenue, New York, New York 10016

Oxford is a registered trademark of Oxford University Press.

Library of Congress Cataloging-in-Publication Data
Maris, Barbara English.
Making music at the piano : learning strategies for adult students
Barbara English Maris.
p.   cm.
Includes bibliographical references and index.
ISBN-13 978-0-19-512326-5
ISBN 0-19-512326-3
1. Piano—Instruction and study.   2. Practicing (Music)
MT220 .M273   2000
786.2'193—dc21   00-020836

5 7 9 8 6

Printed in the United States of America
on acid-free paper

With gratitude, for opportunities
   to share music and learn from each other,
This book is dedicated to the people
   who are a part of it:
          My students,
          My teachers,
          My colleagues,
          My family, and
          My readers.

Preface

Welcome to the world of pianists, pianos, piano music, and piano practice. You belong to a special adult population—people who include time at the piano as part of their regular routine. Perhaps you are an adult beginning piano student, an adult returning piano student who has studied previously, or an adult searching for ways to become more involved with music through the study of piano.

There are many pathways to musically satisfying experiences. In writing this book, I have incorporated ideas and activities that have been useful to me and to my students. I hope you, also, will find some of these strategies helpful. This book is designed to serve as a resource that can supplement your piano teacher and piano books. Piano teachers and authors do not agree on all aspects of training musicians. Ultimately, *you* will discover what information seems useful to you and what material needs to be ignored or put aside until later.

As you explore *Making Music at the Piano*, it may be useful for you to be aware of some of my basic assumptions. I assume that:

- You want to make *music* at the piano.
- You have many interests and commitments. Your time with the piano probably is limited. Efficient use of your practice time is an appropriate goal. Although making music at the piano is a valued enterprise for you, it is not the only meaningful activity in your life.
- All of your previous musical experiences will enhance your future study of music. You have had diverse musical experiences in your home, schools, and social communities. You have encountered a breadth of musical styles that reflect the infinite variety of music throughout time and space. All of that music has been valued and is valuable.
- You have achieved success in many aspects of your life. You are a competent, capable person who has developed numerous talents and skills. You will achieve success in your piano study also.
- You can handle the temporary frustrations that may result from exploring new ways to organize your thoughts and move your body.

- You do not expect to shift careers and become a professional pianist, but you do intend to study piano regularly for at least several months (taking piano lessons in a private studio or participating in piano classes held in a keyboard laboratory environment).

And, finally,

- You *can* use the piano as an instrument for creating music and becoming a more musical person. Making music at the piano can be a highly gratifying activity for you.

In part I, "Pianists and Pianos," you will find five chapters with information about people and pianos. What goals will be feasible for you to consider as an early-level piano student? How do people learn? What can you do at an acoustic or digital piano? How can pianists move efficiently and safely at their instrument? What makes a pianist sound musical?

In part II, "Pianists at Pianos: Productive Practice," you will find numerous suggestions for effective use of the time you spend at the piano. What needs to happen during your practice sessions? What rehearsal strategies can be incorporated into your practice? How can you develop technical and musical skills? What frustrations do adult early-level students frequently encounter, and how might you respond to those? How can performing music become a more gratifying experience? How can your piano study affect all of your musical future?

Throughout the chapters of this book, you will find sections that represent four categories of material:

Concepts to Consider
Activities to Explore
Thoughts about Words
Additional Resources

Scattered through the margins of those chapters, you will find highlights of ideas related to making music at the piano.

The appendixes provide suggestions for building sight-reading skills, beginning a new piano piece, and preparing to perform. They also include an annotated list of published resources.

It is my hope that this book will lead you to increased productivity in your practice and greater personal gratification when you are spending time at the piano. Whether you make music for yourself alone or share musical activities with others, the quality of your experiences can be aesthetically satisfying from the beginning. Even as an early-level piano student, you *can* sound like the sensitive and artistic person you are.

Depending on your personality and circumstances, I suggest that you approach the material in this book in a way that seems helpful to you:

1. Explore topics sequentially (during your early months of study, spend some time each week with one of the thirteen chapters) or
2. Browse (sample materials as questions arise and different headings and reminders catch your attention).

Good Luck, and Happy Music Making at the Piano!

Elizabethtown, Pennsylvania   B. E. M.
December 1999

Contents

PART I PIANISTS AND PIANOS

The opening five chapters of this book deal with people and pianos. Chapter 1, "Clarifying Goals," addresses adults who are at an early level of piano study and emphasizes the fact that—from the very beginning—they can play musically and sound artistic. It discusses a variety of appropriate goals for adult piano students to consider adopting, suggests how they can utilize practice time effectively, and explores the special interactions between piano teachers and adult students. Chapter 2, "Learning about Learning," considers the process of learning, particularly the differences between conceptual learning (understanding a fact) and kinesthetic learning (utilizing a physical skill). Individual approaches to learning and various strategies for strengthening musical memory also are discussed. Chapter 3, "Understanding Your Keyboard Instrument," describes the basic characteristics of pianos, both acoustic and digital. Chapter 4, "Moving Efficiently at the Piano," focuses on developing coordinated, effective, healthy movements at the piano. Chapter 5, "Developing Musicality," explains fundamental characteristics of playing that is considered musical, including the control of subtle gradations of sound, both the length and loudness of tones.

1 Clarifying Goals

CHAPTER OUTLINE

Concepts to Consider
Setting Goals
Making a Commitment to Your Musical Growth
Working with Your Piano Teacher

Activities to Explore
Identifying Personal Goals
Assembling Practice Tools
Experimenting with Sounds: Repeating and Varying Passages

Tempo	Articulation
Dynamics	Rhythm
Register	Repeating Sounds
Pitch	Emphasizing Selected Sounds
Topography	Gestures
Visual Focus	Fingering
Expression	Order of Pitches
Accentuation	Creating Lyrics
Duration	

Thoughts about Words
Should, Must, Need
Pieces for Children
Hard, Difficult

Additional Resources

What are your goals as an early-level student who is starting or continuing the study of piano music? Why do you want to spend time at the piano? Why are you taking piano lessons or participating in a piano class? What are your previous experiences with the piano? As you begin or resume lessons, it will be useful to clarify some basic issues:

- Why are you studying piano now?
- What goals do you want to meet?
- How do you intend to work toward those goals?

CONCEPTS TO CONSIDER

Setting Goals

For most adult piano students, the process of setting goals involves finding a comfortable balance between goals established by the student and goals established by the teacher. As adults, both the student and the teacher have the option of deciding which goals are acceptable to them. Either person can say, "For me, that expectation is not a viable alternative. I don't want to do that. I don't want to place that item on my agenda. I do not intend to meet that request." Such decisions, of course, might carry undesirable consequences, but adults do have choices.

You and your teacher will experience fewer frustrations if you share compatible goals and if both of you are aware of any major discrepancies between your goals. If you only want to practice Bach, but your teacher only wants to hear Chopin, something's gotta give. If your teacher defines *contemporary* music as works by twentieth-century composers such as Igor Stravinsky (1882–1971) and Barbara Pentland (1912–2000), but you use the same word to refer to recordings on this week's popular music charts, acknowledge those different definitions. You may assume that regular practice means you will sit down at a friend's piano for a few minutes once or twice a week right after supper. If, in contrast, your teacher has selected materials and developed weekly assignments with the expectation that almost every day you will work without interruption for at least an hour, soon you and your teacher will encounter a major divergence of goals. When that happens, both of you will become increasingly frustrated as you move further away from shared expectations.

There are two distinct approaches to establishing goals. Consider these questions:

- What do you want to accomplish?—How long will it take to accomplish those goals?
- How much time can you devote to the project?—What goals can be accomplished within that time frame?

Although experienced teachers can speculate about the preceding questions, definitive answers become evident only after goals have been met. With either of the above approaches, it is important to determine how much time you intend to invest in the project. In reality, your responses to those questions will fluctuate: People get sick; work responsibilities shift; income and expenses vary. But, in spite of the realities and crises adults encounter, it will be helpful at the outset of your piano study to consider your own expectations in terms of the time you plan to spend at the piano.

- How often will you practice? For how long? When and where?
- How often will you meet with your teacher? For how long? In what sort of environment: one-on-one weekly lessons in a private studio? piano classes held two or three times a week in a classroom with a dozen digital keyboards used by a dozen students? weekly sessions in a room with one acoustic piano and several computer stations?
- What supplemental activities will be available: monthly gatherings of music students who play for one another in informal, supportive settings? weekly music classes related to theory? a spring recital in the auditorium of a neighborhood school? piano ensemble gatherings held periodically at a music store with students of other teachers?
- What materials will your teacher provide or expect you to purchase?

The preceding questions carry both financial and scheduling implications, so it is useful to clarify expectations from the very beginning of your student/teacher relationship. Today, many piano teachers would describe their work as developing, for each student, an individualized music curriculum that provides a variety of musical experiences and a sequence of gratifying challenges that will lead to a series of predictable successes. Music teachers' current vocabulary and procedures contrast sharply with comic strips I remember seeing when I was a little girl. Today's highly trained professional teachers don't resemble the earlier caricatures of frazzled neighborhood piano teachers who gave half-hour lessons and appeared somewhat witless. Today's adult students are more apt to encounter competent, professional, independent music teachers who base their fees on longer time commitments (comparable to an academic term). Furthermore, in addition to basic lessons, piano teachers may incorporate into their fee structure other educational opportunities such as theory classes, performance workshops, music library borrowing privileges, and access to personal computer equipment that includes educational music software programs.

Many piano teachers no longer think in terms of the question "How much do you charge for a thirty-minute lesson?" They probably don't even "give lessons." (When did you hear of a surgeon "giving an operation" or an attorney "giving a will"?) Instead, teachers teach. Music teachers supervise the educational experiences of their music students. They select and direct appropriate music activities.

Unlike a kidney operation, teaching is not something one does *to* a person. Teaching involves sharing meaningful activities *with* a student. Your music teacher is not a schoolmaster or schoolmarm who will "learn" you to play the piano. Your accomplishments as a piano student will reflect your active involvement in the process of learning.

Learning is an active verb—a very active verb.

Adults today are able to choose from a wide variety of approaches to music study. As you begin this next phase of your relationship with music, I encourage you to clarify your personal goals. Identify your resources (of time, money, energy, and space), research carefully the music study options available in your community, and establish an adult relationship with your teacher. Even when you deal with early-level piano materials, you do not need to revert to childish behaviors and attitudes. Expect your teacher to treat you as a competent adult—especially at those times when you may become a frustrated adult.

Goals are not right or wrong, good or bad, moral or immoral. All goals are valid. Some goals are complete in themselves. Other goals enable you to develop prerequisite tools for meeting future challenges. No matter what your goals are now, I suggest that you reassess those goals periodically as your interests change, skills grow, and commitments shift.

In selecting pieces of music for students to study at any level of advancement, I have found it helpful to direct students to projects they can approach concurrently. It is useful to be involved with both long-term and short-term projects. Students benefit from having a variety of musical challenges, including those that can be completed in the next year, next season, next month, next week, next hour, and next minute. Musical gratification need not be deferred indefinitely. Even if you are just beginning to work with early-level piano music, you can sound like a musical person today.

You do not have to wait for months before you play musically.

Your teacher's experience with other piano students and knowledge of piano repertoire will help determine the difficulty for you of various pieces and the appropriateness of different goals. Your teacher's educational philosophy and pedagogical expertise also will be factors in suggesting how to utilize your time. Often it is helpful to select repertoire that builds on skills you already have developed. Sometimes, however, it also can be beneficial to select a piece that presents new challenges and then use that piece to build additional skills. Both approaches are valid.

The frustrations of adult students usually result from one of the following situations:

- Not understanding some basic element.
- Not yet having control of the prerequisite skills needed to reach certain goals with ease.
- Not allowing sufficient time to accomplish the goals they desire.
- Not knowing how to assess the results of their work and being too vague in setting goals.
- Not experiencing sufficient gratification for their level of investment in the project.

The most common reason that adult music students become frustrated and do not achieve their goals is because they do not establish realistic goals.

The habit of experiencing comfort and ease during piano practice can begin during the first week of your piano study. The best way to achieve your goals is to learn how to establish goals that set realistic and appropriate challenges at every stage of learning. Success breeds success. Comfort and ease in playing a Level One piece this month will lead to comfort and ease in playing a Level Three piece next month (or whenever you reach that level—perhaps next year?). If you create beautiful sounds and establish rhythmic vitality when you play for yourself, you can expect to be able to demonstrate beauty and facility when sharing music with others.

> Achievements lead to more achievements.

Making a Commitment to Your Musical Growth

Performing musicians achieve success only if they invest a considerable amount of time and energy in their mental and physical activities. Playing a musical instrument skillfully necessitates that, on a regular basis, the player will spend a lot of time developing performance skills and building basic musicianship. If you intend to be successful in learning to play the piano, you need to make a definite commitment to that project. If you do not spend adequate time and energy, you are booby-trapping the project and undermining your potential achievements. If that happens, your lack of success will have absolutely no correlation with your talent, intelligence, potential, or musical sensitivity.

Perhaps you can ice-skate as a hobby just on New Year's Day every other winter, but Olympic champions know that they must spend many hours every day in order to maintain existing skills and build new skills. Among concert pianists, there is a common saying: "If I don't practice one day, I know it. If I don't practice two days, my manager knows it. If I don't practice three days, the whole world knows it." If you plan to study piano seriously, you will need to arrange your life so that every day includes a chunk of time for you to rehearse at the instrument. "How long do I have to practice?" is not a question I can answer for you. What you will need to decide is "What do I want to accomplish?" Then you and your teacher need to determine how long it may take to meet your goals.

What is clear is that productive *daily* practice sessions are necessary in order to achieve regular growth of skills. Marathon sessions the night before a language exam and total immersion the weekend before you leave home to visit another country can supplement other work, but "slow and steady" is the key to achieving success when building skills such as conversing in a foreign language, lifting weights, or playing the piano.

Working with Your Piano Teacher

Your piano teacher will be one of your most important resources. To get the most from your piano lessons or classes, be sure that you:

- Understand every assignment, both the final goals and the specific practice procedures that will lead you to those goals.
- Prepare conscientiously for every instructional session. Give your best efforts at every lesson/class. Check yourself for accuracy (of pitch, fingerings, rhythm, articulation, and dynamics) so that careless readings and needless errors do not undermine your progress. Do not insult your own intelligence and musicianship as well as your composers and teacher by presenting sloppy work. Do not expect your teacher to function as a correction officer. Most musical mistakes can be avoided by listening carefully, noticing how your body moves, and paying meticulous attention to details printed in the score.
- Allow yourself at least ten to fifteen minutes of open time both before and after your lesson/class. Beforehand, use that time to stretch, warm up physically, and prepare yourself mentally. Afterward, use that time to stretch again, cool down, and think about things discussed at your lesson/class. Soon after your lesson/class, schedule a practice session so that you can experiment with new ideas while they still are fresh in your mind. The longer you wait before trying new suggestions, the more chance there is that those timely ideas will slip away from you.
- Collect specific questions throughout the week. Write them down and take them to your next lesson/class. During your practice sessions, try to find answers yourself. Then you can say to your teacher, "I have practiced this passage these five different ways, but I'm still having problems. Can you help me figure out the specific problem, what I'm missing, and how I can make that passage seem easier?"

ACTIVITIES TO EXPLORE

Adult students usually experience the most severe frustration when they fail to acknowledge that there are two different kinds of learning: cognitive and kinesthetic.

> *Declarative memory* (cognitive learning) deals with understanding concepts and ideas.
> *Procedural memory* (kinesthetic learning) deals with controlling muscles.

Information about concepts can be imprinted in the brain instantly. ("Aha! I see! I got it.") Muscular patterns, however, need to be shifted from short-term to long-term memory. Kinesthetic knowledge (which necessitates muscular responses) must be repeated many times before it can be transferred to the portion of the brain that controls automatic muscular responses. Adults often become frustrated because kinesthetic control of information is not instantaneous. After you understand something, you will need to experience it many times and in many ways before that skill becomes an automatic response.

Throughout this book I have included activities designed to help you explore different aspects of learning, including procedural learning. I hope you will explore some of these activities and then adapt them to your own music study materials. Let the activities in *Making Music at the Piano* serve as models for developing your own practice procedures. Remind yourself that remembering a concept and being able to talk about it will not guarantee that you can demonstrate or utilize that information. If at first your muscles do not respond as you would like, please do not chastise yourself ("Dumdum!" "Nincompoop!"). Just allow yourself *more time* to repeat, experiment, and develop facility in utilizing the concept.

The various activities at the end of each chapter are intended to supplement piano study assignments but not to replace actual music. Although I hope you will find that these activities help you become more comfortable musically at the piano, I do not consider them prerequisites to making music. I encourage you to approach these activities with a sense of childlike playfulness and curiosity. Treat the explorations as ear teasers, experiments in sound, intriguing puzzles, or challenging games. Please do not turn these activities into oppressive tasks. Allow yourself to have spirited fun with them! As you spend time at the piano making music I hope you will encounter some new ways to use your muscles and will discover some new ways to listen to sound. Enjoy!

ACTIVITY 1.1 *Identifying Personal Goals*

1. Although adult students need to be involved in establishing their own priorities, the following list includes goals I consider appropriate and realistic for adults to pursue during early months of piano study. Use this list to help clarify goals that are most important to you.

2. In front of each goal listed, assign a number to represent the importance of that goal *to you* at this stage of your life. If you realize that you have additional goals, add those to your personal list and rank them also. There are no right or wrong answers with this exercise. Simply ask yourself, "For me, right now, is this goal . . ."

Top priority. Extremely important. A worthwhile investment of my time. (1)

Somewhat important. Seems like it might be useful. I'll give it a try. (2)

Not very important. Probably does not deserve much time or effort. (3)

Totally unimportant. An absolute waste of my time! (4)

3. Suggested goals:

_____ Make music at the piano.

_____ Enjoy your piano studies.

_____ Think and behave in musicianly ways. Let each practice session be filled with musical artistry, physical comfort, and emotional satisfaction. Train yourself to behave as a musician who is responsible to herself/himself, to the composers of the music, to the instrument, and to the listeners. Train yourself to identify reasonable goals that can be achieved within the practice time available to you. Develop rehearsal routines that will be productive and gratifying.

_____ Learn to analyze the causes of pianistic problems and accumulate a collection of useful practice strategies that will help you solve specific problems—perhaps by counting aloud, clapping or tapping rhythmic patterns, working with hands alone, practicing in "slowmo," or verbalizing information. (See chapter 8, "Using Musical Activities.")

_____ Utilize your practice sessions as opportunities to experiment with a variety of sounds and gestures. Keep asking yourself, "What would it sound like if I . . . ?" and "What would it feel like if I . . . ?"

_____ Learn to use your instrument, creating and controlling a wide variety of sounds.

_____ Learn to use your body in appropriate ways. Maintain a balanced position at the piano, with your feet planted on the floor so that they support your body; develop a firm arch of the knuckles; retain flexibility at the wrist/elbow/shoulder/waist; align fingers with the long muscles of your forearm; transfer weight from one finger to the next. Avoid stiffness, slumping, and other habits that can lead to pain or injury. Avoid playing too long, too loud, or too fast.

Remember that playing the piano should be an enjoyable activity. Playing the piano should involve a sense of joyousness and incorporate the ease of *play*.

_____ Demonstrate a steady but flexible musical pulse. Learn to count rhythmically, with accuracy and expressiveness. Become comfortable counting aloud the rhythmic patterns in your pieces. Be able to tap easily the rhythmic patterns you encounter.

_____ Explore and understand basic systems (both pitch and rhythm) of notating sounds and silences.

_____ Explore and understand basic systems, both harmonic and formal, of organizing sounds.

_____ Train yourself to understand and utilize all information and musical symbols that appear on a page of music: title, notes, dynamics, clef signs, tempo markings, fingerings, articulation, rhythms, foreign terms, note values, pedal indications, expressive cues, and so on.

_____ Learn to play certain piano pieces and share them with others at specific times.

_____ Learn to play several familiar songs (including "Happy Birthday") for sing-alongs at informal gatherings.

_____ Play piano duets with a friend or relative.

_____ Become involved in communal music-making activities with singers, dancers, and instrumentalists.

_____ Listen to performances (both live and recorded) of music for instruments and for voices. Listen to early-level music you are learning to play and also to advanced repertoire played by fine pianists.

_____ Continue refining material even after you have learned to play it well. Spend time with new and with old pieces. Maintain a collection of pieces you enjoy sharing. By returning to earlier projects and experimenting with a wider range and subtlety of sounds, you will increase your musicianship and enhance the expressiveness of all of your piano playing.

_____ Record your playing and listen carefully to yourself.

_____ Write reminders to yourself about questions or problems you encounter during your practice sessions. Use your teacher as a resource for removing confusion or clarifying ambiguity. Get help in determining what skills or bits of information you are missing. Remind yourself, as often as necessary, that "there are no stupid questions." Your questions will help clarify your confusion and will provide your teacher with opportunities to discover how you process information. Questions from students help teachers pace and sequence information and activities.

_____ Indulge in musical babbling. Use part of your practice time to explore piano sounds on your own terms. Play by ear. Improvise. Move freely all over the keyboard. Experiment with special effects the pedals can provide. Use your imagination. Spend some time each day making music informally, without reference to printed notes. Fool around with musical material that is not notated. Use the piano to make creative, expressive statements. Let the piano become an extension of your voice. Let the piano speak for you. Use your instrument to communicate.

_____ Use your entire body to move rhythmically and internalize musical concepts.

_____ Use your voice as a tool for demonstrating musical concepts and strengthening technical competence.

_____ Explore music of various styles and periods.

_____ Spend time alone at the piano, making music for your own enjoyment.

4. Discuss your personal goal priorities with your piano teacher. Especially be aware of the goals you identified as "Top priority" or "Totally unimportant." If your teacher has given you a class syllabus or studio policy, study it carefully. Find out what goals and expectations your piano teacher has. Although this will be especially important if your lessons or classes are part of the piano requirements for a specific college degree or a certification program that you do want to complete, the same principles will apply even if you are studying primarily for fun and personal enrichment. If you find that there is a wide discrepancy between your goals and those of your teacher, expect to encounter frustrations at various stages of working together. It will be helpful for both of you to be aware of divergent goals and, if feasible, negotiate some compromises.

ACTIVITY 1.2 *Assembling Practice Tools*

1. Create an inventory of basic materials that you will need to use during your practice sessions. This checklist probably will include:

_____ an acoustic or digital piano in good condition
_____ a sturdy piano bench
_____ music books or other instructional materials
_____ pencils and eraser
_____ metronome
_____ music dictionary
_____ calendar or appointment book

_____ piano lamp

_____ tape recorder (for playing cassette tapes and also recording yourself) and blank tapes

_____ clock or watch

_____ notebook (for writing assignments, noting rehearsal plans, and compiling questions to ask your teacher)

2. Gather your practice tools and rehearsal materials. Establish a convenient place to keep them between practice sessions.

3. Identify items you do not have now. Consider how you might obtain them for occasional use—borrow from a teacher or friend, check out of a library, barter for purchase on sale or at a pawnshop, or rent. Investigate the cost of things you want to obtain eventually. Create a Want List and mention those items when someone asks, "What would you like for your next birthday?"

ACTIVITY 1.3 *Experimenting with Sounds: Repeating and Varying Passages*

This activity is designed to guide you in exploring a huge variety of sounds. By making small adjustments in controlling the loudness and duration of individual tones, pianists learn to create thousands of musical sounds. Just as artists experiment with various combinations of colors from a paint box, pianists learn to control tone colors and build a rich palette of sounds. *Note:* Even if your dominant hand is your left hand, I suggest that you begin by experimenting with the right hand. The RH finger pattern 1 2 3 4 5 reinforces the pitch pattern of the first five notes of a major scale.

1. Place your right hand (RH) on your right leg. Using the sequence "thumb / little finger / pointing finger / middle finger / thumb" (described by pianists as RH finger numbers "1 5 2 3 1"), press each fingertip against your leg; lift each finger up and down gently. Repeat the pattern several times without stopping.

2. Move your RH to any set of five adjacent white keys.

3. Using the same sequence of fingers (1 5 2 3 1), create many variations of the pattern. Just before you begin the pattern, take a breath, representing a fresh start. Notice:

How the motion *feels* (easy/difficult, natural/awkward, fun/not fun);
How the hand *looks* (relaxed/stiff, smooth/jerky);
How the pattern *sounds* (even/uneven, confident/apprehensive, musical/unmusical).

4. Within each of the categories listed in the following text, create several variations of the basic pattern. As you experiment with sounds and gestures, keep asking yourself three questions:

How does it sound?
How does it look?
How does it feel?[1]

Tempo

Play the pattern at a natural, ordinary tempo. Then play it a bit faster. Play it a bit slower. Play it a lot faster. Play it a lot slower.

Dynamics

Play the pattern with a natural, ordinary tone quality: *mezzo forte*, comparable to your regular speaking voice. Play it louder: *forte*, projecting the sound. Play it softer: *piano*, as if you were speaking to someone sitting beside you on a park bench. Play it extremely loud: *fortisssimo*, as if you were calling to a neighbor across the street. Play it very softly: *pianissimo*, as if you were whispering a private message to your best friend.

Register

Play the pattern in the middle portion of the piano keyboard. Then lift your hand and move it a few inches to the right; play the pattern higher. Play the same pattern in the very highest register. Play it in the very lowest register. *Note:* When you shift register, lean your entire body to the right or left so that you can easily deliver the hand to the new set of notes. Do not merely stretch your arm toward those keys. Deliver your hand to the keys you will use.

Pitch

Using the right hand, only with white keys, begin the pattern (1 5 2 3 1) on the G above middle C (G D A B G). Then repeat the pattern beginning on the next key higher, A (A E B C A). Continue, using only white keys, and play the pattern starting on B (B F C D B). Begin the pattern on C. Start it on D. Begin it on E. Begin it on F.

Topography

Using the same fingering pattern (1 5 2 3 1), explore sounds that result from combining white and black keys.

C	A	D♯	F♯	C
C	B♭	E	G	C
C	A	D♭	F	C
C	C	G	A♭	C
D	A	E	F♯	D

As you experiment with different combinations of keys, notice your hand's varying levels of physical comfort.

Visual Focus

Each time you play the pattern, select a specific target on which to focus your visual attention. Look at your wrist. Observe the muscles on the back of your hand. Look at your elbow. Look at the first joints of your fingers. Look at your shoulder. Look at the music rack. Look at the highest keys of the piano. Look at the lowest keys of the piano. Look at the ceiling. Look out the window. Play the pattern with one eye closed. Play it with both eyes closed. Imagine the sound without playing it.

Expression

Each time you play the pattern, create a different expressive mood—representing an emotion, dramatic character, or activity. Let the sounds represent people you know, such as your Great-Aunt Matilda or Cousin Ben, or characters in stories, such as Winnie-the-Pooh or Godzilla. Create sounds that represent various ways of moving—creeping, jumping, or sliding, for example—and different emotions, including anger, joy, pride, or apprehension.

Accentuation

Without changing the rhythm, vary the loudness of the sounds. Make your thumb (1) louder. Make your little finger (5) louder. Make your pointing finger (2) louder. Make your middle finger (3) louder.

Duration

Without changing the rhythm (the start of each sound), vary the duration of the sounds. Between each pair of notes, listen for more or less air space (silence). Make the notes sound more connected (*legato*). Make the notes more separated (*staccato*). Leave each key as soon as possible (*staccatissimo*). Stay with each key as long as possible, overlapping the sounds (*legatissimo*).

Articulation

Separate some notes (•) and connect (⁓) or sustain others (-):

$$
\begin{array}{ccccc}
\overset{\bullet}{1} & 5 & 2 & 3 & 1 \\
1 & 5 & 2 & \overset{\bullet}{3} & \bar{1} \\
1 & 5 & 2 & 3 & 1 \\
\bar{1} & \overset{\bullet}{5} & \overset{\bullet}{2} & \overset{\bullet}{3} & \bar{1}
\end{array}
$$

Rhythm

Create several rhythmic patterns, with various amounts of space between the sounds, such as:

1		5		2	3	1
15					2 3	1
1	5			2	3	1

Repeating Sounds

Vary the pattern by repeating certain keys, such as:

```
1   1   2   3   1   3   2
1   1   1   5   2   3   1
1   5   5   5   2   3   1
1   5   5   1   5   2   2   3   1
1   5   1   5   2   2   2   3   1
1   5   1   5   1   5   1   5   2   3 1
1   1   5   5   2   3   1
```

Emphasizing Selected Sounds

Make some sounds slightly louder, such as:

```
1   5   5   1   5   5   2   2   3   1
1   5   5   1   5   2   2   2   3   1
1   5   1   5   2   3   3   1
```

Gestures

Start with the thumb and fingers placed lightly on the surface of the keys. Begin again with the hand about two inches above the keys. Then initiate the motion with the entire arm dropping from about eight inches above the keys. Use a slow motion. Use a rapid motion. Lift and drop each finger separately, being aware of the motion from the knuckles. Allow the energy (momentum) of a single hand motion to create all five sounds: drop the wrist as you play the first "1," and float off the keyboard as you play the final "1." Using the hand as a single unit, prepare for each set of notes by moving the wrist. Keep your elbow close to the body. Move the upper arm away from the torso so the elbow can float easily. Try each gesture several times, and notice what it looks like and feels like when you intentionally exaggerate the motion. Play on the finger pads using gently curved fingers and maintaining a firm arch of the knuckles. Play with flat, straight fingers and little or no arch at the knuckles.

In the next two categories, experiment with both the right hand and left hand. When you use the same fingering pattern with the right hand and left hand, the fingers mirror each other. Although the patterns will feel the same, the pitch patterns will not sound the same.

Fingering

Begin with the same cluster of keys (G A B C D) and fingering (RH: 1 5 2 3 1/G D A B G; LH: 1 5 2 3 1/D G C B D). Then experiment, substituting different combinations of fingers with the same pitch pattern:

1	5	2	3	1
1	3	2	3	1
3	3	3	3	3
1	1	1	1	1
1	3	1	3	1
2	4	3	4	2
1	2	1	5	1

After you feel comfortable playing the RH and LH patterns separately, play them hands together.

Order of Pitches

With five fingers over five neighboring keys (RH: thumb on G—G A B C D / 1 2 3 4 5; LH: thumb on D—D C B A G / 1 2 3 4 5), using only four different pitches, experiment with different sequences of those pitches:

1	5	2	3	1		
5	1	3	2	1		
1	2	3	1	5		
3	2	1	2	3	3	3
3	3	3	3	3	3	5 1 2 3

Creating Lyrics

Read various lyrics with expression. Replace each word or syllable with a single pitch. Discover keyboard sounds that will reinforce expressive moods.

How are *you* to-day?
Do you want some *pie?*
Look! Your tire is flat!
Some-one stole my hat.
Did you hear that owl?

THOUGHTS ABOUT WORDS

When you speak to yourself during practice sessions, whether aloud or in your private thoughts, I suggest that you select your words with care. Words carry many messages, and sometimes words are accompanied by a good deal of garbage. Periodically throughout this book, I will share thoughts about vocabulary that sometimes results in misunderstandings or elicits nonproductive reactions.

Should, Must, Need

When *should, must,* and *need* control your life or your piano practice, you risk losing spontaneity, creativeness, and personal satisfaction. I encourage you to remove those words from your piano-practicing vocabulary. Find other ways to refer to the goals you establish for yourself.

Pieces for Children

The German word *kleine* can be translated several ways, including "short," "little," and "easy." Some publishers have labeled collections of "short piano pieces" as *Pieces for Children* or *Easy Pieces for Piano.* A composition that is described as little, such as a one-page prelude, actually could be quite difficult even if it is shorter than a six-page prelude by the same composer. It is OK to enjoy some of the wonderful shorter works by composers whose longer piano works last many minutes rather than several seconds.

Robert Schumann's set of pieces known as *Kinderszenen* (Scenes from Childhood), Op. 15, was not composed for children to play. Instead, these short piano pieces—which are musically challenging even to advanced pianists—were intended as pieces for grown-ups to play so that children could listen to them. The pieces also provide adults with sonic reminders of what certain childhood experiences felt like, for example: riding a hobbyhorse ("Knight of the Rocking-Horse") and daydreaming ("Traümerei").

Early one summer evening several years ago, I took a toddler for a walk around her grandfather's farm. As we neared the fence at the western edge of the property, we noticed that the setting sun was creating immense shadows on the grass. Although this little girl was less than three feet tall, her shadow stretched at least fifteen feet. Her discovery of shadows and our play with shadows was an exciting experience for both of us. Naïveté brings fresh insights, and when we can see with the eyes of children or hear with the ears of children, our lives are enriched.

Small does not mean unimportant. Great works of art are found within small picture frames as well as on huge canvasses. Beautiful blossoms and lovable pets come in many sizes. Similarly, early-level repertoire composed for piano includes many miniature masterpieces. The realization that such music has been performed by people who are younger than you need not prevent you from enjoying the same pieces.

Hard, Difficult

I have two objections to these words. The adjective *hard* conveys the sense of harshness and undermines the goal of producing beautiful, rich, musically satisfying piano sounds. *Difficult* implies that the challenge is beyond one's capacity. Instead of hearing, "That's hard," or,

"That's difficult," I have found it is more helpful to hear different observations, such as:

- "I will need more time to solve that problem."
- "I'm not yet ready to tackle that composition with ease."
- "That certainly is a challenging passage."
- "I'll come back to work on that section later, when I'm fresh."

ADDITIONAL RESOURCES

Books

Adams, Noah, *Piano Lessons: Music, Love and True Adventures* (New York: Delacorte, 1996). At age fifty-two, the longtime host of "All Things Considered," National Public Radio's award-winning program, answered a lifetime call to learn to play the piano and provided a month-by-month account of his experiences.

Booth, Wayne, *For the Love of It: Amateuring and Its Rivals* (Chicago: University of Chicago Press, 1999). Based on the author's experiences with the cello, starting at age thirty-one. Although Booth realized "he would never 'master' it," he found that he loved practicing cello and being involved with music study.

Cooke, Charles, *Playing the Piano for Pleasure* (Westport, CT: Greenwood, 1941; reprint ed. New York: Simon and Schuster, 1960). In this small book, written more than a half-century ago, Cooke, then a staff writer for the *New Yorker* magazine, shared his strategies for indulging an intense love of music and spending an hour a day at his piano.

Holt, John Caldwell, *Never Too Late: My Musical Life Story* (New York: Delacorte, 1978; reprint ed. New York: Perseus Press, 1991). Insights from an educator who took up cello in midlife. Holt's many books include *How Children Fail* (New York: Pitman, 1964) and *How Children Learn* (New York: Dell, 1967; reprint ed. New York: Seymour Lawrence, 1989).

Tapscott, Don, *Growing Up Digital: The Rise of the NET Generation* (New York: McGraw-Hill, 1998). Considers the educational implications in the digital age of the shift from "teacher as transmitter to teacher as facilitator."

Wilson, Frank R. *Tone Deaf and All Thumbs? An Invitation to Music-Making* (New York: Vintage Books, 1986). Written for "late bloomers and non-prodigies." A useful, humorous book by a neurologist who became a beginning piano student and an amateur pianist. Wilson concludes that "music making doesn't just belong to people with talent; by biologic heritage it belongs to everyone."

Pamphlets

"Yes You Can! Learn to Play a Musical Instrument as an Adult" (Carlsbad, CA: American Music Conference, 1990). Brochure addressed to the adult student.

"The Possible Dream" (Dallas: National Piano Foundation, 1992). Encouraging words to adults who want to begin music study.

Videotape

Piano for Quitters by Mark Almond (Turnwater, WA: Pacific Communications, 1996), videotape #54996, 90 minutes. Almond speculates that most of the 36 million Americans who have taken piano lessons and quit never stopped loving music and still want to play. Throughout the ten "chapters" of this videotape, he emphasizes the importance of improvising on basic chords and encourages adults to enjoy themselves at the piano.

2 Learning about Learning

CHAPTER OUTLINE

Concepts to Consider
Learning to Play the Piano
Older Students
Aspects of Memory
Short-term and Long-term Memory
Declarative and Procedural Memory
Brains and Computers
Right Brain—Left Brain
Whole—Part—Whole
Mental Presets
Movement
Learning Styles

Activities to Explore
Chunking and Encoding
Focusing on the Object
Playing with a Rhythmic Pattern
Recognizing *Same* and *Different*
Observing Learning Styles and Preferences

Thoughts about Words
Don't
Students Who Understand or Speak More Than One Language
Practice Makes Perfect?
That Was Good; That Was Right

Additional Resources

Perhaps you already have heard the story of the little boy who was given a turtle and so decided to visit his neighborhood library in order to learn more about his new pet. The friendly librarian was extremely helpful and carefully showed the boy how to use the card catalog and computer to locate a variety of encyclopedias, storybooks, videotapes, research publications, magazine articles, and Web sites. Two hours later, as the little boy sat surrounded by stacks of materials with thousands of words and pictures about turtles, he looked at the librarian, stood up to leave, and, in his most grown-up voice, said with a mournful sigh, "Thank you very much for your help, but I think that's more about turtles than I will ever want to know."

In recent years, extensive research has been done on the physiology and psychology of music and the biomechanics of music performance. For the purpose of this book, however, I will deal only briefly with a limited number of concepts that have a direct connection with ways that you, as an adult piano student, might choose to use your time at the piano. If you want to explore further the fascinating studies of physiology, psychology, and biomechanics, you can delve into those topics on your own.

CONCEPTS TO CONSIDER

Learning to Play the Piano

First of all, playing the piano should be just that: a playful activity. It should feel good to play the piano. Playing the piano can be a joyous, freeing experience. It can serve as a source of pleasure for you. The movements you need to use when you play the piano are comfortable, flowing, efficient, natural, and painless ones. Although some bodybuilders and athletes have followed the slogan "No Pain, No Gain," I believe that it is crucial for pianists to learn to interpret pain as a warning signal. Pain conveys an important message that the person is abusing the body through misuse or overuse. The presence of pain or discomfort during piano practice or performance should not be ignored. Pain provides useful information.

Playing the piano should not hurt.

Since pain can result from playing too long, too loud, or too fast, you need to be aware of this as you plan your practice sessions (see chapter 7, "Planning Effective Rehearsals"). Pain also can result from using muscles inappropriately (such as employing the larger muscles of the full arm in a rapid passage, rather than using the smaller muscles in the hand; poking a key, rather than depressing it gently; locking the wrist; raising the shoulders; jutting the head forward; or misaligning muscles). In addition to my concerns about physical discomfort and pain, I worry about piano students who inflict psychological pain or discomfort on themselves. That, too, is counterproductive.

> *Practicing the piano should not be an abusive activity, either physically or emotionally.*

At all stages of your piano study, you will need to be sensitive to your physical and emotional responses to practicing. Would you tolerate teachers or coaches who screamed at you or your children, undermining confidence and self-esteem? Yet too often students—and especially adult early-level students—behave in ways that undermine their own sense of comfort and competence. Please do not treat yourself that way. On a daily basis, you need to function as a sensitive, caring person who provides encouragement and paces rehearsals in satisfying ways. You will need to learn how to structure practice sessions so that when you leave the piano you already look forward to resuming your work. At the close of each practice session, you need to feel that you have been challenged and have accomplished something worthwhile and want to return to the piano.

Although people may talk about training muscles, in reality we do not train our muscles in order to play the piano. Instead, in order to control our muscles, we must train our brain. Only by strengthening the connections between brain cells do we gain control of muscular activities. The number of human brain cells is not static. It changes throughout life. What makes those cells so powerful, though, is not the sheer quantity but, instead, the fact that each cell is able to make connections with thousands of other cells. It is the strength of the connections between neurons that determines the effectiveness of those cells.

Older Students

During the process of aging, humans experience some decrease in the number of neurons in the brain. (But don't worry. Scientists have determined that by the age of three, you had lost half of the neurons you had at birth. You still have more than 100 billion neurons to utilize.) Although certain studies show poorer learning performance in some older students, it is unclear whether the poorer performance is the result of the aging process or merely a side effect of a long break in serious learning activities. At every age, involvement in serious learning activities improves learning performance. So there is yet another reason to make a commitment to studying piano. Activities associated with studying piano will increase and strengthen the connections between neurons in your brain. That, in turn, even as you continue to age, will strengthen your ability to learn.

When one compares learning traits of adults and children, several characteristics often are evident:

- Older students benefit from being able to self-pace their own learning activities. In contrast, fast pacing dictated by an instructor often results in an increased level of anxiety and a lowered level of achievement.
- Older students benefit from using more mediators—words, analogies, comparisons, and pictures that link words—to create stronger retrieval cues.
- Adult students are more reluctant to get into situations where their pride is at risk. They also are more reluctant to respond unless they are confident that they have the correct answer or can make an appropriate response.
- Adult students have a tendency to make premature judgments (jumping to wrong conclusions) and then find it more difficult to relinquish a wrong interpretation.
- Adult students benefit from longer learning sessions. However, for all students, it has been found that learning is more efficient when practice time is distributed rather than massed. Thus, it is useful to punctuate periods of practice with periods of rest.
- Learners become more visual as they get older. Clear written instructions often are useful to adult students.
- Adult students benefit from learning activities that incorporate the process of discovery.
- Even for those older students who find that it takes longer to learn something, once the new information is firmly registered in their long-term memory, the retention of that information or skill and the accessing of it will be very secure.

To remember something, three distinct activities need to occur. The information needs to be acquired (obtained), stored (retained), and accessed (retrieved). The process of remembering is similar to taking a dozen eggs out of your refrigerator. Before you can make an omelet, first you must obtain the eggs (acquire), then you must store them in your refrigerator (retain), then you must be able to locate and remove them (retrieve). Often when someone announces, "I've forgotten," the real problem is not in retrieving the information but reflects difficulties at an earlier stage (when acquiring or storing information). If you never bought the eggs or did not place them in the section of the refrigerator where you usually keep eggs, they will be inaccessible when you want to retrieve them.

Aspects of Memory

Short-term and Long-term Memory

Scientists distinguish between two time frames related to remembering. Short-term memory allows for recall of information over a period of seconds or minutes. Long-term memory enables the recall of information over a period of hours, days, weeks, or even a lifetime.

Short-term memory functions as a holding station or buffer zone but can store only a limited amount of information (five to seven chunks). In the process of remembering, information is first held in short-term memory and then shifted to long-term memory. However, by learning to organize material and create larger chunks of information, one can store more information in short-term memory. For example, a string of random letters (IBMFBILSDUFO) would represent twelve bits of information. The twelve bits of information, however, can be compressed into four chunks, if those twelve letters are grouped into sets of letters that have meaning for an individual (for example—IBM: International Business Machines; FBI: Federal Bureau of Investigation; LSD: Lysergic Acid Diethylamide; and UFO: Unidentified Flying Object). You could organize the information further by creating a single scenario ("My parents work for IBM; my spouse and I work for the FBI; my neighbor to the west of my home uses LSD; and my neighbor on the east side has reported seeing a UFO.")

Similarly, by learning to recognize groups of musical notes you will enhance your ability to organize and control musical information. A chain of twelve random pitches (CEGFACGBDCEG) represents more information than we can process in short-term memory. But when the same pitches are organized into groups of notes (chords) that represent a familiar harmonic pattern frequently used in European and American folk music (I IV V I: tonic, subdominant, dominant, tonic), the same series of pitches is condensed to only four chunks (CEG, FAC, GBD, and CEG). Going a step further, the twelve original bits of information become one chunk when described as "a I IV V I chord progression in the key of C major."

Studies of short-term memory indicate that some people retain information better (encode it more securely) when they both hear it and see it. Thus, you might find it helpful in your practice to describe aloud the information you want to remember, thereby adding another layer of cognition to the process of visualizing. As you do something, talk to yourself. Listen to your description of what you are doing.

Declarative and Procedural Memory

Declarative memory provides the recall of facts (dealing with concepts). Procedural memory represents the ability to perform skills automatically (controlling muscles). Using declarative memory, a physicist can *explain* what happens in space when a skater does a triple-axel. Procedural memory is what enables Olympic skaters to *perform* triple-axels successfully. Their muscles have been trained to respond in a specific way. The information has been placed into long-term memory, and the actions have become automatic.

Content and skills are two distinctly different types of learning. One of the greatest frustrations for adult piano students at all levels is the fact that they can understand a concept long before they can utilize that concept. Although adults often understand something the very first time it is explained (eliciting the "Eureka!" response), before they will be able to internalize and demonstrate the concept their muscles will have to experience it repeatedly. The pathways that control the sequence of muscular responses have to be reinforced many times.

Content primarily involves the mind and focuses on characteristics of the material being learned. Skills, however, primarily involve muscles and call for actions that are applied to the material being learned. Content and skills are interdependent and, like a lock and key, do not function alone. Understanding (content) is a mental concept that involves the mind; doing (skill) is a physical concept that involves sending messages to muscles. Although content-related information is learned quickly, skills are acquired over time and become automatic when processed in the cerebellum (the automatic pilot of the brain). Once developed, the control of physical skills remains accessible unless it is removed by an injury to the brain or the body.

Too often we allow ourselves to become inordinately frustrated when we make a mistake. Sometimes the brighter the student and the more quickly she or he understands a concept, the greater the level of frustration in not achieving instant control of muscular processes:

> Two minutes ago my teacher told me that I will need to use an F♯ in that chord. Why do I keep playing the white key, F♮? Wasn't I listening to my teacher? I must be a real dummy! I am so embarrassed.

After scolding ourselves and undermining our sense of self-esteem, we continue berating ourselves:

> I'm obviously too old/too dumb/too uncoordinated/too untalented to be able to do this; I'm totally incompetent; I might as well quit now and save myself further embarrassment.

We may also issue dire predictions:

> My teacher and friends will lose all respect for me; I'll never get this right; I'm going to lose my scholarship and flunk out of school; I will never get a good-paying job, and I will never be able to afford to move out of my parents' house and rent my own apartment.

Years ago, when my daughters were young and taking music classes on Saturday mornings, I decided one semester to redirect an hour of my parental waiting time and enroll in a ballet class for adult beginners. Although, as an adult, I had enjoyed many hours of folk dance, modern dance, and social dance, I had not participated in a ballet class since I was seven years old. Suddenly I found myself in the middle of a large room, standing on the wooden floor of a dance studio encased by mirrors. I was wearing new ballet slippers, knowing that my right arm was supposed to go to the right, my left hand was to do something else, and I was to land on my right leg before pivoting in the opposite direction and then shifting my weight to my left leg. Although I wanted to be in that class, I liked the teacher, I really had listened carefully to the instructions, and I could explain what I wanted my body to do, it simply would not respond appropriately. As I watched my reflection in those relentless mirrors, I *felt* like a jackass on crutches. Perhaps today I would have more patience with myself than I did twenty-five years ago as I painfully observed the mirror image of that miserable creature wearing a black leotard. In any case, as you pursue your piano studies I urge you to acknowledge the difference between knowing concepts and demonstrating skills. Show patience to yourself as you develop control of new muscular patterns.

Now I understand better how one learns a physical skill. Now I realize that, instead of chastising myself in that beginning ballet class for adults, I needed to acknowledge the fact that, in order for a muscular pattern to become comfortable and automatic, it has to be repeated many times. That is simply the way the human mechanism works. We need to allow ourselves time to experience new patterns and to encode many repetitions of a muscular action before we can expect it to enter the automatic realm of our brain. We have to practice physical motions, not simply understand the concepts behind them. *When we need more time to repeat a motion,* that does not mean we are dumb. It simply means *we need more time to repeat that motion* before it enters the cerebellum and becomes an automatic response to a cue.

> *Knowing* what (*declarative memory*) *and knowing* how (*procedural memory*) *call for different learning responses.*

Brains and Computers

The human brain is often compared to a computer, and there are many similarities between these two complex mechanisms. Both are designed to process very complicated information, and both are capable of breaking down when overloaded. Both have the capacity to save information and then recall it if it has been saved appropriately and can be accessed properly. There is, however, one very important difference between brains and computers, and this difference needs to affect the way you practice.

When you make a mistake at the computer keyboard, such as writing "hoppy" instead of "happy," it is very easy to replace the *o* with an *a* and then save that correction. Instantly, easily, and permanently, the wrong letter is removed and replaced. If you save the correction, close the file, shut off the computer, and come back next week, the corrected version

Example 2.1
Perceiving mistakes:
* = mistake occurs;
x = mistake is heard.

will reappear on your screen. The correct version has been saved, and the error has been replaced. At the computer keyboard you can type "H O [Oops! Backspace. Delete.] A P P Y" and end up with the word "HAPPY."

In your piano practice, however, if you intend to play "D F-sharp A" and by mistake you play "D F-natural [Oops!] F-sharp A," you are not correcting that passage. Instead you are creating a detour. Your brain, in contrast to your computer, retains the original imprint of any information, even if you realize later that you provided incorrect information (that is, *made a mistake*). Once you send something to the brain, it stays there even if you decide to correct the message later. When you send a correction to the brain, the new information is added to your storehouse of information, but the original imprint cannot be removed. If your initial reading of a melody omits an F-sharp and substitutes an F-natural, the brain retains the first image even after a later reading includes the F-natural. Even after numerous correct readings, the initial error remains encoded in your brain. Although you can program your brain to reroute the circuits, you can never actually erase that initial impression.

> *To avoid mistakes, avoid making mistakes.*

In establishing efficient neural pathways, it is important that you avoid creating unnecessary detours. When you play "D F-natural A" instead of "D F-sharp A," the mistake is not in *depressing* the F-natural key. The mistake is in *traveling* from D to F-natural (white key to white key) rather than D to F-sharp (white key to black key). The mistake *occurs* before the mistake is *heard* (see Example 2.1). The player makes a mistake (*) that results in an error that the listener perceives later (*x*).

Right Brain—Left Brain

Much research has focused on understanding that different parts of the brain control different activities. The left side of the brain controls the right side of the body, and the reverse is true. Therefore, a stroke that results in loss of muscular control on the right side of the body demonstrates damage to a portion of the left side of the brain.

The two hemispheres of the brain also control different aspects of perception and emotion. The left hemisphere deals with verbal and analytical skills. Its primary mode of operation is sequential, rather than simultaneous, and it enables us to take things apart and deal with one aspect at a time. Left-brain thinking is analytical, logical, linear, and detailed.

In contrast, the right hemisphere of the brain deals mainly with nonverbal considerations, intuition, perception, spatial orientation, facial recognition, imagery, emotion, aesthetic responses, and overall patterns of relations. It seems to process information simultaneously rather than sequentially. Although traditionally educators have emphasized activities that develop the left brain, more recent research acknowledges the value of developing both spheres. By training both your left brain and right brain, you will gain more complete access to your entire brain.

Whole–Part–Whole

There is strong evidence that effective learning sequences should begin with the whole and move to the parts, rather than the other way around. When you have a sense of the *Gestalt* (totality, the whole picture), then you have created a grid onto which you will be able to attach specific details. With a given template or skeletal framework, it becomes easier to encode additional information (see Activity 2.1, "Chunking and En-coding"). As a result, you will find it easier to assimilate more informa-tion and then relate it to previous experiences.

Many students find it helpful, very early in the process of learning a composition, to obtain an overview of the complete work. Before deal-ing with isolated bits of information, establish a sense of the complete structure. Before breaking things into smaller parts, obtain an imprint of the final goal (visually scanning the entire piece or listening to a per-formance of the complete work).

Some researchers go a step further and recommend that we system-atically create a learning sequence that involves a three-stage process: whole part whole. Rather than starting "at the very beginning," as Maria suggested in *The Sound of Music*, you may find it more helpful to create three distinct stages for yourself when you begin to learn a piece:

1. Introduction (whole: overview of the complete project)
2. Application (part: specific study of separate sections)
3. Reinforcement (whole: greater understanding of the whole)

Mental Presets

Barry Green and W. Timothy Gallwey transferred many effective practice techniques from tennis courts and golf courses to music practice rooms.[1] These authors suggested specific steps for achieving a more useful learn-ing style that eliminates negative habits of self-doubt, frustration, and se-vere judgment. Green and Gallwey recommended that we remove our judgmental self from the act of learning and, instead, focus on the object to be learned. They described four distinct modes of focusing:

1. Pay attention to *sight*—notice all the visual elements, including notes on the score, hand position, and keyboard topography.
2. Pay attention to *sound.* Listen intently to aural elements: for tennis players, this would include the *ping* of a ball bouncing in the court; for musicians, it would include such concepts as

high/low, loud/soft, fast/slow, major/minor, long/short, tonic/dominant, legato/staccato, sound/silence, thick/thin, brass/strings, and various vocal qualities.

3. Pay attention to *feelings*. Attend to your own emotional reactions to playing the music. for example:

Comforted: My parents sang this lullaby to me.
Fearful and resentful: My previous teacher yelled at me and hit my hand with a ruler when I played wrong notes in this piece.
Happy: This melody was used in a cartoon I watched at my nephew's third birthday party.
Proud: I worked hard and have learned to do this!

4. Pay attention to what we already *know* about the piece, such as stylistic characteristics, events of the time period, composer's intentions, theoretical analysis of the harmonic language, and meaning of the title.

It is easy to translate these recommendations into specific activities that might occur during a practice session (see Activity 2.2, "Focusing on the Object.") When you have problems with a passage, do not waste time judging your results or criticizing your unsuccessful attempts. Instead, make observations rather than judgments. Accumulate further information by asking yourself:

- What do I see?—What does this passage look like on the page and on the keyboard?
- What do I hear?—What does this passage sound like?
- What do I feel?—What are my physical and emotional responses to playing this music?
- What do I know about this music?—What knowledge do I have that relates to this music?

Movement

After you experience something with your large muscles, it will be easier to control a similar activity with your smaller muscles. Systematic psychomotor experiences—including creative movement, body rhythms, and hand gestures—greatly enhance the ability to develop strong rhythmic perceptions. For example, after you have stepped a rhythmic pattern across the courtyard or tapped a challenging rhythm on your lap, it will be easier to control a similar rhythm on the keyboard with your fingers (see Activity 2.3, "Playing with a Rhythmic Pattern").

Learning Styles

Much recent research has focused on the fact that different people approach learning experiences in different ways. Some students are most comfortable when every detail is laid out sequentially, step-by-step. Others prefer to bounce around, exploring a variety of ideas and experiences. Some students are inner-directed and prefer to work alone. Others flourish in social situations and learn more from working with friends and explaining a concept to another person. Some people function most successfully when they can follow specific directions from a commanding officer or other recognized leader. Others respond best to the discovery approach. Within different cultures, professions, and age groups there also may be distinct patterns of learning styles. Not only do students have different learning styles, but teachers have different teaching styles. Ideally, students and teachers will be sensitive to such differences and will learn to accommodate each other through compromise (see Activity 2.5, "Observing Learning Styles and Preferences").

Learning styles can also be categorized by preferred modes of perception: aural, visual, and kinesthetic. Often the vocabulary that students use will provide clues to help teachers identify diverse ways of perceiving information: "I *see* what you're saying." "I *hear* you." "Finally I *feel* like I know what's going on."

Another variable of learning styles relates to spatial considerations and social interactions. Within all environments (both human and animal), creatures become uncomfortable when others intrude on their space. Among different people, there is a wide range of acceptable comfort zones. In rain forests and on plains as well as in studios, classrooms, offices, and other learning environments, space can become an issue related to safety and comfort. Sometimes this is expressed silently, through body language, as teachers and students move toward or away from each other during a verbal exchange. Sometimes the protection of space relates to establishing or avoiding eye contact.

I encourage you to do four things related to various learning styles:

1. Become more aware of your own inclinations.
2. Become more aware of your teacher's tendencies.
3. Be willing to stretch a bit and to explore learning styles or strategies that may be outside your previous experiences.
4. Reassess periodically the value to you of various learning modes. When feasible, select those that you find the most helpful to you, but be willing to expand your collection of learning strategies.

ACTIVITIES TO EXPLORE

ACTIVITY 2.1 *Chunking and Encoding*

1. Study the chain of notes in Example 2.2.
2. In the blanks that follow, write the letter name of each note in the sequence in Example 2.2.

Example 2.2
Chain of notes

3. Omitting the second and fourth note of each line above, copy the remaining letter names.

4. Using the middle finger of the right hand, play only the first note of each line and the final note in step 3. Notice that those notes create a G major chord (see Example 2.3). Using the vocabulary of musicians, those four tones can be referred to as "G B D G" or "1 3 5 8" or "root third fifth root" or "*do mi sol do.*" On a music staff, that set of notes would look like Example 2.3.

5. Go back the chain of sixteen notes. Using the right hand, play the notes in Example 2.2, with the following fingering pattern: "3 4 3 2 1."

6. Notice the color of the keys—that is, the pattern of white and black keys—you just played.

7. In ordinary language, describe the location of the ornamental notes—the ones you played with fingers 4 and 2—in relation to the first notes.

8. Play this passage several times, using different speeds, different levels of dynamics, and different rhythms.

9. Look at the four keys that provide the four chord tones of the G major triad (G-B-D-G). As you play those four notes individually, hum the pitches. Then sing those four chord tones in ascending order (left to right on the keyboard), using various vocabulary (see step 4: letter names, scale numbers, functional names, and solfège syllables.

10. Without depressing the keys, imagine yourself playing very quickly the first five pitches in the chain. Then, without looking at the score, play the complete set of sixteen notes at a comfortable speed.

11. Look at the score again (see step 4), and play the notes slowly, observing each one separately. Then play the set more quickly,

Example 2.3
G Major chord

perceiving each group as the embellishment of a single note made fancier by adding neighboring tones.

12. Notice how many times you need to repeat the phrase before it feels facile.

ACTIVITY 2.2   *Focusing on the Object*

1. Reread material under "Mental Presets."
2. Select a piece of piano music that you can play. Isolate a short passage that seems awkward or uncomfortable.
3. Work your way through four distinct modes of focusing on the material. Play through the same passage several times. Following the guidance of Green and Gallwey, remove your judgmental self from the scene. Do not allow yourself to receive negative messages such as: "That was awful. I really messed up. At best, my teacher would have given me a grade of D–." At least twice in succession, focus on each of four different aspects (sight, sound, feelings, and facts). Each time you play the passage, describe some of the things you notice. Talk to yourself (in a loud, clear, confident voice), making observations (what do you see, hear, feel, know?).

ACTIVITY 2.3   *Playing with a Rhythmic Pattern*

This activity reinforces the feeling of a basic pulse and a specific rhythmic pattern (see Example 2.4.):

1. Talk the counting of the rhythm (**1** + 2 **+ 3** + **4** +). Emphasize the numbers that coincide with a note (**1** + **3** **4**), but also feel the pulse divisions (+ 2 + +) that come between notes.
2. Step the pulse at a comfortable pace (M.M. ♩ = 110–120). While stepping the pulse—Left Right Left Right—talk the rhythm: "Long– –Short Long–Long").
3. With both hands on your thighs, slowly and energetically tap the rhythm.
4. Using a faster speed and lighter gestures, tap the pulse with the left hand and the rhythm with the right hand. Create an energetic and steady pulse. Repeat the pattern many times.
5. With both hands on a flat surface, such as a table, desktop, or closed lid of the keyboard, tap the pulse with the left hand and the rhythm with the right hand.

Example 2.4
Feeling pulse and rhythm

Rhythm	$\frac{4}{4}$ ♩.	♪ ♩	♩
Pulse	x	x	x	x
Divisions of pulse	x x x x	x x	x x
Counting	1 + 2 +	3 +	4 +

---

6. At the keyboard, tap the pulse with the left hand and play the rhythm with the right hand's fingers. Describe the sequence of motions ("Both–Left Right Both–Both").

RH: Play rhythm	1	3 2	5	
LH: Tap pulse	x	x	x	x
Feel subdivision of pulse	x x x x x x x x			

ACTIVITY 2.4 *Recognizing* Same *and* Different

1. At the piano, locate and play the following pairs of notes. Read them from left to right (low to high).

D and A	F and C	D and C	G and E	C and F
C and G	E and B	C and E	G and D	A and E

The first pair (D-A) does represent the interval of a fifth (notes/keys: D-E-F-G-A; RH fingering: 1-2-3-4-5). See Example 2.5.

2. Play each pair again, describing the interval either as "a fifth" or "not a fifth." Notice how the pairs look, sound, and feel.
3. At random, anywhere on the keyboard, create pairs of notes that are not fifths.
4. Locate several pairs of notes that are fifths.
5. Verbalize (say aloud) your own definition of a fifth.
6. Improvise a short piece based on fifths, either solid or broken. Explore fifths in a variety of registers, dynamics, speeds, and rhythms.
7. Look for fifths in your piano music. The interval may be either vertical (solid) or horizontal (broken). Notice that the interval of a fifth will involve either two space notes or two line notes (see Example 2.6.). *Note*: Odd-numbered intervals (unison, third, fifth, and seventh) always are alike: either a pair of line notes or a pair of space notes. Even-numbered intervals (second, fourth, sixth, and octave) always involve unlike notes: either a line note and space note or a space note and line note.

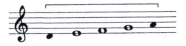

Example 2.5
Interval of a fifth

Example 2.6
Fifths (space-space and line-line)

ACTIVITY 2.5   *Observing Learning Styles and Preferences*

1. Become more aware of your own preferences in learning situations. Identify three things you notice about your own approach to learning something new.

   A. _____

   B. _____

   C. _____

2. Become more aware of your piano teacher's tendencies. Identify three things you notice about his/her approach to students and study assignments.

   A. _____

   B. _____

   C. _____

3. Be willing to stretch your boundaries a bit and to explore learning styles or strategies that may be outside your usual procedures. Identify three possible choices.

   A. _____

   B. _____

   C. _____

4. Select one strategy to explore several times during the next few days. Describe your reactions to those explorations.

   _____

   _____

   _____

   _____

5. Notice various learning attitudes and approaches employed by your friends and by other teachers. Describe them.

   _____

   _____

   _____

   _____

THOUGHTS ABOUT WORDS

Don't

If you ever have tried to train a dog or talk with a toddler, you probably know that any phrase starting with the word *don't* conveys the opposite message. When a two-year-old hears, "*Don't* cross the street," the message actually received is "*Cross* the street!" When your puppy hears, "*Don't* bite," the action directive is "*Bite!*"

Most adults have developed the ability to process the concept "not," but you still might find it useful to replace "don'ts" with positive reminders. Instead of "Don't hold that quarter note through two pulses," substitute "Lift [that is, "do lift"] the finger before the third pulse" or, even better, "Listen ["do listen"] for the silence that arrives on the third pulse." Instead of thinking "Don't rush here," remind yourself, "Do maintain a steady pulse throughout this passage." Instead of "Don't leave out the F-sharp," remind yourself you will need to "place the middle finger on a black key in order to create a D major triad." Instead of "Don't get tense there," remind yourself, "I will need time to take a big breath before I begin that passage."

Students Who Understand or Speak More Than One Language

If you are comfortable in more than one language, you have some options to explore during your piano practice sessions. If you are an early-level adult student who is a nonnative speaker of English, you might find it helpful to talk to yourself (verbalize messages) in your original language. Perhaps, on the one hand, when you were very young your grandparents spoke to you lovingly in your childhood language. Now, as an adult, would you enjoy hearing supportive words in the same language? If, on the other hand, you have unhappy memories of music lessons as a child, perhaps you would prefer to avoid your childhood language and hear messages in the language of your successful adulthood.

Practice Makes Perfect?

When I was a little girl and someone told me, "Practice makes perfect," my mother the piano teacher would always add quietly, "Only when it's perfect practice." If your practice involves repeating errors, then you are not learning how to eliminate mistakes but how to repeat them.

That Was Good; That Was Right

The opposite of good is bad. The opposite of right is wrong. When you tell yourself, "That was right. That was very good," you are using vocabulary associated with moral judgments. If you are good today but make mistakes tomorrow, does that mean that when you make mistakes you are bad and can expect to be punished? In providing feedback to myself and my students, I have found that it is more useful to utilize descriptive, nonjudgmental phrases. Be specific in describing what happened that resulted in a more successful play-through. Here are some examples:

"That was an accurate reading of the rhythms in the score."
"I got rid of the intrusive bumpy spots in the melody."

"That phrase was a bit more flexible in time, and it sounded more musical."

"My hand floated off the keyboard. That time, the final note of the phrase didn't sound clipped."

"I released the pedal more gradually and eliminated that disruptive whooshing sound."

"That time I heard the F-sharp. Just before I played that passage, I saw my third finger ready to depress the black key."

"I maintained a steady pulse throughout that section."

"I gave myself a bit more time at the end of the phrase. That enabled me to move easily to the new hand position and made it much easier to control the passage."

Acknowledge your accomplishments. Cheer yourself.

"I achieved my goal."

"I heard a difference."

"I felt more secure that time."

"Hooray! I got it."

ADDITIONAL RESOURCES

Books

Green, Barry, with W. Timothy Gallwey, *The Inner Game of Music* (Garden City, NY: Anchor/Doubleday, 1986). Gallwey's insights into natural learning principles, originally published in the 1970s to enhance performance in tennis and other sports, were transferred to the world of musicians by Green, a double bass player.

Uszler, Marienne, Stewart Gordon, and Elyse Mach, *The Well-Tempered Keyboard Teacher* (New York: Schirmer, 1991). A book about teaching and learning. Written primarily for piano teachers, it includes much information that is useful to adult piano students. Note especially chapter 3, "A Survey of Learning Theories"; chapter 7, "The Adult Student"; and chapter 11, "The Transfer Student."

3 Understanding Your Keyboard Instrument

A t your lessons and practice sessions, you may be playing an acoustic piano or an electric, digital keyboard. Acoustic pianos are those that are not plugged in (comparable to a traditional guitar, either classical or folk). Acoustie pianos do not depend on electricity to deliver or enhance the sound. Pianists—unlike singers, flutists, and harmonica players— usually do not take their own acoustic instrument with them when leaving home. Instead, they learn to adjust to the wide variety of instruments they encounter and do the best they can with whatever piano is available.

> *As a pianist, you will have opportunities to work with both acoustic and electric instruments.*

CONCEPTS TO CONSIDER

Keyboard Instruments

The phrase *keyboard instrument* is a generic term. It includes harpsichords, clavichords, and organs—including those used in cathedrals, churches, homes, theaters, baseball stadiums, and skating rinks. It also includes twentieth-century reproductions of pianos built in the eighteenth and nineteenth centuries (including wooden-framed instruments referred to as fortepianos), harmoniums (such as pump organs), player pianos, acoustic pianos (including spinets, consoles, studio uprights, and grands of various lengths), digital instruments (including those with eighty-eight keys, full-size touch-sensitive keyboards, and a wide variety of technical specifications), synthesizers, MIDI (Musical Instrument Digital Interface) keyboards, music work stations, and toy pianos (including those with as few as eight miniature keys).

Although music keyboard instruments may look similar (with the same configuration of keys), there are many differences between various keyboard instruments and the performance techniques required to use them effectively. Consider the following analogy: Two people may have the same family name, but when you interact with them, it is useful to be aware of both their similarities and differences. If you expect Smith (Harry) to behave exactly like Smith (Mary), your expectations probably will create complications. The same principle applies when you interact with Piano (Acoustic) and Piano (Digital). In spite of family similarities, those keyboard instruments represent significant differences, just as Harry and

Mary Smith do. It is important for pianists to become aware of such differences and adapt to various instruments.

Historically, the traditional piano is an acoustic stringed instrument designed with a separate set of strings for each pitch. The strings actually are made of wire. Coordinated with each pitch is a lever (key) connected to a small hammer. When a key moves down, the attached hammer is tossed toward the strings. After hitting the strings, the hammer immediately falls away from the strings, which continue to vibrate (thus, the acoustic piano is a *stringed percussion instrument*). Later, when the key is released and returns to its original position, a device called a damper drops against the string and stops the vibrations (damping the sound).

The immediate keyboard predecessor to the modern acoustic piano was the *gravicembalo col piano e forte* (harpsichord with soft and loud). That instrument was created in the late seventeenth century by Bartolomeo Cristofori (1655–1730), an Italian harpsichord builder who worked in Florence at the court of the Medici. In contrast with earlier keyboard instruments, including the organ and harpsichord, Cristofori's piano was touch-sensitive. That enabled performers to control a variety of dynamic levels—a range of loud and soft sounds—by the way they moved and depressed the keys, rather than by adjusting various knobs and levers. The change in technology coincided with a change in musical aesthetics. Music composed specifically for the acoustic piano incorporated subtle gradations of dynamics comparable to inflections of expressive speech. As has always been the case, composers influenced instrument makers, and new inventions inspired composers.

In 1925, Walter J. Turner, a music critic in London, wrote, "It would not surprise me if in another fifty years the pianoforte were an extinct instrument along with the viol and harpsichord."[1] Turner's dire prediction has not come true. The vast repertoire of music composed for acoustic piano continues to be studied, taught, performed, and broadcast by professional and amateur musicians around the world. And, even today, composers are writing music specifically for the acoustic piano.

At the beginning of the twenty-first century, although the plugged-in, digital piano has earned a significant place in the music world, the acoustic piano has not been discarded. It is likely that the two instruments will coexist for many years to come. Whether you practice on a digital piano or an acoustic piano, it will be useful to understand the basic principles of the acoustic instruments for which Mozart, Beethoven, Schubert, Schumann, Chopin, Liszt, Brahms, MacDowell, Grieg, Tchaikovsky, Rachmaninoff, Ravel, Debussy, Kabalevsky, and many others composed. Although much of their piano music can be transferred to or arranged for other instruments (such as marimba, harpsichord, saxophone quartet, violin, brass band, or digital piano), the acoustical effect will not be the same. The melodies, harmonies, and rhythms of piano music can be shifted from an acoustic piano to another instrument, but the timbral essence of the piano depends on resonance that results from sympathetic vibrations. On an acoustic piano, when you play middle C, every other note tuned to C also resonates—whether or not those other seven C keys are depressed. This increased resonance enhances the total effect of the acoustic piano. Furthermore, whenever you depress the damper pedal, eighty-eight complete sets of strings vibrate sympathetically.

Artists can depict a sunrise in many media, but the artistic effect of scenes created with watercolors or chalk or oil paints will be different from that of mosaics or stained glass or crayons. Visual artists select various media on the basis of their own skills, subject matter, and artistic intentions. They also make choices in response to requests from patrons and the availability of materials. In visual arts as in language and music, subtleties often are lost in translations.

Characteristics of Acoustic Pianos

It is helpful for pianists (even early-level pianists) to understand the basic mechanism of the acoustic piano. As noted earlier, the sound of the acoustic piano occurs when small hammers strike strings. The dynamic level of the sound results from the speed at which the key descends and the hammer strikes the strings. Speed also is affected by the mass (size and weight) of the tool (such as hand, arm, full body) used to depress the key. When the piano hammer travels faster, it hits the strings with more energy and creates a louder sound. The dynamics of acoustic piano sounds are correlated with speed (that is, the speed of the key's descent and the corresponding speed of the hammer's journey toward the strings). In this context, speed does not relate to tempo (the pacing of musical pulses) or rhythmic activity (the tones between pulses).

The speed of the key's descent controls the speed of the hammer.
The speed at which the hammer travels to the strings determines the loudness of the sound.

After a key is depressed, greater force or finger pressure on it does not affect the volume of the piano sound. Once the key has traveled to the bottom of the key bed (the full depth of the key), additional finger motion on the piano key will not affect the sound. Although a violinist or clavichord player can move a finger very slightly and create a richer, more vibrant sound, when a pianist pushes harder against the piano key or wiggles around on it the movement has no effect on the piano's sound. Such unnecessary motion represents wasted energy and inhibits the pianist's ease in traveling to the next keys.

Pushing the key harder or longer does not affect the loudness of the acoustic piano's sound.

As soon as the hammer strikes the string, the sound of the acoustic piano begins to decay—that is, to get softer. Acoustic pianists, unlike singers and wind players, cannot increase the level of volume of a single tone after the sound begins.

Music is an art form that deals with relationships of sounds changing through time. A single note on the printed page represents the beginning of a tone that has a life span. Throughout a note's duration, the sound changes. Each tone has a distinct and predictable shape, known as an envelope pattern, that includes a beginning, middle, and end. Key punchers merely press a lever. They initiate an event and that is the end of their task. Such a technique works at a computer keyboard, but at the piano keyboard punching keys does not result in sensitive music making.

The sound of an acoustic piano tone immediately diminishes in loudness.

Parenting provides an appropriate analogy. The birth of a child marks the start of parenting, not the end of that responsibility. Effective parents remain responsive to changing needs throughout the lifetime of their child. A sensitive musician accepts responsibility for the entire duration of a tone.

When a series of notes results in tones that have exactly the same dynamic level, the result often is described as punchy. The predictable sameness of a single dynamic level creates a mechanical, unmusical effect (see Figure 3.1). Fine pianists, however, are skillful in allowing the beginning of each new note to relate to the ending sound of the previous note. By matching tones, you actually can create the illusion of a *crescendo* or a *diminuendo* (see Figure 3.2).

Using Acoustic Pianos

The Italian musician and writer Ferruccio Busoni (1866–1924) served as a prophet of new music early in the twentieth century, but he also was an outstanding pianist in his own day. With the voice and intensity of a true romantic, he extolled his favorite performance instrument:

> Respect the Pianoforte! Its disadvantages are evident, decided, and unquestionable: The lack of sustained tone, and the pitiless, unyielding adjustment of the inalterable semi-tonic scale. But its advantages and prerogatives approach the marvelous. It gives a single man command over something complete; in its potentialities from softest to loudest in one and the same register it excels all other instruments. The trumpet can blare, but not sing; contrariwise the flute; the pianoforte can do both. It embraces the highest and deepest practicable tones. Respect the Pianoforte.[2]

What can pianists do at an acoustic piano? There are many possibilities.

1. Control the texture (number of distinct lines):
     Play a single melody: monophony.
     Play several melodic lines simultaneously: polyphony.
     Play groups of notes that represent chords: harmony.
     Play melody and accompaniment at the same time: homophony.
2. Create special acoustical effects by using various devices controlled by pedals:
     Left: soft pedal, *una corda*
     Middle: sostenuto pedal
     Right: damper pedal

Figure 3.1
Diagram of the Decay
Pattern of Piano Tones

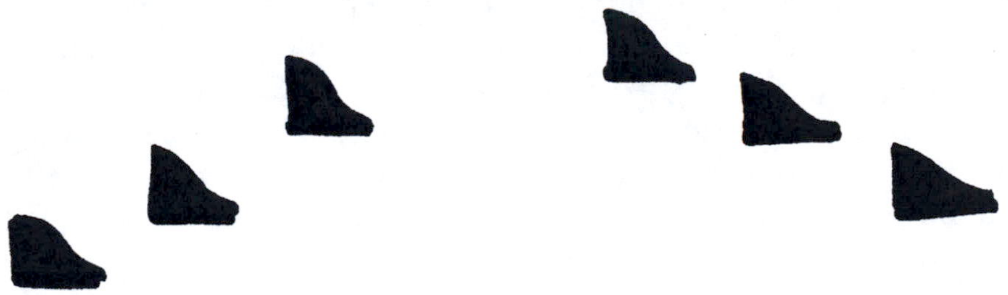

Figure 3.2
Gradations of Piano
Dynamics

3. Control dynamics in several different ways:

   Create a very wide range of dynamic levels: from extremely soft to extremely loud.

   Control dynamics horizontally: combine individual tones into musical phrases and shape melodic lines to provide inflections of sound.

   Control dynamics vertically: vary the dynamic level of different notes played at the same time.

4. Control a wide variety of articulations: sustain and separate notes in different combinations.

5. Control a wide range of sounds: as high and as low in pitch as the sounds of almost any musical instrument.

6. Shift easily from one pitch register to another.

7. Utilize any of twelve different pitches as a home tone (tonal center). Transpose musical material into other keys/tonalities while using similar fingering patterns.

8. Function alone and with other musicians:

   As a solo instrument: drawing on an extensive repertoire of music composed for piano.

   As a duet instrument: with two people at one piano playing music for four hands, original piano pieces as well as arrangements of music composed for other instruments.

   As an accompanying instrument: playing pieces composed for piano in combination with virtually all types of voices and musical instruments.

   As a chamber or ensemble instrument: with small groups of instruments or singers.

   As a solo instrument with symphony orchestra: performing the solo piano part of multimovement compositions that feature piano with orchestra.

9. Provide music for a wide variety of activities: at work and play, when worshiping and studying, in secular and sacred celebrations.

Pedals of Acoustic Pianos

Although musical instruments sometimes have been made to order and delivered with different options (similar to automobiles and computers), the standard acoustic grand piano has three pedals that affect the interactions of the strings and dampers. These pedals are described in the following three sections. To decide how to use pedals effectively, pianists need to consider many factors. The variables include the pianist, the specific instrument being used, the acoustical characteristics of the performance space, the composer, and—especially—the music: tempo, texture, harmonies, articulation, dynamics, and phrasing.

Left Pedal: Soft Pedal, Una Corda

The pedal at the left of the set of three pedals is attached to a shifting mechanism. As early as 1725, Cristofori had introduced a shifting device on one of his pianos. When the shifting pedal was depressed, there were two distinct resting places. At the first stage of depression, the keyboard shifted slightly and the hammers, instead of striking all three strings, made contact with only two strings (*due corde*). When the pedal was depressed a bit deeper, the keyboard was shifted even more so that the hammers would strike only one of the three strings (thus the name *una corda*). On today's acoustic grand piano, the left pedal still controls a shifting mechanism, but it is designed without stopping points. The use of this pedal mechanism affects both the quantity and the quality of the piano's tone. When the hammer strikes only one or two of the three strings, the other strings still vibrate sympathetically. With the *una corda* pedal you can increase the variety of tone color and even minimize the percussiveness of the piano's sound. This device colors and changes the basic piano sound in much the same way that a mute affects a string or brass instrument.

The *una corda* pedal, however, is not a crutch for playing softer. Many pianists consider it inappropriate to depend on the left pedal to create softer sounds, even though sometimes it is referred to as the soft pedal. I agree with the concept that the pianist's control of *pianissimo* must be in the arms and fingers, not in the foot. I suggest that you reserve the *una corda* device for special expressive effects. Use it when you want an unusual, muted sound or a dramatic change of tone color. Use it selectively to create expressive sounds and establish a soft, magical atmosphere.

Note that with an acoustic upright piano, the left pedal does not shift the whole keyboard. Instead, it moves the entire set of hammers closer to the strings. The result is that when the hammers travel a shorter distance and at a slower speed, the impact of the blows is minimized and the strength of the tone is diminished.

Middle Pedal: Sostenuto

The middle pedal is a tone-sustaining pedal. The invention was introduced in 1844, at the Paris Exhibition, in a piano built by a French manufacturing firm. Later this pedal mechanism was patented in the United States by the American Steinway Piano Company. Soon other American piano manufacturers incorporated the invention in their grand pianos and also in their better-quality upright instruments. European builders, however, did not adopt this pedal as standard equipment. Even today some of the finest European-built concert grand pianos do not have a sostenuto pedal.

To control the sostenuto pedal, first depress selected keys and then depress the pedal while the keys are still down. As long as the pedal remains down, the selected dampers will stay up and only those sets of strings will vibrate even after you let the key come up. If you depress other keys *after* the pedal is down, the sounds of those additional strings will not join the original collection of sounds. If you depress the sostenuto pedal before you depress any keys, the device will not accumulate any sounds.

Some uprights have a pedal device (placed in the middle of the three pedals) that controls a sound silencer, sometimes called an apartment pedal. Some piano manufacturers, however, include a middle pedal that does not affect the piano sound in any way; it is only for show.

Right Pedal: Damper

The pedal on the right lifts the damper mechanism away from the strings. The damper pedal has been described as the soul of the piano. When the foot depresses the damper pedal of an acoustic piano, the dampers move away from the strings, allowing them to vibrate freely. The strings continue to vibrate until the pedal is released and the dampers fall back against the strings (damping the sound). Chopin cautioned his students that learning to use the pedal appropriately is a lifelong study. Although on today's acoustic piano you will use your right foot to control the damping device, ultimately you need to learn how to pedal with your ears. Your decisions regarding the use of the damper pedal require sensitive monitoring of the sounds that accumulate when you depress the right pedal and lift the dampers away from the strings.

> *The damper pedal of an acoustic piano is not an on/off switch.*

It may be useful to think of the damper pedal as a variable control rather than a digital device. Just as a rheostat dial allows gradual changes in the intensity of light, the damper pedal affects the amount of resonance created at the piano. The piano's damper pedal is similar to the car's gas pedal. When you are driving a car, the amount of pressure you direct to the pedal affects the amount of gas that is sent to the motor. On the piano bench, as in the driver's seat, it is important to control the depth of the pedal, fluttering it sometimes.

When using the damper pedal, you should not create extraneous noises. To avoid such disruptive sounds, remember:

Place the heel of your shoe on the floor.
Keep the sole of your shoe in contact with the metal of the pedal.
Move your entire foot from the ankle joint, not from the knee or hip.
Monitor carefully the speed at which the foot moves the pedal.
Avoid making gestures that result in noises.

**Figure 3.3
Pedal Zones**

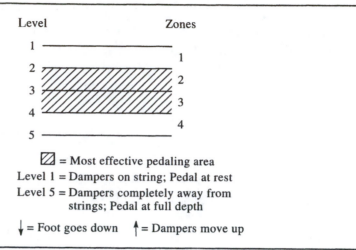

Level Zones

= Most effective pedaling area
Level 1 = Dampers on string; Pedal at rest
Level 5 = Dampers completely away from
strings; Pedal at full depth

↓ = Foot goes down   ↑ = Dampers move up

The depth to which you depress the damper pedal is an important variable in controlling the sounds of the acoustic piano. You may find it helpful to visualize the downward journey of the right pedal, learning to monitor five resting points for your foot, thus creating four pedal zones (Figure 3.3).

Level 1. Foot and pedal are at rest: dampers are on the strings; foot has not yet started moving down. Zone 1 is between levels 1 and 2.

Level 2. Foot and pedal are down a very small distance: dampers begin to move away from the strings. Zone 2 is between levels 2 and 3.

Level 3. Foot and pedal travel down a bit farther:dampers have left the strings, allowing the sound to vibrate freely. Zone 3 is between levels 3 and 4.

Level 4. Foot and pedal travel farther: dampers are farther away from the strings, allowing greater resonance and creating a richer sound. Zone 4 is between levels 4 and 5.

Level 5. Foot and pedal are down as far as possible: dampers are completely away from the strings.

You will have the greatest control of resonance when you work within pedal zones 2 and 3. Many times inexperienced pianists move their right foot at appropriate times yet still accumulate muddy sounds. When your foot remains within pedal zones 1 or 4, even when you move it slightly the dampers may not affect the vibrating strings sufficiently. As a result, conflicting harmonies will resonate as you create a thick pileup of sounds.

The timing of depressing the damper pedal also is an important variable in the control of resonance. The damper pedal can be depressed before the keys go down, at the same time the keys are depressed, or after the keys are down.

1. Right foot first; then hands.

1. *Anticipated Pedal.* When you lift the dampers before you depress the keys, all of the piano strings are ready to begin

resonating immediately. This creates a richer, more immediate tone quality from the first sounds.

2. *Rhythmic Pedal.* This represented the standard pedaling technique until about 1870. It was used to emphasize and define rhythms, mark accents, and support melodies.

3. *Syncopated Pedal.* This became the standard pedaling technique after about 1870.

> 2. *Hands and right foot move down simultaneously.*

> 3. *Hands first; then right foot.*

Because pedaling decisions involve several variables and are affected by individual instruments, many composers do not provide specific pedal indications in their scores. Sometimes they simply tell pianists to utilize the damper pedal (play with pedal: *con pedale*) and assume that each performer will make his or her own specific judgments about depressing and releasing the pedal.

During your practice sessions, you need to plan the pedaling choices you expect to use with a piece. Each time you play a piece, however, you will need to respond to the actual sounds you hear. Be ready to adjust your plans. The pedaling that worked effectively in a rehearsal, on your practice piano, may not resolve the musical problems when you play the same piece on a different instrument.

> *Fine pianists learn to pedal with their ears.*

Sometimes editors of piano music, with the best of intentions, try to help students by presenting their own guesses for solving a pedaling question. When you use an edition that has pedaling suggestions from an editor rather than the composer, approach those ideas with caution and perhaps even apprehension. The aesthetic intentions of editors and composers do not always match and may lead to different sounds and different pedaling decisions. Reimar Riefling, a twentieth-century Norwegian pedagogue, suggested that "*most* piano music presents inaccurate indications of when to use the damper pedal." He recommended that pianists "experiment with *reasonable* illegalities"—that is, experiment with pedaling that seems to be consistent with what we know about the composer's musical style (texture, instrument, phrase delineation, and sound)—even if that pedaling was not written in the score by the composer.[3] Pedaling decisions—like most performance decisions—will need to be based ultimately on the performer's understanding of the composer's style and the pianist's own sense of good taste. Would you expect apple pie to taste like beef stew or chili? Piano music by Mozart should not sound like it was composed by Ravel or Rachmaninoff.

Using Pedal at a Digital Piano

The pedals of digital pianos look very much like the pedals of acoustic pianos. However, the two types of keyboard instruments create very different acoustical effects. With an acoustic piano, the damper pedal lifts all of the dampers and allows us to hear overtones of strings vibrating sympathetically (see Activity 3.3, "Exploring the Overtone Series"). With digital keyboards (electric pianos), however, the damper pedal can collect the sounds of the keys that have been depressed but cannot accumulate additional resonance from overtones and sympathetic vibrations.

When using pedal at an electric piano, I recommend that you begin with the same basic pedaling technique that you would use with an acoustic instrument: keep the heel of your shoe on the floor; keep the sole of your shoe on the metal both when traveling down and when coming back up. Then, as you shift between different types of pianos, you will experience fewer problems. You need to realize, however, that with some digital pianos, the pedal functions as a trigger mechanism that accesses other kinds of mechanical responses from the instrument (such as initiating a recorded rhythmic pattern, changing the envelope pattern of a sound, or controlling only a portion of the keyboard).

Changing Technology of Musical Instruments

Throughout the history of instruments, people have made adjustments in design and sought to improve various aspects of their tools. Often the changes represent differences rather than improvements. Although the twentieth-century metal-framed pianos can create louder sounds (those with more decibels) than Mozart's lighter, wooden-framed pianos, his eighteenth-century instruments provided greater clarity of articulation and more control of sounds in the extremely soft range. "Bigger, louder, faster" does not necessarily represent artistic improvements. Technological differences reflect changes in cultural and aesthetic values. With every technological gain, though, there is a trade-off. If you travel from New York to San Francisco on a jet plane, you will arrive in California in less time than if you pedal a bicycle across the continent. If you fly to California, you may have more time to visit with your daughter and son-in-law. However (and here are some trade-offs), during the flight in a pressurized cabin you will hear fewer songbirds, see fewer sunsets, and get less exercise.

Instrument manufacturers, composers, and performing musicians continue to experiment with procedures that utilize the special capabilities of new technologies. Although I wrote this chapter near the close of the twentieth century, your involvement with the piano will take place in the new millennium. You will encounter many options that were not available to composers writing music in the nineteenth century and pianists trained in the twentieth century. Even while you explore music for the acoustic piano, I encourage you to investigate developments associated with other keyboard instruments. The National Association of Music Merchants (NAMM) meets annually and brings together thousands of music product manufacturers and dealers. An innovative product that is introduced one year probably will be adapted and altered by many other manufacturers before the next NAMM show twelve months later. For timely information about developments in keyboard technology, visit various Web sites on the Internet, explore articles and other publications from the music industry, study advertisements in current periodicals, talk with technologically involved musicians, listen to new recordings, and spend time experimenting with items in the display rooms of music merchants.

Using Digital Pianos

What can pianists do at a digital piano? (Note that not all digital pianos are capable of producing all of the effects described here.) When selecting a digital instrument, you will need to ask, "At this specific instrument, will I be able to do this?"

- Control the output of the piano's sound by directing it to internal or external speakers or to earphones, just as you do with radios and television sets. When you use earphones, you will be able to practice the piano in privacy, without others in the room hearing the sounds you hear.
- Control dynamics by varying the speed and pressure of the key's descent. *Note:* There is a wide variety in the degree of touch sensitivity associated with various digital keyboards.
- Accumulate pitches (collect groups of keys depressed) by using a sustaining pedal.
- Change tonal characteristics by adding vibrato, bending pitches, altering the acoustic piano's decay pattern (replacing diminishing sounds with ones that grow in intensity), and reproducing the acoustical effect of resonance created in concert halls of different sizes.
- Select from various prerecorded sounds that replicate different sonorities, such as electric piano, grand piano, harpsichord, strings, trumpet, choir, barking dogs, and so on.
- Access various tuning systems used in other times or places.
- Access prerecorded harmonic or rhythmic patterns that support single-line melodies or reinforce accompanying notes.
- Transport the instrument easily.
- Record and play back passages and pieces. Record your playing at one speed and then listen to the piano reproduce the same material at a different speed, faster or slower.
- Transpose digital information so that a pattern played in one tonality, such as C major, can be played back in any other major key. If you want to hear a passage in C♯ or A♭ or B major, OK! It's all the same to the digital piano.
- Interact with educational software, designed for students of all ages and stages. Many piano method books and other instructional materials now are issued with a computer disk or a compact disc recording.
- Use prerecorded disks, encoded with digital information, that enable you to access or ignore various combinations of recorded tracks (such as right hand material alone, left hand

material alone, instrumental accompaniments, underlying clicks of a metronome, rhythmic patterns, and harmonic backgrounds). Create your own disks to use in practice or performance. Record musical material, creating successive layers and building complex textures of sound.

- Use a built-in metronome.
- Follow guidelights, placed behind each key, to see which keys will need to be played next.
- Look at visual displays on a small screen built into the piano. Follow song lyrics, graphics, or text information, in English or another language of your choice.
- Establish direct connection with a personal computer; use computer software or download files from the Internet.

Manufacturers predict that today's technology will become obsolete before the piece of equipment is worn out. Technological developments create many new opportunities for musicians, but the value of any tool depends on the way it is utilized. Musicians are not obsolete, and both acoustic and digital pianos continue to be useful musical instruments. Making music at the piano is not an antiquated activity.

ACTIVITIES TO EXPLORE

Activities 3.1–3.5 are to be explored at an acoustic piano.

ACTIVITY 3.1 *Listening for Sympathetic Vibrations*

1. At an acoustic piano (spinet, upright, or grand), using the palm of the left hand (flat, with extended fingers), depress silently the very lowest white keys on the piano. While those keys are depressed, the corresponding dampers will be away from the strings, allowing them to vibrate freely and to create a resonant, echolike quality.
2. With the right hand, experiment by playing a random selection of pitches, intervals, or chords. Use a variety of dynamics, registers, and touches. Listen carefully to the resulting sounds. Because strings vibrate sympathetically even when not set in motion by the hammer, the overtones of the keys you depress silently will continue to vibrate even after the dampers of the notes you play have returned to the strings.

ACTIVITY 3.2 *Playing "Red River Valley"*

1. With your left hand (using an open hand, with your palm against the keys), depress silently and then hold down a cluster of the lowest keys, both white and black. Then, with your right hand, play slowly the song "Red River Valley" (see Example 3.1).

Example 3.1
"Red River Valley"

Red River Valley

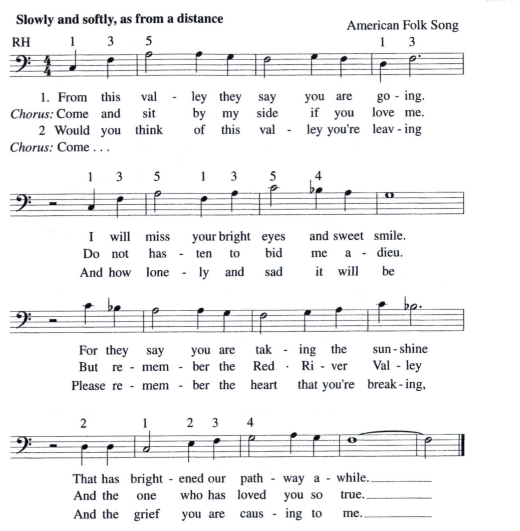

Slowly and softly, as from a distance

American Folk Song

RH   1   3   5   1   3

1. From this val - ley they say you are go - ing.
Chorus: Come and sit by my side if you love me.
2 Would you think of this val - ley you're leav - ing
Chorus: Come . . .

1   3   5   1   3   5   4

I will miss your bright eyes and sweet smile.
Do not has - ten to bid me a - dieu.
And how lone - ly and sad it will be

For they say you are tak - ing the sun - shine
But re - mem - ber the Red · Ri - ver Val - ley
Please re - mem - ber the heart that you're break - ing,

2   1   2   3   4

That has bright - ened our path - way a - while._____
And the one who has loved you so true._____
And the grief you are caus - ing to me._____

2. Listen for the pileup of sounds and the nostalgic, distant quality of the tones. Create the expressive, mournful mood of someone whose beloved friend has gone away. Although you are not using the damper pedal, the dampers connected with those low notes (keys in the bass register) will be away from the strings and thus allow them to vibrate sympathetically.

ACTIVITY 3.3   *Exploring the Overtone Series*

Whenever a string vibrates its full length, it also vibrates in segments, called partials. Each musical sound has a specific pattern of overtones; the relative loudness of certain overtones results in sounds that are characteristic of a particular kind of instrument such as piano, clarinet, or harp. The first seven overtones of the tone C are given Example 3.2.

Example 3.2
Overtone Series

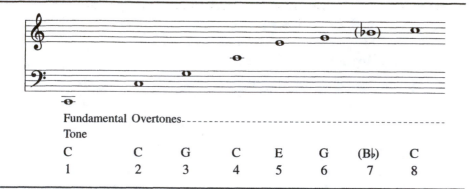

Fundamental Tone	Overtones						
C	C	G	C	E	G	(B♭)	C
1	2	3	4	5	6	7	8

1. At an acoustic piano, silently depress the key for a single low-pitched C—continue holding that key down; do not depress the damper pedal.
2. Play the C an octave higher—strike it abruptly and energetically. This pitch represents the first overtone, which is the second pitch in the overtone series. Listen to the sounds that will continue to vibrate sympathetically even after the damper drops back onto the strings.
3. Experiment by playing loudly and abruptly other individual pitches in the overtone series. Listen carefully to the sounds as they change.

ACTIVITY 3.4 *Exploring the Depth of the Damper Pedal Mechanism*

1. At an acoustic piano, depress slowly the right pedal (that is, damper pedal) until you sense that it has reached the bottom of the mechanism and can move no farther.
2. Depress and release the damper pedal several times, learning to gauge the distance from the resting position (Level 1) to the deepest point (Level 5).
3. Experiment by depressing the pedal various depths. Go from Level 1 to 2, 1 to 3, 1 to 4, 1 to 5, 4 to 2. Become aware of four pedal zones.
4. Play a set of notes, either a broken or a solid chord. Use the damper pedal to collect those sounds. While remaining within neighboring zones (such as between 2 and 3), flutter the pedal slightly. Notice how the sound changes as the dampers move nearer the strings.
5. Play a G major scale (GABCDEF#G) in double octaves: play, very slowly and loudly, four notes together using an octave in each hand (LH:51; RH:15). Change the pedal with each scale tone. Experiment by depressing the damper pedal to different depths. Notice the variety in the sounds you create.
6. Notice how long you must allow the dampers to remain on the strings in order to stop the vibrations and avoid creating a

muddy sound. To stop the sound completely, you will need to allow the pedal to return to its resting place long enough that the dampers drop back onto the strings.

7. Play the double octave scale at various dynamic levels (*pianissimo* to *fortissimo*). Notice how the amount of sound you create (level of loudness/quantity of decibels) affects the pileup of sound. When you play *fortissimo* and use a deep pedal, you are more likely to accumulate dissonant sounds. When you play *pianissimo* and use a shallow pedal, you can keep the pedal down for a longer time and create a shimmering sound quality.

ACTIVITY 3.5   *Creating Percussive Effects with the Pedal*

The pedal mechanism of an acoustic piano is capable of making extraneous percussive sounds. Sensitive and skillful pianists avoid creating distracting sounds with the pedals. To avoid making noises, it is useful to learn how to create undesirable effects intentionally. The pedal mechanism of each piano is slightly different. When you play a new instrument, you will need to adjust to it quickly. By learning how to create noises intentionally, you also will discover what motions to avoid when you encounter a noisy pedal mechanism.

1. *Slapping.* Lift your shoe away from the pedal. Drop the foot very quickly so that the shoe creates a slapping sound when it reaches the metal.
2. *Stomping.* Lift your entire leg. Stomp on the pedal (as if you were keeping time energetically at a Saturday night square dance).
3. *Whooshing.* Depress the pedal very quickly, so that a whooshing sound results as the dampers travel away from the strings abruptly.
4. *Thudding.* Depress the pedal as deeply as possible, creating a clunk when you hit bottom.
5. *Echoing.* Depress the pedal as deeply as possible, then release it abruptly. Notice the extraneous noises that occur when the dampers drop abruptly onto the strings.

Activities 3.6–3.8 are to be explored at both acoustic pianos and digital pianos.

ACTIVITY 3.6   *Controlling Layers of Dynamics*

1. Depress the same key several times. Experiment in controlling variations of volume (1 = very soft; 5 = very loud). Monitor the dynamics according to the number assigned to each pitch.
2. Use the sets of notes in Example 3.3. The directions of stems represent left hand (stems down) and right hand (stems up).

> *To avoid a percussive sound and have greater control of the pedal, keep the sole of your shoe on the pedal and the heel of your shoe on the floor. Lift the foot from the ankle joint.*

> *You will have greater control of the pedal if you move your foot from the ankle joint rather than your entire leg from the hip joint.*

> *To avoid a whooshing sound, depress the pedal with a slow, gentle, even movement of the foot.*

> *To avoid a thudding sound, be sensitive to where the bottom of the pedal is. Be aware of where the lowest zone ends. Do not attempt to travel beyond that deepest point.*

> *To avoid an echoing effect, keep the sole of the shoe on the metal of the pedal; release the pedal slowly so that the dampers return gently to their resting position and do not create new vibrations that echo.*

Example 3.3
Controlling Levels of Sound:
1 = *pp*, 2 = *p*, 3 = *mf*, 4 = *f*, 5 = *ff*.

5 2 4 1 4 1 3 3 2 3 1 1 2 1

The numbers below the notes represent various levels of volume (1–5, very soft–very loud).

3. Repeat this activity on several different pianos, using the damper pedal to sustain the notes.
4. Using the same combination of notes, experiment with different combinations of dynamic levels.
5. Using a piece you are working on, experiment by choosing different dynamics for specific tones. Notice how the sound of a single note affects the sounds of other tones.

ACTIVITY 3.7 *Timing the Descent of the Damper Pedal*

1. Set the metronome at M.M. ♩ = 80. Using an acoustic piano, play a scale in double octaves or use a series of chords, such as a chorale hymn, four-part harmony exercise, or chordal piano piece. Assign eight ticks for each scale or melody tone.
2. Experiment with the various sounds that result when you depress the pedal and lift the dampers at different times. For example:

| 1 | 2 | 3 | 4 | 5 | 6 | 7 | 8 |

PLAY

Pedal \——————————/

PLAY

Pedal \—————/

PLAY

Pedal \————————————————————/

3. Repeat the activity several times using a variety of dynamic levels (*pianissimo* to *fortissimo*) and a variety of speeds.
4. Repeat the experiment using pitches in different registers of the piano (very low to very high).

ACTIVITY 3.8 *Using Damper Pedal with a Piano Piece*

1. Using a piece of music composed for the piano (see Example 3.4), experiment with various levels of dynamics and with choices

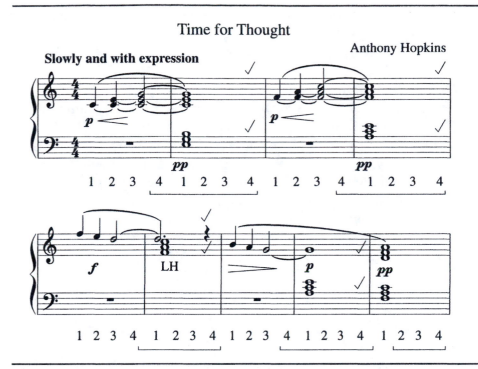

Time for Thought

Slowly and with expression

Anthony Hopkins

Example 3.4
Hopkins, "Time for Thought."
Numbers added below
indicate beats in a measure.
Pedal indication shows when
to depress and release the
damper pedal. Checkmarks
indicate when to lift the
hands and move to the next
location. From *For Talented
Beginners*, Book I (Oxford,
1963). Used by permission.

of timing and damper pedal depth. First, play the excerpt without using any damper pedal. Then try the suggested pedaling.

Then experiment with your own variations of pedaling.

2. Play the same excerpt on different pianos.

3. Experiment in using the damper pedal with your own pieces of piano music. With your foot, vary the depth, speed, and duration of pedal, thus controlling the dampers in relation to the strings. With your hands, on the keyboard, vary the amount of sound you give to different tones.

THOUGHTS ABOUT WORDS

Keys, Notes, Tones

Although the words *keys*, *notes*, and *tones* sometimes are used interchangeably, each word has a special meaning for pianists. If you consider how you perceive information regarding these three nouns, it will be easier to distinguish between them.

Keys represent objects you *touch*: the piano has eighty-eight keys, which are black or white.

Notes represent symbols you *see*: the printed notation of rhythmic patterns uses many values, including quarter notes and half notes; note heads may be white or black, depending on the time value assigned to the note.

Tones represent sounds you *hear*: the tones produced by drums and bells create different qualities of sound.

Tension, Intensity

For musicians, these two similar words represent two very different conditions. *Tension* refers to a physical state of tightness or rigidity. In order for an acoustic piano or guitar to sound in tune, the strings must maintain an appropriate degree of tension. If the strings are pulled too tight, they will snap. Excessive muscular *tension* or stiffness is a state that musicians need to avoid at all times.

In contrast, musical *intensity* in a performance describes an expressive characteristic valued by insightful musicians. Musical intensity is characterized by concentration, caring, and commitment.

Digital, Acoustic

The term *digital* carries different meanings. *Digital dexterity* refers to one's ability to move fingers (that is, digits) with ease and speed. *Digital information*, however, refers to data that is represented by numbers, a sequence of zeros and ones (0s and 1s). Computers and digital pianos process information that has been formatted digitally.

Digital instruments use electricity and are plugged in. *Acoustic* instruments resonate within themselves and are not plugged in.

Strike, Hit, Pound, Beat, Poke, Jab, Bang

When you *strike* the keys or *hit* that chord or *pound* out the rhythm, you create harsh and abrasive sounds. When you use the words *beat, poke, jab,* and *bang,* you are employing verbs associated with inflicting pain. I encourage you to substitute words that represent gestures more appropriate to creating beautiful piano sounds. Consider using such alternative phrases as *depress the keys, bring out that chord, emphasize the rhythmic energy, enter with confidence, caress the keys,* and *start on the first pulse.*

Up and Down, High and Low, In and Out

In working with children, I have become aware of the confusion they often encounter when the same word is used to describe different concepts or actions. As an adult, you know what directional words mean. However, I am never surprised when adults make incorrect associations between words and motions, just as they might have done when they were children. If you find that certain directional words confuse you, be ready to adjust your vocabulary and describe the concept with whatever words make sense to you. Watch out for the following potential confusions at the piano.

Turn the volume down usually means turning a radio dial to the left (counterclockwise) or touching a television volume control device until the sound gets softer. At the piano, though, simply moving to the left or pushing against a key will not change the volume of the sound.

At the piano, *get higher* means selecting keys located toward the right end of the keyboard. On the cello, however, the same directive tells the cellist to move the left hand down (in the direction of the floor) in order to shorten the length of the vibrating string and create a higher pitch.

When pianists move from the notes F to F♯ to G, they travel chromatically (by half steps). But in order to create that series of ascending pitches (which are getting higher), one must move from a white key to a black key (which is farther from the floor) and then back down to another white key.

Low can refer to keys in the deeper pitch register (to the left end of the keyboard). It also can refer to volume (quantity of loudness) and mean soft sounds.

Pianists refer to "F-sharp," but perhaps we should describe the note as "sharpened F"? The F♯ *sign* appears to the left of the note on the staff, but the black *key* that controls the sound of F♯ on the keyboard is to the right of the key called F.

In counting lines of a five-line staff, musicians count from the bottom up. (The fifth line of the staff is the highest line and represents a higher pitch.). In counting staves on a page, however, musicians count from the top down. The first staff is the highest one on the page. It is possible for notes on the first staff to be lower in pitch than notes on the fifth staff.

On the music staff, because of the traditional use of clef signs, octave symbols, and ledger lines, a note head that is placed lower on the staff actually may sound higher in pitch (see Example 3.5).

When you play piano duets, the person using the right half of the keyboard (the treble) is said to have the higher part. That material is also referred to as the Primo and is sometimes printed on the right-hand page of the music book. Some duet arrangements, however, may require the person playing Primo to move a hand down to keys that create lower pitches. Some editors place the Primo and Secondo parts together on the same page, so that both players can easily watch their partner's part (above or below their own).

Because pianists use a fingering system that mirrors the two hands (in this country, pianists' thumbs are always represented by the number 1), when using fingers 1 2 3 4 5 with the right hand you create an ascending pitch pattern. In contrast, fingers 1 2 3 4 5 with the left hand create a descending pitch pattern (see Example 3.6). When you use fingers

Example 3.5
Pairs of notes (higher and lower in pitch). With each pair, the first note is higher in pitch than the second note.

Example 3.6
Fingering directions: Shows notes moving in contrary motion when the same fingerings are used in right hand and left hand.

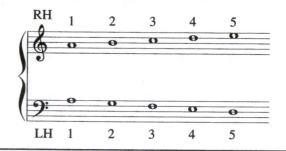

Example 3.7
Pitch directions: Shows left hand shifting location and creating ascending pitchers.

3 2 1 in the left hand, you create a pattern that rises in pitch (see Example 3.7). (To cause even more confusion, today's string players—as well as nineteenth-century piano players in England—do not number their thumb; for them, 1 represents the pointing finger.)

The words *in* and *out* are used in several different ways. They can refer to the movement of the elbow toward or away from the side of the body, the movement of the hand toward or away from the wooden fall board behind the keys, the placement of the fingers on the white and black keys, the movement of the torso toward or away from the keyboard, the movement of the foot forward on the pedal or changing position under the keyboard, and the movement of sets of notes toward or away from each other.

Too Much Pedal, Too Little Pedaling

Acoustic pianists often are accused of using *too much pedal* and creating thick, muddy sounds. This can result from depressing the pedal too far, holding it down too long, misjudging the acoustics of an unfamiliar space, or not allowing the dampers to remain on the strings long enough to stop the vibrations before raising the dampers again. Many times the unmusical effect described as *using too much pedal* actually results from *doing too little pedaling.* Pianists need to learn to monitor the depth, timing, and duration of pedal movements. Small movements with the ankle can result in significant changes in the resonance controlled by the damper pedal.

ADDITIONAL RESOURCES

Books

Banowetz, Joseph, *The Pianist's Guide to Pedaling* (Bloomington: Indiana University Press, 1985). Although this work is directed to advanced pianists, Banowetz presents clear explanations of basic concepts related to pedaling. The author includes separate chapters dealing with different pedaling traditions of keyboard composers from various stylistic periods.

Blake, Dorothy Gaynor, *First Steps in the Use of the Pedal* (Cincinnati: Willis, 1925). Written more than seventy years ago, this small volume is still in the publisher's catalogue. Underneath the left hand's part notated on the lower music staff, Blake provides a rhythm line for the right foot, showing when the damper pedal needs to be depressed and released.

Carden, Joy, *A Piano Teacher's Guide to Electronic Keyboards* (Milwaukee: Hal Leonard, 1988). A practical guide to digital pianos.

Crombie, David, *Piano: A Photographic History of the World's Most Celebrated Instrument* (San Francisco: Miller Freeman, 1995). More than 200 photos that feature more than 150 pianos.

Dubal, David, *The Art of the Piano: An Encyclopedia of Performers, Literature and Recordings* (London: I. B. Tauris & Co., 1990). Reference book divided between pianists and composers of piano music. Also includes lists of exceptional recordings.

Fine, Larry, *The Piano Book: Buying and Owning a New or Used Piano*, 4th ed. (Boston: Brookside Press, 1994). Provides helpful suggestions for purchasing and maintaining a new or used acoustic piano.

Gill, Dominic, ed., *The Book of The Piano* (Ithaca, NY: Cornell University Press, 1981). Written by twelve authors; includes extensive chapters on various periods and styles. Wonderful diagrams and pictures. Presents short biographies of many famous pianists.

Guy, Suzanne, and Donna Lacy, *The Music Box* (Lawrenceville, VA: Brunswick, 1998). A short story (historical fiction, for children of all ages) that explains how Bartolomeo Cristofori, an Italian boy who liked to explore sounds, grew up to become the inventor of the acoustic piano.

Holland, Sam, *Teaching toward Tomorrow: A Music Teacher's Primer for Using Electronic Keyboards, Computers, and MIDI in the Studio* (Loveland, OH: Debut Music Systems, 1993). Although written for piano teachers, this publication serves as a valuable resource for adult piano students.

Loesser, Arthur, *Men, Women and Pianos: A Social History of the Piano* (New York: Simon and Schuster, 1954: reprint ed. New York: Dover, 1990). Loesser presents a fascinating and highly readable study of the cultural history of musicians. Shows how the function of the piano and the roles of pianists have changed during the past three centuries.

Neely, Blake, *Piano for Dummies* (Foster City, CA: IDG Books Worldwide, 1998). An abundant resource that is very user-friendly. Includes a compact disc with musical excerpts prepared on a digital piano. Part of a series of general reference books "written for those frustrated and hard-working souls who know they aren't dummies." "But," as one reviewer noted, "a book is no substitute for a qualified human instructor."

Palmieri, Robert, and Margaret W. Palmieri, eds., *Encyclopedia of the Piano, vol. 1131.* (New York: Garland Reference Library of the Humanities, 1996). Presents more than 600 articles by seventy-seven contributors. The American pianist André Watts observed that this book will make "dedicated pianophiles feel like children let loose in the world's most fabulous candy store."

Parakkilas, ed., *Piano Roles: Three Hundred Years of Life with the Piano* (New Haven, CT: Yale University Press, 2000). A comprehensive study of people who have manufactured, composed for, or performed on pianos.

Videotapes and Digital Files

The Anatomy of a Piano: How Your Grand Piano Works (Kansas City, MO: SH Productions), videotape #54996, 75 minutes. Prepared by master piano technician, John Serkin, whose father, Rudolph Serkin, was a master musician and internationally celebrated concert pianist.

The History of the Pianoforte: A Documentary in Sound (Bloomington: Indiana University Press, 1999), videotape #47404, 90 minutes. Script prepared and narrated by Eva Badura-Skoda. Piano music performed by Paul Badura-Skoda, Malcolm Bilson, and many others playing more than thirty historic keyboard instruments from European and American museums and private collections. Traces technical developments related to controlling subtle changes of dynamics and resonance. Demonstrates how changes in keyboard technology affected composers and performers.

An Overview of Electronic Instruments (Westbury, NY: J. D. Wall Publishing, 1988), videotape, 40 minutes. Produced by Joseph Muro and Don Muro in association with Korg, USA.

The Pianist. Collection of recordings of several hundred pieces from standard piano literature. These performances can be played back using a MIDI system or the sound card of a computer. Available in disk format for Yamaha Disklavier and on compact disc (CD-ROM) for use with personal computer. It is possible to watch the score unfurl on the computer screen while listening to the playback of the musical sounds,. The technology allows the user to stop, pause, or repeat sections. It is also possible to make changes of tempo and volume (without affecting pitch) and to transpose the material from the tonality recorded originally. Volumes 1–5 include more than 800 compositions for solo piano.

There are many periodicals directed to piano students and teachers. They often provide specialized articles related to pianos and present information designed to keep readers aware of issues related to new keyboard technology. These publications include *American Music Teacher, Clavier, Keyboard Companion, Piano and Keyboard,* and *Piano Today.*

Several piano manufacturers publish magazines, catalogs, and newsletters that incorporate current information regarding their keyboard instruments. At this writing, some of the major manufacturers of digital pianos are Baldwin, Kawai, Korg, Kurzweil, Roland. Technics, and Yamaha. Some of the major manufacturers of acoustic pianos include Baldwin, Bösendorfer, Boston, Kawai American Corporation, Mason & Hamlin, Samick, Steinway & Sons, Yamaha Corporation, and Young Chang America. Most of these companies also maintain Web sites.

4 Moving Efficiently at the Piano

When I was a little girl, one of my first piano books was John Thompson's *Modern Course for the Piano: Teaching Little Fingers to Play*.[1] Later I learned that we do not really play the piano with our fingers. Instead, our hands and arms, as extensions of our bodies, deliver our fingers to the keys that function as levers in sending energy to the piano mechanism. The secret to effective piano technique is not in isolating fingers or building muscular strength but in learning how to coordinate and synchronize the parts of the body. Interdependence of muscles enables the stronger ones to help weaker ones. Constant adjustment of the body eliminates rigidity in the muscles and joints. For pianists, rather than training fingers or strengthening muscles, it is more important to refine one's hearing and become more sensitive to sounds created at the piano.

CONCEPTS TO CONSIDER

The Parts of Your Piano-Playing Mechanism

Even at an early level of piano study, it is useful to be aware of the different components of the body that we use when playing piano. These components function in coordination; adjusting one affects all.

- Fingers and hand—connected at the knuckles
- Hand and forearm—connected at the wrist
- Forearm and upper arm—connected at the elbow
- Upper arm and torso—connected at the shoulder joint
- Torso and legs—connected at the hip joint
- Legs and feet—connected at the ankle

Each of the connecting points needs to remain flexible. For pianists, flexibility is a condition to seek; rigidity is a state to avoid. Tendons function as elastic bands that link adjoining bones and stretch gently to allow easy movement. When tendons move freely and when muscles maintain an appropriate balance between contracting and extending, sufficient oxygen reaches the muscles. Then movements feel fluid and comfortable. In contrast, when tendons become trapped and swollen, when there is an imbalance between contractions and extensions, muscles do not get sufficient oxygen. When that happens, pain or injury may result.

Playing the piano should not hurt. In an earlier chapter I voiced my strong opposition to the slogan "No Pain, No Gain." I want to repeat that concern. Playing the piano, at all levels of advancement, can be a freeing experience. Playing the piano should be a source of pleasure, both physically and emotionally. Pain is a warning signal to be taken seriously.

Establishing a Balanced Body Position

"The role of notation is to change the noun 'music' into the verb 'music'."
— *Toru Takemitsu*

Music takes place in time, and sound waves travel through space. Music symbols placed on a page create an object you can touch, but music as sound results from actions that set sound waves into motion. The twentieth-century Japanese composer Toru Takemitsu (1930–1995) observed that "notation is simply the drafting of a contract to be entered into by composer and performer for the benefit of listener."[2]

The transformation of the word "music" from a noun to a verb requires mobility, not force or rigidity. Unlike a stone statue, a musical composition is not a static work. When you make music at the piano, you need to constantly move your body, adjust your relationship to the instrument, and alter the shape of your hand as it encounters various combinations of black and white keys. When you walk along a rocky beach, your feet adjust to the topography of the ground. When you play the piano, your fingers need to adjust to the topography of the keyboard.

Beginning keyboard textbooks sometimes present a picture to show students "*the correct position* to assume when you play the piano." Such pictures usually represent only one position—when the person is resting or frozen in motion. It is more helpful to view such pictures as frames from a motion picture rather than representing a single position you should maintain at all times. When you play the piano, instead of trying to lock yourself into "the correct position," seek to develop a consistent feeling of balance and readiness.

One day a very talented and conscientious student came to my studio and said, "I'm having trouble in this passage. How should I be holding my hand?" His question provided an important clue for resolving the difficulties he was having with that passage. In the process of trying to fix things, he had asked the wrong question. The question he needed to ask was, "How can I move with ease in order to play the notes in this passage?" The solution was not to identify a single, rigid position ("How should I hold my hand?") but to discover and maintain a balanced relationship while traveling with ease all over the keyboard. A slightly different question, "What's preventing me from moving with ease?," led him to a solution. The answer to the puzzle became evident when he allowed piano technique to function as an active verb, something in motion, rather than a compound noun.

Various Elements of a Balanced Body

I suggest that, during the process of establishing a comfortable, balanced piano-playing position, you develop greater awareness of the following parts of your body. Become more aware of how they interact.

Lower Body

Pelvic bones—supported by a firm, stable bench, balanced on both sit-bones.

Feet—placed firmly underneath the keyboard, on or close to the pedals, ready to press against the pedals or the floor, to support the body, and to provide balance when you need to shift from one part of the keyboard to another, right foot usually placed slightly in front of the left foot.

Knees—under the front edge of the keyboard.

Legs—bent at the knees but positioned so that your feet have room to fit comfortably in front of your knees (not folded behind them).

Upper Body

Torso—floating within the pelvic bones and ready to lean forward or backward, to shift to either the left or right, and to twist slightly in either direction.

Head—floating easily on the top of the spine (chin not sticking out).

Mouth—relaxed but closed (jaw not clenched).

Back—straight (but not stiff), spine stretched so you feel like you are sitting tall.

Chest—uplifted, ready to receive a full supply of air into the lungs.

Shoulders—relaxed (not stiff, rolled forward, or hunched up toward the ears).

Upper arms—suspended loosely from the shoulder sockets, hanging easily (and slightly away from the body).

Elbows—floating freely (not locked).

Forearm—away from the body slightly, retaining alignment between the fingertips and the elbow.

Hand

Hand—placed on the keys so that the fingertips are balanced on the finger pads and the muscles that cross the wrist at the carpal tunnel remain aligned with the muscles of the forearm, thus avoiding needless stress caused by misalignment.

Thumb—curved gently, with tip tilted slightly toward the pointing (second) finger. For ease and efficiency, lift the thumb with the muscle at the base of the thumb near the palm of your hand. (Do not lift the thumb by turning the whole hand.)

Fingers—finger pads (fleshy portion behind the fingernails) touching the keys; firm finger joints (not collapsing at either the first or second joints); fingers slightly curved, with a slight bend at each joint (not flat or straight). On the surface of the keys, the pads of the five fingers need to create a gently curved line (not a straight line).

Fingernails—trimmed short and shaped so that you will not hear clicking sounds when you touch the keys.

Knuckles—highest part of the hand, creating a firm, bony arch for the hand.

Wrists—relaxed and flexible (not locked), free to move up and down, pivot, or move the hand in small circular motions.

Pay special attention to your joints at the shoulder, elbow, and wrist. These joints need to remain buoyant, free, and flexible. Check them frequently: How do they look? How do they feel? Be sure that no tension settles into those joints. You need to be able to move them easily in several directions.

Body Alignment

To use muscles efficiently when we reach for an object, we place ourselves in close relation to the thing we want to affect. Throughout the day, we automatically make subtle adjustments in the position of our body. Before lifting a heavy suitcase, we move near it. When painting the side of the house or cleaning the gutters, we shift the ladder periodically rather than stretch beyond the range of safe balance. When playing racquetball, we try to anticipate where the ball will bounce and travel toward that spot. When embracing someone, we move within hugging distance. When playing piano, move to the keys you will need.

To play the piano with ease and efficiency, the entire body needs to remain balanced and aligned. But to maintain a balanced relationship it is necessary to adjust the body's position almost constantly. This is especially important in terms of protecting the muscles of the hand and forearm. If the natural alignment is lost and the tendons are pulled away, you will place unnecessary stress on the playing mechanism. You then risk causing serious damage to your body. Depending on the keys being used—the combination of notes, their location on the keyboard, dynamic level, and speed—the hand and arm need to be ready to adjust their position to maintain an efficient alignment that creates a balanced relationship (see Figure 4.1).[4] When the thumb (1) plays, the elbow can be nearer the body. When the outside fingers (4 and 5) are in use, the elbow needs to float freely, away from the torso.

Relationship of Body and Piano

In addition to maintaining balance within the body itself, you need to have a balanced relationship between your body and instrument. Ease

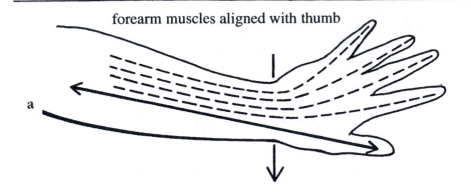

forearm muscles aligned with thumb

Figure 4.1
Alignment of muscles in the hand and arm. From *On Piano Playing, Motion, Sound, and Expression*, 1st edition, by G. Sandor © 1981. Reprinted with permission of Wadsworth, a division of Thomson Learning.

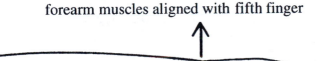

forearm muscles aligned with third finger

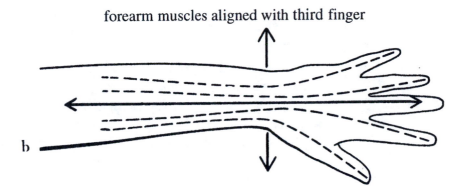

forearm muscles aligned with fifth finger

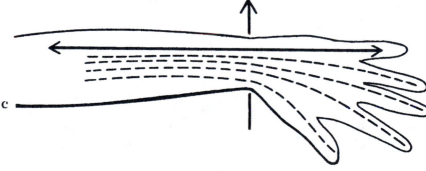

and efficiency of movement are important goals. Check the following variables.

Stability of Bench

To provide your body with a strong base of support, the piano bench must be firm so that it does not jiggle, sway, or shift in any direction. Your body needs to be placed so that your weight rests mainly on the center of the bench. Although piano benches should not wobble, piano players need to be able to shift their body weight with ease. By directing some weight to your feet and using them to balance the body, you will be free to move in any direction: to the right/treble or left/bass and toward or away from the fall board covering the keys.

Height of Bench

This is an individual matter, determined primarily by body proportion (relationship of the trunk to the upper arm) rather than by height. If you have a long trunk and short upper arms, you will need to sit on a lower bench or chair. If you have a short trunk and long upper arms, you probably will have more control if you use a higher seat. Usually the pianist's forearm needs to be about the same level as the keyboard itself.

Distance between Bench and Piano

Many early-level adult piano students constrict their movements by sitting too close to the piano keyboard. (I promise you that those eighty-eight keys will not run away!) When you play the piano, you need to be able to reach farther and deliver more energy than when you work at a computer. If you limit yourself to the physical range of a computer keyboard, you will constrict the portion of the piano keyboard you can control easily as well as the variety of pitches and dynamics you can create.

At the piano keyboard, you will need to be able to reach farther than when working at a computer keyboard.

Place the piano bench far enough away from the keyboard so that your forearm and upper arm feel free, not constrained. Usually this means that your hands will be slightly extended, reaching forward. You need enough space for your elbows to move in front of your body without being blocked by your rib cage.

Placement of Body on the Bench

Instead of sitting all the way back on the piano bench, I suggest that you sit on the front portion. To check your position, make two fists and put your hands behind you. Between your buttocks and the back edge of the bench, there should be room for your fists. You will be able to shift your body weight more easily if the front edge of the bench is not directly behind your knees.

Velocity and Power

When playing the piano, you need to correlate speed and weight (mass). When you want to achieve greater speed (more velocity), use the smallest available tool. For example, it is easier to play scales that sound fast and light when you use the muscles that control the fingers and transfer weight to the next finger rather than pumping your arms. If your teacher ever tells you, "Curve your fingers," that is a reminder to utilize the most efficient set of muscles.

In contrast, when you want to create more sound (loudness), select a different set of muscles that will enable you to combine speed and weight. For example, when playing chords that need to be loud and slow, utilize a gesture that involves the arm and torso, not just the hand or forearm. Tack hammers and sledgehammers are designed for different tasks. When playing piano, as when tapping tacks and driving spikes, select the device that works most efficiently.

Energy and Rhythmic Movement

Since most piano music is based on patterns of predictable pulses, it is helpful to relate virtually all of your keyboard sounds to rhythmic motions. It is a waste of time to punch keys in a sporadic, jerky, haphazard fashion.

> *Whatever you do at the piano should feel rhythmic and sound musical.*

The sounds you create can result from controlled energy that is correlated with predictable pulses. Even when you play only a few notes, you can place those sounds into a musical context. Establish a tempo before you depress a single key. Be aware of a continuity of pulse throughout a musical phrase.

Feel Pulses	**X**	X	**X**	X	**X**	X	**X**	X	**X**	X
Play Keys			C		E		G			

Finger Activity

Although the ability to control individual fingers is a skill you will use when playing the piano, technically it is not helpful to lift fingers extremely high. When individual fingers tap gently on a tabletop, you will become more aware of each digit. That is useful. But if you isolate individual fingers and lift them extremely high, you are apt to create noisy, percussive sounds when the finger returns to the key. That exaggerated gesture also creates unnecessary stress on the muscles.

When you walk, your feet remain near the surface of the floor or ground, and you simply transfer your weight from the heel to the toe of one foot and then to the heel and toe of the other foot. (If you have ever walked through a field filled with thick mud or deep snow, you probably have experienced the frustration of needing to pull your feet out of the mud or snow before taking the next step.) When moving with ease, you do not waste energy lifting the previous foot. After one foot makes contact with the ground, there is a momentary push-off or springing motion. The completion of one step actually prepares the body to take the next step. At the keyboard, your fingers make similar motions when transferring weight from one fingertip to another. As that happens, you may feel like your fingers are dancing across the keyboard.

Defensive Posture

The body's defensive posture was once needed for protection against dangerous wild animals. Such a posture leads to elevated shoulders and tension in the neck and shoulders. When the shoulder bone is lifted, the elbow tends to move closer to the body. Although that automatic response protects the heart and lungs and helps you make a fist and punch an aggressor, raising the shoulders makes it more difficult to play the piano with ease. When the elbow is pressed against the body, arm motions are constrained and interfere with a natural alignment of the hand and forearm muscles. The result is that it is more difficult to produce rich, full piano sounds. Playing the piano does not require defensive responses. When you sit on a piano bench, you are not at risk of attack from tigers. When you establish and achieve appropriate piano goals, the problem of defensive posture is minimized.

> *Let your shoulders remain relaxed (not hunched).*
> *Allow your elbows to be away from the body.*

Oxygen

In order for muscles to function efficiently, they need to receive a sufficient supply of oxygen. Muscles work in pairs, shortening (contracting) and lengthening (stretching) in alternation. When the muscles receive enough oxygen, they can function for long periods of time. When they do not receive sufficient oxygen, however, they tighten, work less efficiently, cramp, and may cause pain.

Besides needing to deliver oxygen to your upper body, you also need to send oxygen to your brain. Singers, wind players, and brass players have to breathe regularly because they use currents of air to create vibrations in their vocal cords, reeds, or metal tubing. String players, percussionists, and keyboard players, however, actually are capable of creating instrumental sounds even when they do not breathe regularly.

Several semesters in succession, I heard the piano exams of a talented student who would begin securely but, after playing a few minutes, always encountered serious performance problems. One summer when her teacher was going to be away for several weeks, the young woman and her teacher asked me to schedule some lessons with her. During the time we worked together, I realized that she experienced the same basic problem with every piece. Pages 1 and 2 were fine, but on about the third page she fell apart—even at her lessons. If she took a short break, however, and then started on page 3, she played that material with ease but ran into problems two pages later. Eventually I noticed that this student was in the habit of holding her breath when she concentrated. Whenever she started playing, she stopped breathing regularly. It became clear that although she worked hard, knew the music, and could demonstrate technical control of each and every section, when her brain was deprived of oxygen (that is, after she started playing and stopped breathing) it became almost impossible for her to perform a long piece with comfort. She had blamed her performance problems on nervousness and had sought to minimize her performance anxieties. She discovered, though, that when she took a breath at the end of each musical phrase (in response to thinking the melody, singing, or counting aloud), she *did* breathe regularly and most of her so-called technical problems disappeared.

Excessive Tension

When you become aware of tightness in your body, contract your muscles or move your joints. You can do that before and even during a piece, between phrases and during rests. If your body feels constrained, frozen in one position, move it gently, turning first in one direction and then in the other. Do not try to make your muscles do something. Instead, allow muscles to stretch. Permit them to relax.

Singers and wind players know that they must take a breath before they begin a musical phrase. Conductors provide their musicians with a small but energetic upbeat before giving the downbeat. Similarly, piano students need to learn to let their wrists breathe and to create preparatory motions before the start of a phrase. When you see someone playing piano with a tight, locked wrist, you probably will hear harsh, ugly sounds. Words such as *elastic, cushioned, resilient, flexible, synchronized,* and *supple* often are used to describe the playing mechanism of artistic pianists who create beautiful piano sounds.

ACTIVITIES TO EXPLORE

ACTIVITY 4.1   *Finding the Moving Parts*

Observe the ways your body can move.

1. Notice how the parts feel at their points of connection.
     Wiggle your fingers: with your other hand, touch the knuckles.
     Wave your hand: touch the wrist.
     Pump your forearm: with your other hand, touch your elbow at the funny bone.
     Lift your entire arm as a single unit: touch the top of your shoulder.
     Bend your torso: put your hands on your hipbones.
     Lift your legs: touch your hipbones.
     Kick with your foot: touch your kneecap.
     Rotate your foot: touch your ankle bone.
     Wiggle your toes: feel your foot at the base of your toes.
2. Experiment by moving various parts of your body at various speeds. What does it feel like when you wiggle your fingers quickly? How does it feel when you try to move your entire arm at the same speed?
3. Set the metronome at M.M. $\quartno = 60$. Isolate different parts of your body. Then, while maintaining a steady pulse, move each body unit rhythmically—tap a single finger or the entire hand, knock with the fist, move your forearm, swing your full arm, step, and jump.
4. Experiment with different speeds. Change the metronome setting and determine a comfortable tempo to use with each unit of your body.

ACTIVITY 4.2 *Shaping Your Hand*

For greatest ease and efficiency, the position of your hand at rest should be slightly curved, with firm finger joints, a strong bridge created by the knuckles, and a very flexible wrist. Try each of the following suggestions for finding an appropriate hand position. Identify the suggestion that is most useful to you in establishing a balanced hand position.

1. Place your hand over your kneecap. Let your kneecap provide a mold for shaping your hand. Move your hand to the keyboard, retaining a strongly defined arch.
2. Place your hand on the top of your head, separating the fingers slightly. Without changing the shape of your hand, move your hand to the keyboard as a single unit.
3. While you stand comfortably with your arms hanging loosely and your hands cupped gently, let your fingertips touch the side of your leg. Without changing the shape of your hand, move it to the keyboard.
4. While seated at a table, place your entire arm on the wood. Begin with all fingers stretched out, flat against the wood. Gradually slide your fingertips toward the palm of your hand, creating a bony arch at the knuckles. Notice that the fingertips will create a slightly curved line (not a straight line). Let your thumb move close to the pointing finger. Without changing the shape of your hand, move it to the keyboard.
5. With one hand, make a fist. Place the fist under the other hand and use the knuckles to mold the other hand. Without changing the shape of the hand being molded, move it to the keyboard.
6. Take a regular chicken egg and place it in the palm of your hand with the larger end of the egg nearer your thumb.
7. Place all five fingertips on a flat surface. Lift fingers 3 and 4. Position a pencil underneath those fingers, supporting it with fingers 2 and 5.
8. Pick up a pencil and hold it vertically, with the tips of all five fingers (2-3-4-5 side by side, along one side; 1 balanced on the opposite side). Turn your hand so that the palm is down. Notice the bridge created by your knuckles. When you move your hand to the keyboard, you will need to move the thumb out from under fingers 2 and 3, but maintain your strong arch.

ACTIVITY 4.3 *Finding Your Thumb's Muscle*

1. Place your entire forearm on a flat surface, such as a table or desktop or piano fall board. Shape the hand so that the five fingertips are in a curved, balanced position.
2. Using fingers 2 and 3 as a single unit, tap the rhythm of an energetic song such as "Yankee Doodle."
3. Using fingers 2, 3, 4, and 5 as a single unit, repeat the song.

Example 4.1
Diminished Seventh chord

4. Using just the thumb as your unit, repeat the song. The motion should involve lifting and dropping the thumb with the muscle at the base of the thumb. Watch that muscle. Do *not* turn the entire forearm in order to lift your thumb. The tip of the thumb should be near the tip of the second finger, curving toward your little finger.

ACTIVITY 4.4   *Aligning Your Fingers and Forearm*

1. Work with the notes C, D-sharp, F-sharp, A, and C to create a diminished seventh chord. Place one finger on each key (RH: 1-2-3-4-5. LH: 5-4-3-2-1; see Example 4.1).
2. Beginning with either hand, play one note at a time. Use slow, separate, descending arm gestures and listen for full, rich, separate (staccato) sounds. Allow the weight of the arm to drop onto each finger pad, so that you feel centered on each key. Notice where the pad of the finger is on the key. Check the alignment: Is there an unbroken line from the fingertip, across the wrist, through the center of the forearm, and then continuing all the way to the shoulder? Does your fingertip feel like it is connected to your shoulder? *Note*: As you move from fingers 1 to 5, your elbow will shift away from the side of your body slightly, in order to maintain the alignment of the muscles.
3. Play pairs of notes (C/D♯, D♯/F♯, F♯/A, A/C) together, as solid intervals (see Example 4.2). Notice how you shift the alignment of the hand and forearm as you use different pairs of fingers. Maintain the feeling of being balanced between two fingers, as if you were standing firmly on two feet rather than balancing yourself on only one foot.

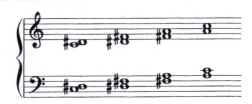

Example 4.2
Pairs of notes from a
Diminished Seventh chord

Example 4.3
Parallel sixth intervals in the right hand. With this chart, white note heads represent white keys; black note heads represent black keys.

ACTIVITY 4.5 *Adjusting to the Keyboard's Topography*

1. Play a series of solid sixths (RH, with fingers 1 and 5: [F/D, F♯/D♯, G/E, A♭/F, A/F♯, B♭/G, B/G♯, C/A, C♯/A♯, D/B, E♭/C, E/C♯, F/D], moving up chromatically (by half steps). With each new pair of notes (always using fingers 1 and 5), shift the hand slightly in order to maintain a sense of balance (see Example 4.3; in this figure, white keys are indicated with white note heads and black keys are indicated with black note heads).

2. Using the left hand, play a series of descending sixths [D/B, D♭/B♭, C/A, B/G♯, B♭/G, A/F♯, A♭/F, G/E, G♭/E♭, F/D, E/C♯, E♭/C, D/B], moving down chromatically (by half steps; see Example 4.4). With each pair of notes, shift the hand to a new balanced position.

3. Combine hands, playing parallel sixths with both hands. *Note*: By beginning with both fifth fingers on a D and moving outward in contrary motion, you ensure that the color patterns of these pairs of sixths mirror each other. Continue moving out for two octaves. With each pair, adjust the balance so that the middle of the hand remains aligned with the forearm. Notice when the thumb moves closer to the fall board and when the fifth finger moves closer to the fall board.

4. Within the interval of a sixth, add one note. RH: A added to F and D creates an inversion of a D minor triad; LH: G added to D and B creates an inversion of a G major triad (see Example 4.5). Using these three-note chords, play a series of triads, moving out by half steps. With each chromatic shift of the entire hand, adjust the alignment as necessary to maintain a sense of balance with all three fingers.

ACTIVITY 4.6 *Strengthening Your Fingers' First Joints*

When you play piano, the finger joint nearest the nail needs to be firm—that is, it should not collapse easily. The following isometric exercise has helped students of all ages. Repeat it away from the piano, several times each day.

1. Using one hand, let the tip of your thumb touch the tip of each finger in succession: 1 2, 1 3, 1 4, 1 5. Press the fingertips against each other firmly as you create *O* shapes, such as doughnuts, knotholes, or OK signs.

2. With the other hand, tap gently against the first joint.

Example 4.4
Parallel sixth intervals in the left hand.

Example 4.5
Inverted triads.

3. Then press slowly and more firmly against the first joint; do not poke at the joint or push it hard. To keep the joint from collapsing, press the fingertips against each other firmly.
4. Sing a familiar energetic song, such as "Yankee Doodle" or "Jingle Bells." As you sing the melody, tap the rhythm quickly and lightly with your fingertips—that is, doughnuts created by various pairings of the thumb with another finger.

THOUGHTS ABOUT WORDS

Comfortable, Natural, Familiar

The words *comfortable*, *natural*, and *familiar* are not always interchangeable. I have noticed that after someone experiences something repeatedly, it becomes *familiar*. Then it may be described as feeling *comfortable* and be thought of as *natural* even when the body is out of balance and the muscles are not working in coordination. Although the route you usually take to work seems familiar, it might not be the safest or most efficient way to get there. Do not let the familiarity of a gesture prevent you from exploring other ways of moving that might result in more efficient motions and greater comfort at the piano.

Evenness of Sound, Evenness in Time

The concept of evenness is problematic for many piano players. As an expressive pianist, you will need to make a distinction between *evenness of sound* (volume) and *evenness in time* (space). Evenness in volume and time represent two totally different effects. If you speak with no vocal inflections ("WHERE ARE YOU GO-ING?"), you will sound like a robot. If you play with no gradations of volume, your playing will sound mechanical. Whenever you play a series of notes of the same rhythmic value, it will sound more musical if the dynamics are inflected (shaped very slightly). Basic evenness in time is an important goal for pianists at all levels. Absolute evenness in dynamics rarely creates a musically satisfying effect.

The following row of *X*s represents sounds that are even in size but not in space:

X   X   X   X X X   X   X

The following row of *X*s represents sounds that are even in space but not in size:

X   x   x   **X**   **X**   x   X   x   X   X   x

The following rows of *X*s represent sounds that are even in space and also in size:

X   X   X   X   X   X   X   X   X   X   X   X

x   x   x   x   x   x   x   x   x   x   x   x

x   x   x   x   x   x   x   x   x   x   x   x

Most musical playing creates a sense of regular pulses but also incorporates very slight gradations of sound. This results in expressive groupings of sound rather than an uninterrupted series of predictable beeps. The following group of *X*s represents a triple meter (such as $\frac{3}{4}$ or $\frac{3}{8}$ time signatures):

X   x   x   **X**   x   x   **X**   x   x   **X**

while the next set represents duple meter (such as $\frac{2}{4}$ or $\frac{2}{2}$ time signatures):

X   x   **X**   x   **X**   x   **X**   x   **X**

When a series of pitches is exactly the same in volume, it sounds mechanical, unmusical, and nonexpressive. This sort of evenness is sometimes described as "note-y" playing, and it conveys the emotional level of a robot. I urge you to avoid that aspect of evenness in your playing.

Relax!

Keep your fingers curved. Keep your elbows out. Don't let the finger joints collapse. Remember to use the correct fingering. Sit up straight. Keep counting. Don't stop! Keep your eyes on the music. Maintain that articulation. RELAX! "Relax *Relax*. RELAX. I *told* you to RELAX!" Now there's a message guaranteed to create tension in any person, adult early-level piano student or not. As we discussed earlier, the goal for musical pianists is not to maintain a specific position but to keep their body in balance with itself and in alignment with the instrument.

When speaking to yourself, consider using supportive, neutral directives, such as:

Allow yourself	Discover
Notice	Feel
Listen for	Balance
Find	Explore
Consider	Observe
Float	Enable yourself
Choose	Select
Experience	Imagine
Enjoy	Be aware of

ADDITIONAL RESOURCES

Book and Article

Mastroianni, Thomas, "Technique: Born Free," in *Piano Quarterly*, No. 134 (summer 1982), 56–59. A succinct summary of basic concepts of healthy piano playing.

Newman, William S., *The Pianist's Problems: A Modern Approach to Efficient Practice and Musicianly Performance*, 4th ed. (New York: Harper, 1950; reprint ed. New York: Da Capo Press, 1984). A compassionate and insightful book directed to adult piano students, both amateur and professional. Originally published more than half a century ago, Newman's book is available in many libraries and as a reprint.

Videotapes

Freeing the Caged Bird: Developing Well-coordinated, Injury-preventive Piano Technique (Winston-Salem, NC: Wingsound, 1996), videotape, 150 minutes. A video guide written and produced by Barbara Lister-Sink. Explores body and piano mechanisms, considers myths and mysteries of piano technique, describes potentially harmful technical habits, and presents a five-step training program for developing healthy coordination at the piano.

Nelita True at Eastman. Technique through Listening (Kansas City, MO, SH Productions, 1991), videotape #501. Volume 3 of a series of four videotapes filmed before an audience of piano teachers. True emphasizes the importance of students monitoring their sounds and gestures by listening carefully to the sounds they create.

YOUR NOTES

5 Developing Musicality

CHAPTER OUTLINE

"But," you say, "I'm only a beginner! I'm just starting. How can I sound like a musician? How can I make my playing sound musical? Aren't you expecting too much? Doesn't that have to happen much later?" With confidence, I offer you my answers: "No. I am not expecting too much. No! You do *not* have to wait until much later in order to sound musical."

The tale is told of the little girl who performed her piano exam piece with great confidence. She played no wrong notes or rhythms, but she also demonstrated no sense of musicality. Later, when the evaluator spoke with her and suggested that some slight variations in her loud and soft sounds would have made the note-perfect piece sound more musical, the child responded cheerfully, "Expression is extra, and Mummy can't afford that." But musical expression is not extra. Expression presents the essence of music, and I believe that playing expressively is an essential priority for all musicians, not a luxury reserved for a few.

CONCEPTS TO CONSIDER

Early-Level Musicians

Musicianship is not something to tack onto your piano playing after you learn to depress certain keys in a certain sequence and move in specific ways. Musical playing does not result automatically because of studying piano a certain length of time. In fact, some people take piano lessons for decades and still approach the piano unmusically. However, pianists of any age who are studying early-level materials can sound musical. Even during your earliest phases of piano study, you should be able to enjoy hearing yourself play. True musicianship starts at the very beginning, and ultimately all musical training is *ear*-training.

The ability to show kindness is not a trait tucked inside a diploma and handed to students on Graduation Day. Becoming a sensitive, kind person is a gradual process that begins in childhood. Becoming a sensitive, musical person also is a gradual process that needs to begin early. If you can say three words (such as "I love you") meaningfully, with vocal inflections (slight gradations of sound), you will be able to play three notes musically.

> *If you can speak expressively, you will be able to play expressively.*

When you were a child learning to speak, you listened to others, imitated them, babbled (experimented in making various sounds), and organized your vocal sounds in order to communicate (see Activity 5.1, "Speaking Expressively"). To make sense out of sounds, you grouped ideas into units. You learned to vary pitch, making some syllables a bit higher or lower than others. You learned to vary intensity, making some words a bit louder than others. You learned to pace your words and to modify the quality of your voice, creating sounds that represented the dogs and cats, frogs and bats, hogs and rats in your storybooks. Whether you lived in Brooklyn or Boston, Seattle or Savannah, Paris or Peoria you learned to pronounce certain words the same way as the people around you. You became aware of your own family's responses to subtle aspects of language and behavior. You learned how people reacted to certain messages (such as "No!" and "Stop!" and "Hot!" and "I won't!") and discovered the magical power of some words (like "Thank you!" and "Pleeeze?").

Now, as an adult creating sounds at the piano, you can do exactly the same thing you did a long time ago, when learning to talk. To make sense out of musical ideas, you can group sounds into meaningful units and vary the dynamic inflections. How will you learn to do this? The same way you learned to speak. By listening to yourself, listening to others, repeating what you hear, noticing how other people react to what you do, and experimenting with your keyboard instrument. Gradually you will decide what sounds you want to emphasize and what sounds to keep in the background. You will learn to create different kinds of sounds, make loud and soft sounds, play notes faster or slower, group tones in meaningful patterns, give special importance to specific sounds, and emphasize some sounds by surrounding them with silence.

> *All sounds are important, but not all sounds need to receive the same degree of emphasis: alllettersareimportantbut notalllettersneedtoreceive thesamedegreeofemphasis.*

Listening Carefully

Once upon a time (or so I was told), there was an adult student who practiced every day and went to all his lessons but made very little progress. As weeks went on, his playing continued to sound hesitant, his range of tone colors was limited and lacked vitality, and his results were bland and unmusical. At lesson after lesson, the teacher tried to help the student develop a greater sense of musical continuity and create richer, fuller sounds. The results were frustrating to both the student and his teacher. One day this student mentioned something about turning on the radio before he practiced. "Why in the world would you want to do that?" his teacher asked in amazement. Responding with pride and with the tone of a responsible citizen, the student explained, "Well, I certainly wouldn't want my neighbors to have to hear what I sound like when I practice!" The irony of this tale is that learning to play the piano musically requires careful listening (even when your neighbors are home). Unless you monitor the sounds you make and experiment with ways to move at the instrument, you will not learn to utilize the piano as a musical instrument.

But if, when you practice, you keep asking yourself the three basic questions discussed in chapter 1, you will gather valuable information that will help you become a more musical person:

- How does it sound?
- How does it feel?
- How does it look?

When playing piano, as in speaking, you can create sounds that are timid or tired, confident or cranky, bouncy or blustery, sullen or soothing. You can utilize the piano to express your emotions.

Characteristics of Musical Performances

Why does one person sit down at the piano and sound musical, but another person plays the same notes in the same sequence and sounds unmusical? What does one performer do at the instrument that grabs your attention and squeezes your heart? Why are there some performers you really would prefer not to hear again? Why can two performances be clocked at the same speed and yet Performance A has excitement and vitality and Performance B seems dull and plodding? What are some of the common characteristics found in performances that seem musical?

Inevitability

When I hear a fine performance, everything seems *inevitable*: Everything fits; all the musical decisions make sense to me and seem to come from an understanding and love of the music itself. The performer has control of the instrument; there are no disturbing surprises. But a fine performance is not *predictable*. That is, it does not sound mechanical, dull, or humdrum. When I hear a performance that is merely predictable, my response is probably, "Oh, my! Why keep listening to this? I already know what's going to happen." In contrast, when listening to a performance that is musical, I find myself asking, "What will happen next?" I want to experience that musician's insights, to hear what that person will share.

> *When I hear a performance that is musical, I want to keep listening.*

Integrity

Another characteristic I always find in a musically satisfying performance is integrity, or honesty. As I listen, I am convinced that the performer is presenting valid musical ideas (his or her own or those of the composer). When someone offers you the best that is available, that represents a special sharing. Skaters don't fall down on purpose. Receivers don't plan to drop passes in the end zone. Performers don't make mistakes intentionally. They share their best efforts and do the very best they can at that time in their life.

Conviction

In a satisfying musical performance, I hear pitches that match my pitch memory (if I have heard the piece before) or coincide with my harmonic expectations (if the piece is new to me). I am not jostled by the appearance of wrong choices of either pitch or rhythm. Curiously, though, fine musicians often can play a wrong note—the wrong pitch or the right pitch arriving at the wrong time—and then follow it with other notes that, in retrospect, make everything sound OK, even the mis-taken note. Fine musicians can turn a wrong pitch into an expressive *appoggiatura* or a wrong rhythm into an exciting *syncopation.* When there are surprises, they are presented with such conviction that I am confident that the performer is playing a valid version of what the composer wanted us to hear.

Expressiveness

In a musical performance, the performer conveys the message, "Listen! This is great stuff, and I want you to hear it. I've discovered something wonderful, and now I want to share it with you. My life has been enriched, and I would like to enrich your life as well." The performing musician risks not being heard—or being heard and rejected—but the musician feels something and is willing to risk sharing those feelings. This attitude is evident whether the person performs at Carnegie Hall for hundreds of ticket-buying listeners or plays alone or with one other person in the room.

Organization of Musical Sounds

Not all poetry rhymes. Not all poetry is metric, with singsongy word patterns (such as *JACK and JILL went* **UP** *the HILL* . . .). Not all music is metric, based on predictable pulse patterns. Music can be rhythmic even if it is not metric. Not all music is grounded on a harmonic system that has a single pitch functioning as a tonal center. Music can be organized in many ways besides a formula based on two or three chords. At various times in history and various places around the world, people have created and valued music that is neither metric nor tonal. Our own cultural customs are not the only meaningful and honorable ones. Having established that caveat, I want to share some observations about music that is metric and tonal. If you understand these musical characteristics, then when you do experience nonmetric or nontonal music you also will understand it better.

Most of the music presented in our time and country—that is, at the start of the twenty-first century, in the United States—is both tonal and metric. It is grounded on long-established and predictable relationships of pitch and duration. It is likely that most of the music you encounter, either in performance or in print, developed out of Western European musical traditions prevalent during the seventeenth to twentieth centuries. The following information deals with music that is characterized by a strong tonal center and a regularity of pulse.

Creating Musical Templates

When I travel to a new city, I find it helpful to obtain information related to the geographic and temporal aspects of that place. I look at a map and determine where I am in relation to geographic sites such as rivers or mountains. I create for myself a sense of stability by learning which direction I face when I leave the hotel. I observe facts regarding that city's system of numbering streets. I feel more at home when I know where I am. In becoming accustomed to a new environment, I want to know what time zone I am in and whether I will need to adjust my watch to match local time.

For musicians dealing with tonal and metric music, just as for travelers exploring new cities, it is helpful to be aware of geographic and temporal aspects of the musical environment. I use the term *geographic aspects of music* to refer to the location of the keys on the piano keyboard; these include specific pitches used in a piece, topographic landmarks, and ways that various notes relate to each other. I suggest the term *temporal aspects of music* to include organizing procedures related to timed events such as time signatures, note values, metric patterns, and rhythms. At the computer or drafting board, a template helps us compile and organize information. It provides a procedural plan and reminds us of what we need to incorporate in a report or design. At the piano, geographic (harmonic) and temporal (rhythmic) templates help musicians be aware of predictable patterns of sounds that relate to each other in terms of pitch or time.

There are many resources that explain various harmonic and rhythmic systems. Therefore, I am not including that information in this book. Instead, I simply want to emphasize the value of obtaining such basic information even during the early stages of piano study. If you understand ways in which musical sounds relate to each other, many aspects of learning and playing music will become easier. As a result of studying music theory, you will accumulate many shortcuts for learning piano music.

Aspects Related to Pitch

In a musically satisfying performance of tonal music, the pitches maintain a predictable relationship with each other. With a small group of pitches (sometimes fewer than eight different pitches for an entire piece), the sounds establish one specific tonal center, move away from it, and then return to it. One particular set of pitches, forming a chord, functions as home base. Other chords interact with that tonal center in predictable ways.

The relationship of pitches within a musical system of tonality can be compared with a family that might include eight individuals who are related to one another by birth or marriage. The most basic interactions among those family members (perhaps including mother, father, oldest child, infant, paternal grandparents, and maternal aunt and uncle) will remain constant whether they live in Illinois or move to New Hampshire or take a vacation in North Carolina. When anthropologists are able to identify individuals and determine each one's role within a family unit, it becomes easier for them to observe and understand personal interactions. Within the social group, each individual functions in different roles whether interacting with a parent, grandparent, spouse, child, sibling, or other relative. All the family members are important, but their interactions will be different from those of eight randomly selected, unrelated individuals.

Most of the music heard in the United States is grounded on a harmonic template. If you are aware of certain predictable relationships between pitches, you can better understand how notes relate to each other. Basic harmonic relationships will remain the same whether a tonal piece is in the key of C major or moves to the key of A-flat major. When you can anticipate certain patterns within a piece, it is easier to read quickly and to learn new music. And when you encounter passages that do not meet your expectations, you can enjoy those surprises and take delight in musical jokes. In describing harmonic templates, musicians use words such as *scales, chords, intervals, inversions, pitch tendencies, tonic, dominant,* and *leading tone.* Explorers use stars and compasses to navigate and find their way home safely. Musicians, when exploring tonal music, remain aware of the location of notes in relation to the tonal center (the home tone).

Tonal music identifies a single pitch, called the tonic, as the tonal center for the music. In tonal music, the tonic provides a sense of stability. Within a specified group of pitches (a scale), different tones and sets of pitches (chords) have tendencies to move up or down. Most tonal music establishes a tonality, moves away from the tonic, explores other harmonic areas, and eventually returns home (reestablishing the tonic). Other chords represent varying degrees of dissonance and instability. Dissonance is usually reinforced with slightly louder sounds; consonance is emphasized by gentler sounds.

Complex chains of chords characterize much of the tonal music we hear regularly. Musicians learn to anticipate where a single pitch or a specific chord probably will move (resolve). When the expected resolution is not heard, that moment is perceived as a surprise and may be described as a deceptive cadence. Sections of music are set off by moments of repose (cadences) created by predictable chord patterns. Through the nineteenth and twentieth centuries, composers used more and more dissonance. In the twentieth century, some composers chose to negate tonality completely, avoiding traditional Western European sound patterns and assigning equal importance to all pitches.

It is useful to be aware of certain aspects of pitch organization. When you approach a piece of tonal music, consider these questions:

- What is the tonal center?
- How is the sense of tonality established?

- What pitches and chords are used?
- What chords function as tonic (I) and dominant (V)?
- What closing patterns (cadences) are used?

Aspects Related to Time

In a musically satisfying performance of metric music, the rhythm of the sounds is grounded on a regularity of pulse. The rhythm incorporates a consistency of pulses and predictable groupings and divisions of those pulses. It provides some flexibility, however, allowing a slight stretching of the pulse before a new section or a little extra time to emphasize an expressive moment within a musical phrase.

As I suggested at the opening of this chapter, things that happen in musical performances sound inevitable but not predictable. Performances that sound musical create a balance between rhythmic stability and flexibility. With metric music, the traditional notation of rhythm is based on the expectation that musical sounds will be imposed on a predictable pattern of regular pulses (see Activity 5.2, "Feeling Pulses and Pulse Divisions").

Most of the music you hear is associated with a grid of timed events that involve steady pulses. Frequently those pulses are grouped in regular sets of two or three pulses. In today's standard system of music notation, any note value (such as quarter, half, or eighth) can serve as the basic pulse unit. Although the quarter note most often functions as the pulse value, a statement such as "the quarter note gets one count" is true only when that is the value assigned to the quarter note. "The candy bar costs ten cents" is true only when that is the price assigned to the candy bar. At a movie theater or in a vending machine on the turnpike, the same candy bar might be priced at twenty-five cents or even half a dollar. What remains constant is the relationship of values. Whatever price has been established for one candy bar, it is reasonable to expect that the merchant or machine will charge twice as much for two of the same candy bars. In our system of music notation (as in our monetary system), we expect that certain relationships will be constant. Two quarters (twenty-five cents) always have the same financial value as one half-dollar coin (fifty cents). Similarly, two quarter notes (♩ ♩) always represent the same temporal duration as one half note (𝅗𝅥).

Musical playing that has rhythmic stability and flexibility incorporates:

- Regularity of pulse
- Consistent subdivisions of pulse
- Predictable groupings of pulses
- Slight gradations of sound (volume)

It is possible to have some but not all of those characteristics in a performance.

Regularity of Pulse

It is quite possible to say "one two three one two three" without having the words coincide with a regular series of pulses. Instead of presenting sounds represented by evenly spaced numbers, such as:

$$1 \quad 2 \quad 3 \quad 1 \quad 2 \quad 3$$

the sounds could be unsteady and irregular, such as:

$$1\ 2 \quad 3\ 1 \qquad 2 \qquad 3\ 1\ 2 \qquad\qquad 3$$

Consistent Subdivisions of Pulse

It is possible to have regular pulses and appropriate grouping of pulses but for the rhythm to seem unstable because the subdivisions of the pulse are not consistent. Instead of feeling four predictable subdivisions for each pulse, such as:

$$1\ x\ x\ x\ 2\ x\ x\ x\ 3\ x\ x\ x\ 1\ x\ x\ x\ 2\ x\ x\ x\ 3\ x\ x\ x\ 1$$
$$1 \qquad 2 \qquad 3 \qquad 1 \qquad 2 \qquad 3 \qquad 1$$

the performer might rush through some of the time units and then stretch others excessively, thus creating an irregular and unstable rhythmic grid, such as:

$$1\ \text{xxx} \quad 2\text{x}\ \text{xx}3 \quad \text{x x} \quad \text{x}1\text{xxx} \quad 2 \quad \text{x}\ \text{x}\ \text{x} \quad 3\text{x}\ \text{x x} \quad 1$$
$$1 \qquad 2 \quad 3 \qquad 1 \qquad 2 \qquad\qquad 3 \qquad 1$$

Predictable Groupings of Pulses

By emphasizing certain pulses, we will perceive them as predictable sets. The most common pulse groupings in music are sets of two or three pulses, but pulses can be grouped by any number and combined in different ways. For example:

2:	1	2	1	2	1	2	1	2	1		
2+3:	1	2	1	2	3	1	2	1	2	3	1
4:	1	2	3	4	1	2	3	4	1		
3:	1	2	3	1	2	3	1	2	3	1	
2+2+3:	1	2	1	2	1	2	3	1	2	1	

Slight Gradations of Sounds

The amount of dynamic stress to give to rhythmic pulses is a matter of style and taste. Ultimately that choice reflects the performer's sensitivity and musicianship. Either of the following dynamic schemes might be appropriate, depending on various factors such as tempo, texture, mood, facility, and style:

1	2	3	1	2	3	1	2	3	1
1	2	3	**1**	2	3	**1**	2	3	**1**

The process of deciding how much intensity to give a note is similar to that of deciding how much seasoning to put into a recipe. Specific measurements given in a recipe book may help you avoid total disasters, but expert cooks season food to taste. The same guideline applies to musicians. In fact, Carl Philipp Emanuel Bach (1714–1788) and other eighteenth-century musicians wrote and talked a lot about the importance of helping students develop a sense of *bon goût* (musical taste).

Controlling Available Options

There really are only three things you can do when playing the acoustic piano to control the sound of a notated composition. Once you decide which keys to depress—representing the composer's notes in a piece of piano music—you only have the option of making those sounds (1) louder or softer, (2) longer or shorter, or (3) more or less resonant (lifting the dampers in order to increase the acoustical resonance of the instrument). With digital pianos, you also can push various tone control buttons to access digitized sounds (such as those that simulate the sounds of electric piano, harpsichord, choir, marimba, and applause).

> *Pianists can vary a tone's intensity, duration, and resonance.*

Dynamics

In a musical performance on acoustic piano, dynamics are the primary resource for enhancing various musical aspects such as harmonic contrasts, sectional divisions, changes of texture, and emphasis of certain tones.

> *Pianists can control dynamics three ways: horizontally, vertically, and sectionally.*

Horizontally—shaping a melodic line by using gradations of sound
Vertically—layering various pitches (creating a sense of texture, balancing melody with accompaniment, defining foreground and background material)
Sectionally—creating contrasts of dynamic levels that coincide with changes of musical material

Outstanding musicians develop a huge palette of sounds that they can incorporate at will (see Activity 5.3, "Pacing Changes of Dynamics"). Their musicianship enables them to select a specific color to use for a specific moment in the music. Just as painters learn to create subtle differences in hues and to use minute touches of color for special effects, musicians learn to create a wide range of tonal colors. Visual artists may begin with black, white, and three primary colors (red, yellow, and blue), but they are trained to create an infinite number of different hues. Student musicians may begin with just a few dynamic contrasts (*piano, forte, mezzo forte*), but they, too, learn to create an unlimited number of subtle distinctions. Furthermore, even if a composer indicates that a certain passage is to sound *pianissimo* (to be performed within an extremely soft range), shaping and voicing still are important. Even when an orchestral conductor wants to create the total effect of an entire orchestra playing *pianissimo,* certain players will need to play some tones louder than others. Not every tone should have the same degree of *pianissimo*-ness. It is appropriate to create gradations of intensity within the general environment of very, very soft sounds. Even when you whisper to a dear one, you can emphasize certain words: "I *love* you with all my *heart* and *soul.*"

When I walk in the woods or examine a natural setting, the only straight lines or unvarying colors I see are those of manufactured objects, such as buildings, brick paths, telephone poles, beer cans, and candy wrappers. Natural objects always have some variability and flexibility in shape, size, or color. When you look at a tree trunk or stone wall or bright flower, you will see slight gradations in the shade and/or intensity of the colors. If you examine fifty leaves from the same tree, you will find that each leaf shares identifying traits, but no two leaves will be exactly the same in shape, size, or color. Artistic musicians, like sensitive visual artists, continually try to expand their color palette by increasing the variety and subtlety of their options. In a performance of piano music, dynamics are the most important tools in clarifying relationships between notes. Dynamic gradations can create the impression that every tone is either going toward or coming from other tones. Nothing remains static, but the Now—the immediacy of a moment—always seems to capture the attention of a fine musician. At any given moment, each single tone is considered in relation to the sounds before and after as well as the tones above and below. The challenge to musicians is to create relationships between concurrent or consecutive sounds. Your sensitivity will help you make decisions related to proportions of sound. Very few recipes call for exactly the same quantity of each ingredient. Can you imagine the taste of a cake made with equal quantities of salt, oil, milk, baking power, flour, vanilla, and eggs? When playing the piano, as in baking, selecting an appropriate proportion of ingredients is crucial to the success of the project.

Controlling vertical elements of music is comparable to lighting a dramatic production. Even when several people are onstage at the same time, lighting technicians direct spotlights to different parts of the stage. When characters move, their actions are enhanced by the lights focused on them. Pianists can do the same thing when playing several notes at the same time. When you play several notes simultaneously, ask yourself, "Which notes are now placed stage front and which ones represent supporting characters standing in a corner?" Just as film directors have camera technicians zoom in on a specific person or a single object, fine pianists can direct listeners' attention to an important musical detail.

Duration

The system of notating most piano music identifies the beginning of the sound. The exact duration of a tone is less definite. Even when a composer asks to have notes played staccato (with some silence between notes), the exact amount of air space is left to the discretion of the musician. Minute gradations of duration can result in dramatic differences in sound and expression.

Resonance

By using the damper pedal on an acoustic piano, pianists can vary the resonant quality of selected notes, extending the duration of some tones and affecting the tone color. When skillful use of the damper pedal is combined with effective gradations of intensity, the variety of acoustic options is unlimited. Resonance also is affected by dynamics. When you play certain tones louder, those sounds will be heard longer and you will enhance the total resonance of all the accumulated sounds. With some digital pianos, you can push a button to control the amount of resonance to use in a passage.

The Myth of Perfection in Musical Performance

What is the perfect way to say "I love you"? Poets and peasants, artists and artisans, parents and teachers, friends and lovers have found countless ways to express feelings of love. The successful way to say "I love you" is any way that results in the beloved one feeling loved.

You may have noticed, in the earlier section "Characteristics of Musical Performances" that I did not even mention the word *accuracy*. In music, it is possible to count the number of wrong notes or rhythms and then declare, "This performance had an accuracy rating of 98.6 percent." But in art as in life there is no such thing as perfection. A thermometer reading of 98.6 degrees may indicate that you no longer have an infection that caused a fever, but that measurement of body temperature does not represent human perfection.

> *In music, artistry requires more than accuracy.*

Music expresses something unique. It conveys human feelings and insights. A successful musical performance is not always a perfect performance technically, but it *is* a convincing and committed performance. The performer has found something meaningful in the music and wants others to hear that. Listeners are touched in some special way. Connections between people are established.

In typing a page of words on the computer, it is possible to remove all spelling errors. But the absence of misspelled words does not ensure that the remaining words are meaningful: "House Fred red into asparagus gigantic dances." "Huh?" Today, because of the technology of digital music recordings, it is possible to produce a recorded performance that is 100 percent accurate technically. Inaccurate readings and technical problems that occurred in a live performance or recording session can be removed. Such errors can be replaced so that the clarinet doesn't squawk, the voice doesn't quaver, the violin isn't flat, and the French horn solo doesn't include inaccurate pitches. Recording engineers can replace "wrong notes," adjust the balance of dynamics, and change tempi.

One result of such technological developments (I will not call them advancements) is that professional and amateur musicians begin to act as if technical perfection is possible even outside the recording studio. When performers focus excessively on avoiding mistakes, they tend to avoid making musical decisions that might lead them to more exciting performances—but also might result in noticeable technical errors. For today's students as well as professional musicians, there is a risk that technical perfection may become more important than musical expression.

I encourage you to listen to great performances preserved during the early stages of recording technology, back in the days when a performer's mistakes could not be removed. From famous pianists of the past you can hear spectacular performances with some wonderfully wrong notes. A smudge on the cheek of a beautiful child at play in the garden does not make her or him ugly. The stickiness of a tired toddler's hand, reaching out to a trusted adult, does not negate the warmth of that affectionate gesture. In music as in human interactions, expressiveness is more important than cleanliness. Accuracy of pitch and rhythm is not the most important goal in playing the piano. Accuracy represents one step toward an honorable goal (responsibility to the composer's score), but accuracy alone is not the ultimate goal of fine musicians.

> *Sometimes imperfections and wrong notes simply do not matter!*

Aspects Related to Tempo

When one is selecting an appropriate tempo for a piece of music, several factors come into play:

- The composer's intentions and instructions (as indicated by an expressive word, title, or metronomic marking)
- The specific instrument (including the degree of stiffness or responsiveness of its mechanism)
- The pianist's desired tempo (the target goal)
- The pianist's current abilities (the tempo the pianist can control today considering realities of technical facility, energy, or level of anxiety)
- The acoustics of the space where the music is being presented
- The listeners' abilities to hear distinctions

> *No matter what tempo you choose, your performance speed needs to remain within your comfort zone.*

Within those variables, there is room for considerable variety. Fine musicians learn to make musical sense out of the same set of notes played at different speeds. They learn to maintain meaningful note relationships even at different tempos.

When a pianist has a technical breakdown or changes speed without having valid musical reasons, that unpredictability undermines the comfort of listeners. Sometimes a very slight adjustment in tempo—playing a little bit faster or slower—will make a tremendous difference in terms of technical control and comfort for both pianists and listeners. On icy roads, safe drivers select and maintain speeds that allow them to retain control of the vehicle and to remain within comfortable zones. Experienced musicians also understand the need to remain in a safe speed zone when taking listeners on musical journeys.

Some Additional Information Related to Dynamics

When you read this next section, if you find that it does not make sense to you, I suggest that you put it aside for now and return to it sometime in the future. The musical concepts discussed here are not inaccessible to early-level students, but please do not fret if now does not seem like the appropriate time to utilize this information.

Monitoring Your Sounds

Experienced pianists know that their decisions regarding dynamics will vary with every performance, depending on many factors but particularly on the specific instrument and the acoustical properties of the hall. Although performers in practice need to plan what they will do dynamically, those pregame strategies are subject to adjustments at the time of performance. It is not your task simply to remember and reproduce the muscular responses you rehearsed. Your muscles need to be trained to adjust quickly, and you need to be able to revise your dynamic plan as artistic needs become evident. Football coaches can prepare intricate game plans, but coaches and their players adapt those plans in response to changing circumstances such as weather, injuries, turf, and the strengths and weaknesses of both teams. What you hear when you play needs to influence decisions you make at the time of your performance. You are not a robot.

> *When you play, you need to respond to what you hear* at that moment.

Nonchord Tones

During my college years, when my music theory teachers talked about nonchord tones, I had the impression that nonchord tones (including passing tones, upper and lower neighbor tones, and escape tones) were unimportant notes. When we analyzed harmonies in theory class, it seemed that nonchord tones were considered extraneous. They were ornamental and sometimes even optional. At my piano lessons, however, my piano performance teachers often pointed out certain notes that needed to be played a bit louder. Years later, I realized that often my theory and piano teachers had been talking about the same tones. It was the nonchord tones (those "unessential ones") that needed to be emphasized. If you are aware of chord and nonchord tones, it will be easier to decide which notes are special and need to be emphasized.

Tritones

Within the traditions of music composed in the past four hundred years, there is one interval that is the most dissonant. The interval of a *tritone* (such as C to F♯ or F to B) consists of three whole steps (on the piano keyboard, a tritone always involves seven contact keys). During the medieval period, the tritone was considered an interval of the devil and the Catholic Church prohibited composers from using that sound in music for formal worship. The tritone is an ambiguous interval: it can be spelled as an augmented fourth or a diminished fifth; and, unlike all other intervals, when you turn a tritone upside down, it still is a tritone. Composers often have utilized the interval to represent surprise and mystery, apprehension and uncertainty, dissonance and ambivalence. In most piano music, when you find the interval of a tritone, that represents a special moment. Let those two pitches receive special treatment. Give them a bit more intensity or time. Spotlight the mystery. Emphasize the harmonic moment. Relish the surprise. Treat that dissonance as a very special expressive moment. Make the notes of the tritone a bit louder, and then let the next interval (the one that resolves the dissonance by either expanding or contracting) be a bit softer.

Dynamic Stress versus Durational Stress

Dynamic stress (intensity) is not a substitute for durational stress (time). The rhythmic gesture "Short Short Short Long" is not the same as the dynamic gesture "Soft Soft Soft Loud." Beethoven's Fifth Symphony does not begin with the musical motive "Short Short Short Loud." When you have a series of shorter notes that lead to one longer note, don't pounce on that last note. Do not exaggerate the moment of arrival.

ACTIVITIES TO EXPLORE

ACTIVITY 5.1   *Speaking Expressively*

Read the following sentences aloud. Let your voice convey differences you perceive in the size and shape of the letters. Change the speed, pitch, intensity, flow, and articulation. Experiment with different vocal qualities (such as breathy, nasal, or scratchy) and use various cultural accents (such as British, Texan, and Yankee). Exaggerate your sounds while incorporating diverse body positions and facial expressions.

"How are YOU this morning?"
"How ARE you this morning?"
"How are you THIS morning?"

"HOW ARE YOU THIS MORN - ING?"
"Morning this are you how?"
"This you are how morning?"
"HO WARE YOUTH IS MOR NING?"
"How are ewe this mourning?"
"*How   are **you**   this   morning?*"

ACTIVITY 5.2   *Feeling Pulses and Pulse Divisions*

For this activity, you will need to use a tempo-measuring device (such as a metronome).

1. Begin by finding the speed of your own pulse. Set the metronome so that it ticks once for each pulse beat.
2. Set the metronome at the speed of your own pulse (or at M.M. ♩ = 60). While maintaining a steady speed, talk the following counting patterns:

One tick per count

Tick	X	X	X	X	X	X	X	X
Talk	1	2	3	4	1	2	3	4

Two ticks per counting unit

Tick	X	X	X	X	X	X	X	X
Talk	1	+	2	+	3	+	4	+

Two counting units per tick

Tick	X				X			
Talk	1	+	2	+	3	+	4	+

ACTIVITY 5.3   *Pacing Changes of Dynamics*

1. Select a comfortable group of notes (such as LH:5-1, G-G; RH:1-5, D-B), so that you feel balanced between hands and centered in the middle of the keyboard (see Example 5.1).
2. At a relaxed, slow, steady pulse, repeat the same four-note chord ten times. Use the damper pedal to enhance the basic sound. Change the pedal whenever you want, in response to the sounds that accumulate.

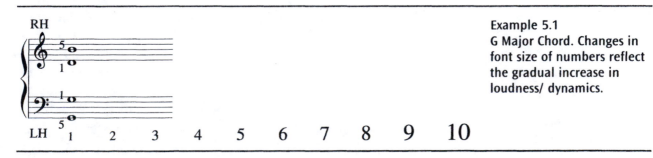

Example 5.1
G Major Chord. Changes in font size of numbers reflect the gradual increase in loudness/ dynamics.

3. Create a long, gradual *crescendo* as you count silently and travel from 1 to 10. Pace yourself and save the greatest increase of energy for the last four chords (7–10).
4. Beginning loudly, control a long, gradual *diminuendo* as you count backward silently and travel from 10 to 1.
5. Build a big *crescendo* and *diminuendo* as you go from 1 to 10 and from 10 back to 1. Pace the dynamic growth so the peak of the long phrase occurs within 9 10 10 9.

THOUGHTS ABOUT WORDS

Artistry

The concept of *artistry* has nothing to do with the level of difficulty of a piece. All musicians, including early-level students, can present artistic performances. In fact, one of the basic characteristics of any musical performance is that it is artistic. An artistic performance captivates the listener and expresses something. It results from caring about the music, caring about the activity of making music, and caring about sharing musical insights with listeners. It requires attentive listening. Trust me when I promise you that if you listen attentively, you can play with artistry even during your early phases of piano study. However, if you do not care about your sounds and do not try to control them, I predict that you never will play musically.

Amateur, Dilettante, and Connoisseur

It is useful to consider the meanings of three words: *amateur, dilettante,* and *connoisseur. Amateur* comes from the Latin verb *amare* (to love). Although the word *amateur* sometimes has been used in a derogatory sense, describing people who lack competence or seriousness, actually it refers to people who love music deeply. *Dilettante* derives from *dilectare* (to delight). We use a related word, the adjective *delectable,* to describe something that is delicious, tasty, or highly pleasing, but the noun *dilettante* often carries negative connotations in referring to someone who has only a superficial or transient interest in something. *Connoisseur* relates to the Latin verb *cognoscere* (to know) and refers to someone who understands and enjoys with discrimination and an appreciation of subtleties.

When Carl Philipp Emanuel Bach, the son of Johann Sebastian Bach, worked in Prussia as a court musician for Frederick the Great, he composed six volumes of keyboard pieces he described as works *Für Kenner und Liebhaber* (for connoisseurs and amateurs). Frederick was an enthusiastic musician who played the flute proficiently, composed many flute sonatas, and supported an excellent orchestra at his court. There is honor in being a person who knows and loves music. You can take pride in being an amateur musician (one who loves music) or a musical connoisseur (one who understands music).

Play It Louder

In some situations and cultures, it is considered rude and vulgar to be loud. If *louder* seems offensive to you, describe the gesture that will result in a fuller sound. Perhaps you would find it more helpful to tell yourself:

"Employ a larger gesture."
"Use a fuller sound."
"Send that melody soaring to the upper balcony so it can be heard by someone who skipped lunch all week in order to buy a ticket to attend this concert."
"Let your entire arm drop into that chord."
"Let that passage sound more regal."
"Create more contrast between the foreground and background elements. Soften the accompanying material."

Play It Softer

In some situations and cultures, it is considered a sign of weakness and powerlessness to speak softly. If *softer* means timid and insignificant to you, perhaps you would find it more helpful to tell yourself:

"Create a gentler sound."
"Use a smaller gesture."
"Begin on the key and depress it more slowly."
"Keep those accompanying notes farther in the background, not so near the front of the stage."
"Turn down the spotlights."
"Imagine you're conveying a sound that began on the other side of the valley."
"Let it sound like musical cobwebs. Create a lighter texture."

Playing Easy Pieces, Playing Pieces with Ease

Backstage one evening, following a wonderful concert that had included some of the most difficult piano pieces ever composed by Franz Liszt, I heard the virtuoso performer respond to an enthusiastic admirer with the comment, "But I only play *easy* pieces at my recitals." Then the pianist went on to explain that until he could play a piece with ease (that is, until the music felt easy to him), he didn't present that piece in a piano recital.[1] His goal was not to play technically difficult music but to discover how he could perform every piece of music *with ease.* That attitude is a useful one for pianists at all levels of advancement. Instead of always trying to conquer harder pieces, seek ways to play every piece with *greater ease.*

Discrimination, To Discriminate

Discrimination—the conscious decision to deprive people of opportunities because of their gender, age, race, religion, physical characteristics, place of birth, or marital status—is abhorrent to people of goodwill. In contrast, the act of *discriminating*—the ability to make subtle distinctions between tones or hues or motions—is essential to the creative work of painters, musicians, and other artists.

Walter Gieseking (1895–1956) was famous for his piano performances and recordings of the French Impressionistic composer Claude Debussy (1862–1918). I do not consider it a coincidence that Gieseking, like his father, was an acknowledged expert in classifying butterflies. The ability to make subtle distinctions in shapes, sizes, colors, and textures is important to pianists as well as to lepidopterologists.

ADDITIONAL RESOURCES

To enhance your ability to hear aural subtleties, spend time looking at visual subtleties. Visit art museums, libraries, and bookstores to study reproductions of paintings or photographs. Become more aware of gradations of color. Notice how light affects two- and three-dimensional works. Observe how an artist can create hundreds of variations of a single color. Study how a speck of white paint or drop of black ink affects the space around it.

To enhance your sensitivity to musical timbres and textures, examine leaves, butterflies, and animals, as well as objects such as fabrics, pottery, and sculptures.

Book

Ames, Joan Evelyn, *Mastery: Interviews with Thirty Remarkable People* (Portland, OR: Rudra, 1997). Interviews with people who are acknowledged experts in diverse fields (including cooking, medicine, sports, arts, and science). Ames focuses on the process involved in mastering something and considers various pathways to mastery. She introduces experts who have approached their work with unusual passion, devotion, and determination and presents accomplished people who are committed to their continued growth, including Indian musician Ali Akbar Khan, operatic soprano Margaret Harshaw, cellist Janos Starker, mezzo-soprano Marilyn Horne, and conductor Gisèle le Ben-Dor.

PART II PIANISTS AT PIANOS
Productive Practice

The first part of this book considered pianists and pianos. The second part of this book presents chapters that deal with *pianists at pianos*. It suggests ways to practice with greater efficiency in order to achieve a higher degree of personal satisfaction as a musician.

Chapter 6, "Learning to Play Piano," considers aspects of learning that relate to playing an instrument by ear and reading music. Chapter 7, "Planning Effective Rehearsals," assumes that it is appropriate for adult students to plan their independent piano practice times with the same care shown by conductors and coaches when they plan rehearsals or practice sessions for groups of people. Chapter 8, "Using Musical Activities," describes a large variety of practicing procedures that divide tasks into small projects and enhance rhythmic and technical comfort. Chapter 9, "Developing Technical Skills," recognizes that, for musicians, all technical problems are musical concerns. It describes strategies for strengthening awareness of musical concepts and developing control of technical skills.

Chapter 10, "Identifying and Diagnosing Problems," discusses ways that adult students can respond to practice difficulties. Chapter 11, "Preparing to Share Music," explores issues related to making music with others and performing piano music. Chapter 12, "Avoiding Common Pitfalls," considers some of the frustrations frequently experienced by adult early-level piano students. Chapter 13, "Looking Ahead," closes this book by suggesting ways that adults can maintain a lifelong involvement with music.

6 Learning to Play Piano

My cellist friend chuckled a bit when she told me about the adventurous and self-confident lad who had gone backstage to talk with her after the symphony concert. The boy already had learned to ride a bike, play chess, do in-line skating, pitch a tent, bake cookies, and use a computer. After hearing the sound of a solo cello for the first time, he told my friend, "I really want to learn how to play that instrument. Will you teach me how to play cello tomorrow afternoon? I could come by your house at three-thirty. My soccer game doesn't start 'til four."

Learning to play piano is very simple in comparison to learning to play some other musical instruments. When you depress a piano key, you get a sound. When you move the same key the same way, you get the same kind of sound. Sometimes playing a digital piano can be a bit more complicated: before you can get any sound from the instrument, it must be plugged in and turned on, and because different designers have placed the on/off button in different locations, sometimes it seems tricky just to locate the switch.

VARIOUS ASPECTS OF LEARNING

Learning to play a musical instrument incorporates aural, visual, and kinesthetic, emotional, and factual components. You can watch musicians do something and then imitate them. You can listen to something and then experiment, discovering ways to create similar sounds. You can have someone move your body in certain ways. You can have someone direct you, step-by-step, telling you exactly what you need to do next. You can be moved emotionally and then strive to reproduce those emotional responses by playing the instrument.

You can even learn how to do something by reading a manual. Soon after my father finished college and began teaching high school math, the school administrator asked Dad to establish and coach a wrestling team as an after-school activity. Dad had never wrestled and had never even seen a wrestling meet, but he was convinced that you could learn anything from a book. So he went to the library, got a book with lots of pictures, and started practicing various wrestling holds and movements on the living room carpet—with his ninety-five-pound bride, who became my mother several years later. Although my father's team eventually won some championships, his approach is not the usual one for wrestling coaches.

Children are able to talk (say words) long before they can read words. Unless they have severe disabilities, whatever language or languages children hear spoken they will learn to understand and to speak before the age of four. Reading and writing (literacy), however, involve different skills than hearing and speaking (conversation). Today and throughout recorded history, many intelligent people speak eloquently but do not know how to write and read letters.

The process of learning to read words actually is an exercise in learning to recognize the graphic representation of sounds one already knows. Babies hear sounds and imitate sounds. Children look at letters, correlate letters with sounds, and learn to draw shapes of letters that represent sounds. When my daughters were very young, they made a game of repeating various combinations of sounds and letters such as "cat, bat, fat, sat, mat." Many times, while I was preparing a meal, they would play in the kitchen, arranging and rearranging brightly colored magnetic letters on the refrigerator door. We spelled words together, and it was very exciting for all of us when they realized the connection between symbols and sounds and could read *The Cat in the Hat*.

Music is an aural language, and some people who are visually impaired have become superb musicians, depending on their ears in place of their eyes. Many people learn to play musical instruments even though they are unable to see. Long before the pianists George Shearing and Stevie Wonder began entertaining audiences, blind organists had served as professional musicians in European cathedrals. I understand that in some African villages blind musicians teach at night while seated on the floor of a dark hut. Their students—unable to see the instrument and unable to watch the master musician's movements—learn to listen intently to the sounds created in that enclosed environment.[1]

People with perfect sight also have learned to play musical instruments "by ear." Although they can play the instrument and create beautiful music, they have not learned to decipher the notation of music for that instrument. They are unable "to read music." In an earlier chapter, I mentioned the importance of piano students experimenting with musical sounds (babbling). Exploring sounds and ways to create sounds is an essential step in becoming musically literate. "Fooling around at the keyboard" is not a waste of time. Instead, it is a means of becoming comfortable with the language of musical sounds.

> Symbols gain meaning when they represent something one already has experienced.

Although it is possible to create piano sounds without seeing the keys or reading musical notation, for literate, seeing adults who study piano, whether in private lessons or piano classes, it is appropriate to combine various aspects of learning. Literate adults will benefit from employing aural, visual, kinesthetic, and factual information. They also will be more productive in their piano study if they approach music as an expressive language, not simply an intricate system of organizing symbols.

Whether individuals tend to be more visual or more aural in their personal approach to learning, it will be helpful for them to explore various modalities and let those reinforce one another. A secure musician looks at notated music and can imagine how it will sound even before touching the instrument. Such a musician also hears music and can imagine how sounds might be notated in terms of both pitch and time. For most musicians, ears and eyes work together. For all musicians, hearing is the most basic component when learning to create and control meaningful sounds. For pianists who are musicians, playing the piano is much more than an intellectual, visual, or tactile activity.

LEARNING TO READ MUSIC

With the possible exception of music for guitar, which provides a ligature or chart that shows where to place each finger, the notation of keyboard music is probably the most logical of all instrumental music notation. Reading the notation of keyboard music is similar to reading a map. Sometimes it is helpful to isolate the elements of pitch and rhythm.

Deciphering Pitch Notation

There is a direct correlation between the musical staff and the piano keyboard. Sounds that get higher in pitch are represented on the page by note heads that move up on the grid of horizontal lines and spaces. Sounds that are higher in pitch are created by depressing keys toward the right end of the keyboard. *Note*: Don't just read about this very basic concept. Go to the piano and experiment with different sounds. Create exploratory activities. Move your hands to different areas of the piano keyboard and notice the sounds you create in different registers. Investigate the correlation between moving to the right and hearing piano sounds that "get higher."

Although your piano keyboard probably has eighty-eight keys, when you identify and locate two pitches you only need to be aware of three options:

1. Are the two notes the same or different?—Do they repeat or change?
2. If they change, do they move up or down? (up = move to the right; down = move to the left)—Is the second sound higher or lower in pitch?
3. Is the new note near or far?—Does it involve a step or skip?

Deciphering Rhythmic Notation

It is useful to realize that the same proportion of timed events can be notated in several different ways. In spoken language, *Sea, See, Si,* and *C*

Example 6.1
Notation of a rhythmic
pattern

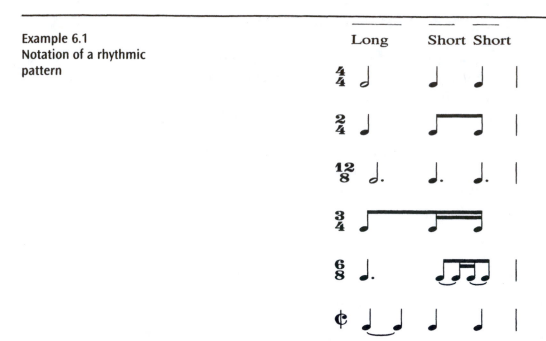

Example 6.2
"Wiggle, Wiggle Wog"

1. Wig-gle, Wig-gle Wog,   Wig-gle, Wig-gle Wog.
2. Wig-gle, Wig-gle Wog,   Wig-gle, Wig-gle Wog.

Wig-gle, wig-gle I'm   a   po - ly - wog.
Wig-gle, wig-gle soon   I'll   be   a   frog.

Example 6.3
Counting "Wiggle, Wiggle
Wog"

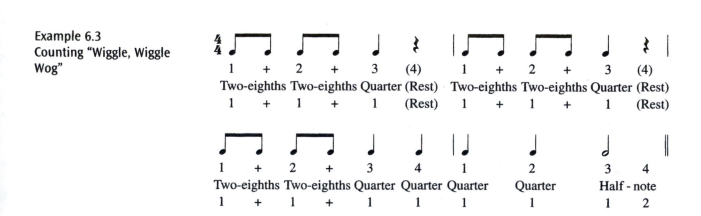

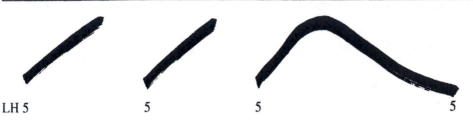

Figure 6.1
Map of "Wiggle, Wiggle Wog"

LH 5   5   5   5

are pronounced almost the same but represent subtle differences of meaning. In notating musical sounds, a very basic pattern (such as _____ __ __ , "Long Short Short") can be represented by several different rhythmic values (see Example 6.1).

ISOLATING PITCHED AND RHYTHMIC ELEMENTS

As I suggested earlier, when deciphering notated piano music it may be useful to separate aspects related to pitch (where?) and duration (for how long?). As an example, study the silly song, "Wiggle, Wiggle Wog"a long-ago favorite of mine (see Example 6.2). If you look carefully at the notation of the nineteen pitches of this four-measure melody, you will see that the entire song uses only five pitches (G A B C D), which represent five white keys. The five notes represent five neighboring keys. To play them, you either move up (to the right by steps) or—in the reverse order (D C B A G)—move down (to the left by steps). The entire melody can be diagrammed with three lines (see Figure 6.1).[2]

The fingering (given here for the left hand) always correlates five fingers with five neighboring white keys. The left hand's fingering pattern steps either up (5 4 3 2 1) or up and down (5 4 3 2 1 2 3 4 5). In becoming comfortable with the pitched elements, it is useful to chunk the notes (play all five at the same time). Then play and play with the pattern: on your leg or a tabletop, at different speeds and levels of energy, and so on.

In exploring rhythmic aspects of this song, experience the pattern in many different ways (see Example 6.3): clap it with both hands, pat it on your thighs, count it, and then verbalize it in other ways (such as "Wiggle wiggle wog," "Going up the hill," "G-Up-Up-Up-Up," "Short Short Short Short Long, " "two-eighths two-eighths quarter (rest)," or "do re mi fa sol"). These and many other rehearsal strategies are explained in more detail in chapter 8, "Using Musical Activities." When you look at a new piece of music, hunt familiar patterns. Isolate the aspects of pitch and rhythm. Become comfortable controlling them separately before you combine them.

KNOWING AND DOING

Knowing how to make a car "go" and driving responsibly are not the same activity. It is not enough for a teenager to have watched a parent drive for sixteen years and noticed how to put the key in the ignition, start the motor, release the brake, push the gas pedal, turn the steering wheel, flip the turn signals, and turn on the radio. Becoming a competent driver requires more than being able to make the car move forward. Becoming a sensitive musician requires more than moving some piano keys down a few millimeters. Competent musicians, like competent drivers, learn how to control their instrument. They become aware of ways they move in relation to their instrument. Literate musicians learn to decipher graphic symbols that represent sounds.

My cellist friend had chuckled because she knew that learning to play a musical instrument would require more than a few moments just before a soccer practice. Although the adventurous lad had been turned on by hearing the cello, learning to play the instrument would require much more than his being shown how to turn it on and make it go.

> *Musicians develop the ability to listen astutely.*

7 Planning Effective Rehearsals

CHAPTER OUTLINE

Concepts to Consider
  Rehearsal Time
  Morale
  Language
  Making Choices
  Developing a Rehearsal Agenda
  Categories of Practice Activities

  Warming Up and Cooling Down   Etudes (Study Pieces)
  Repertoire (Solo Piano Pieces)   Sight-reading
  Ensemble Music   Analyzing and Memorizing
  Exploring Sounds at the Piano   Listening
  Technical Patterns   Activities "Off-the-Bench"
  Planning Your Practice Time

Activities to Explore
  Using Your Time
  Choosing Your Verbs
  Assessing Your Morale
  Planning Your Practice Time
  Listening to Another Person's Practice Session

Thoughts about Words
  Always Do Your Very Best
  Watch the Clock
  Good Enough

Additional Resources

Coaches of sport teams and conductors of music-performing organizations, including choirs, bands, and orchestras, know that they have limited time to work with their groups. You, too, will have limits on the time you can practice the piano. Even if you could spend ten hours a day at the piano, you would be unable to practice twenty-five hours each day.

Successful coaches and conductors have learned how to work effectively within the boundaries of the time available. They understand the need to establish and achieve specific goals within given time frames. When a high school administrator schedules forty-five-minute rehearsals for the band, the conductor cannot extend those sessions arbitrarily, working twenty minutes extra and causing students to be late to their next class. Coaches know that a scheduled event will begin at a certain time—whether or not their players are ready.

CONCEPTS TO CONSIDER

Rehearsal Time

Conductors of professional orchestras realize that the musicians' union monitors rehearsal conditions, including the length of rehearsals. Permission must be obtained to extend a rehearsal. Furthermore, because time represents money, additional lengthy rehearsals affect the orchestra's budget. Before the season begins, prospective subscribers are told what music has been programmed for each date. Subscribers, on the basis of their own musical preferences, then decide what music and performers they want to hear, which concerts they want to attend, and what tickets they will order. In essence, the orchestra's management makes a commitment to listeners, agreeing to present music that has been announced months in advance of a concert.

Professional music organizations face two realities: (1) rehearsal time is limited and cannot be expanded easily; (2) while working within the limits of available rehearsal time, musicians need to prepare themselves to present quality performances of certain works on specific dates. As a result of these realities, conductors select repertoire judiciously, plan their rehearsal time carefully, and work with an eye on the clock. Learning to use rehearsal time efficiently is an important part of the training of successful conductors. I believe that it also will be important in your development as a well-prepared piano student.

Morale

Many factors, both physical and emotional, affect rehearsals.

Conductors and coaches know that they must be sensitive to the emotional and physical needs of their players, whether professional or amateur. Just as band and orchestral musicians tune their instruments before starting to play, directors need to tune their groups and tune in to their players.

Is the temperature of the rehearsal hall within a comfortable range? Do the chairs provide proper back support during extended periods of sitting? Is there sufficient light for reading scores? Are the music stands stable? When will the players need to take a short break? What else is happening in the professional and personal lives of the musicians? Are they thinking about social activities scheduled for next weekend? Is there a flu epidemic in the community? Are quarterly tax payments due the day after the next concert? The answers to such questions will affect rehearsals, and experienced conductors take such realities into consideration. Similarly, as a piano student, you will benefit from being sensitive to your own needs and helping yourself plan practice sessions.

The experience of being involved in organized rehearsals and practice sessions needs to bring sufficient gratification to the participants that they will want to return for the next rehearsal or workout. If individuals lose interest, the group will disintegrate and the leader will have no players to direct or coach. At each practice session, players renew their decision to continue participating in that activity. As a piano student, you need to direct your own rehearsals in ways that result in your wanting to practice the next day. When you leave the piano after a productive practice session, you already can be looking forward to your next rehearsal.

Rehearsals are a time to reinforce your sense of accomplishment, self-esteem, and pleasure in making music.

Rehearsals are a time to learn, experiment, and improve your skills. Effective conductors and coaches learn when to boost and when to boast; when to praise and when to prod; when to chastise and when to energize; when to cheer and when to stay clear; when to insist or persist or desist; when to talk and when to take a walk. As a piano student, working primarily on your own, you need to provide yourself with similar guidance as you direct your own practice sessions.

One of the most important variables in reaching a sense of achievement results from creating realistic goals and setting expectations that you can meet within the given time frame and with the energy resources available for that specific practice session. The establishment of attainable goals and, when necessary, the adjustment of those goals are two essential considerations when structuring successful rehearsals. It is not a cop-out for you to process new information and then redefine your goals for a practice session. When you find that you are not meeting your projected goals within a comfortable time frame, it is not a failure to consider new information and change your plans.

Language

Words carry multiple meanings, and I suggest that you select your verbs judiciously. The way you think and talk about your practice will affect the way you perform, whether in a formal setting or for your own pleasure. When you go to the piano, do you *rehearse* or *practice, play* or *work*?

Vladimir Horowitz (1904–1989), the Russian virtuoso pianist, claimed that he never practiced. Instead, he explained, he merely rehearsed for his performances. Whenever Horowitz was at the piano, he was getting ready to perform. His ultimate goal, concert performance, was always linked with the procedures necessary for him to get ready to share music with an audience.

I have noticed that some people equate *rehearsal* with *work* and link *practice* with *play*. For them, *practicing an instrument* and *playing the piano* may represent leisure or recreational activities that they do not take very seriously (perhaps like playing recreational golf or croquet). During my first year of college, the first-year students in the dormitory were responsible for certain weekly tasks. As a group, we were penalized if those housekeeping chores were not completed by noon Saturday. However, if someone had a class or rehearsal scheduled on Saturday morning, she could be excused from the three-hour group session if she had taken care of her share of duties (which actually required less than thirty minutes) earlier in the week. I soon learned that some of my dorm mates seemed unhappy when I asked to be excused in order to go down the street and practice piano. But when I told them, "Saturday morning I have an eight o'clock *rehearsal* at Smith Hall," the same people seemed quite comfortable with that situation and had no problem with my doing certain tasks earlier in the week. My piano rehearsals, four hours by myself in a practice room, often required independent work on Beethoven sonatas or other solo repertoire. I realized, however, that dorm mates who had assumed that piano practice could be squeezed into a few spare moments respected scheduled rehearsals and understood that those sessions were a necessary part of my meeting university requirements for academic work. By adopting vocabulary understood by friends who were not musicians I was better able to communicate the importance of my work.

Practicing sometimes describes the regular activities of surgeons, attorneys, and religiously committed people. When attorneys practice law, they do the work for which they were prepared during law school; they behave in ways associated with activities of people in the law profession. There are certain things that practicing attorneys are expected to do simply because they are lawyers. Fortunately for patients, when physicians practice medicine they do not merely repeat an activity until, through trial and error, eventually they get it right. Instead, they put to use what they learned as medical students. They look after the health of their patients.

Practicing pianists do things that will result in becoming more effective musicians. I suggested earlier that playing the piano feels easy and joyous. Successful musicians, however, often approach their play with the seriousness of going to work. When they are ready to practice, they may say, "I'm going to do some work now." Or they look at the clock and announce, "Time to get going." Or they might comment to someone at dinner, "This was a very productive practice day. I really accomplished a lot!"

As you explore ways to approach your piano practice, I suggest that you experiment with words. Observe how you and others react to certain verbs, and then adopt whatever vocabulary seems most useful to you. Select words and actions that elicit the support of your friends and enhance your success as a piano student.

One day on a campus, I noticed several posters that announced "rehersals." When I saw that, I smiled a bit, wondering whether the main focus of those sessions would be on the female participants (that is, the *hers*)? The secret to having successful rehearsals (as well as to spelling the word correctly) is to remember that the root of the word rehearsal is *hear* or *rehear*. For musicians, rehearsing is an activity that goes beyond the mere repetition of a motion. Rehearsing requires concentration, careful listening, hearing, and rehearing.

Years ago, an interested musician listened through a closed door to a practice session by Myra Hess (1890–1965), the great English pianist. During more than two hours, the listener heard long periods of silence interspersed with brief moments of sound. Then Dame Myra burst out of the room, exclaiming joyously, "I've just had the *best* practice session!" Locating notes and depressing keys is only a small part of piano practice. Productive practice sessions must also include lots of time to think, study the score silently, plan, listen, and assess what we actually do play.

All too often when novice students practice piano, they simply spend time on the bench, sitting in front of the keyboard, playing through a certain passage or an entire piece and then repeating it again and again and again until they "get it right." Have you ever seen the poster that declares: "Amateurs practice something until they get it right. Professionals practice something until they can't get it wrong"? Pianists usually work on their own, in relative isolation, and often develop the counterproductive attitude that they have an unlimited amount of time available for their work. They need to learn how to incorporate a variety of useful strategies into rehearsals and to decide when they have repeated something a sufficient number of times.

Making Choices

The way you practice needs to vary depending on where you are in the process of learning a composition or developing a skill. Just as you have

> *Playing the piano can be an enjoyable, gratifying, interesting, physically integrated, and emotionally satisfying activity.*

> *Piano students at all levels need to learn how to use time effectively, how to practice, and how to evaluate accomplishments during practice sessions.*

learned to select foods from different nutritional groups, you need to learn to select appropriate practice activities. In going through a cafeteria line or planning a menu you might ask yourself, "At this particular meal, do I want [do I need] to eat potato chips, pizza, peanut butter, pork chops, pickles, pasta, pumpkin pie, or prunes?" Similarly, when planning practice sessions, ask yourself, "At this particular time, what do I need to do? How can I use most productively the time available to me? What am I ready to do now? What do I intend to accomplish?" At a cafeteria or restaurant, you might ask yourself, "How will I expend today's budgeted allowances (financial and nutritional units) of money, calories, salt, caffeine, fiber, and saturated fats?" In the practice room, you need to make comparable choices about using your available allowance of practice time.

The innovative Japanese music educator Shinichi Suzuki (1898–1998) used to tease his young violin students by telling them, "Be sure that you practice *only* on the days when you eat." As an adult piano student, however, you will need to go beyond a commitment to practice every day you eat. Junk foods may satisfy a need to eat (to taste food and to put something in your stomach), but foods with empty calories will not provide the nourishment you need in order to maintain a healthy body. When you have problems with a passage, it is not enough just to keep repeating it. In order for you to spend your practice time productively, you need to be able to decide what you will do during your practice sessions. First you need to decide how to approach a passage in order to solidify the actions that will result in an appropriate set of muscular responses and create the sounds you want. Then you can establish goals, select rehearsal procedures, and analyze the causes of difficulties. *Practice* is an umbrella term. It represents an active verb that covers a variety of specific activities (see chapter 8, "Using Musical Activities").

Developing a Rehearsal Agenda

Piano rehearsals can be structured in many ways. Your piano teacher, on the basis of knowing you and your current needs, may suggest ways for you to organize your practice sessions. Ultimately, though, you will need to experiment and discover for yourself what activities are most helpful to you.

The most important things you can do when practicing will be (1) discover coordinated gestures and (2) create sounds that are musically gratifying. The ways you move when you depress the keys will determine the sounds you make. Whether you are sight-reading new pieces, reviewing pieces you already know, playing scale patterns, or working out specific technical problems, let your goal always be *to sound like a musician.*

I believe that you will benefit from spending some time regularly with each of the ten categories of materials and activities described later in "Categories of Practice Activities." I suggest that you incorporate into your

> How *you depress the keys is far more important than* which *keys you depress.*

rehearsals different kinds of work. Before you begin a practice session, select a limited number of specific, identifiable goals. Before you leave the piano, assess the day's accomplishments and make some preliminary plans for your next rehearsal. Over a period of days, it should be possible to incorporate into your practice sessions all of the categories described here. Instead of simply playing through certain piano pieces, work to develop skills that can be used with every composition.

Categories of Practice Activities

Warming Up and Cooling Down

Just as athletes prepare their bodies for exertion or recovery, many musicians routinely incorporate stretching and other conditioning activities into their rehearsals.

Repertoire (Solo Piano Pieces)

Several different pieces that represent:

Various stages of learning (such as beginning a new piece; analyzing and memorizing; polishing for performance; reviewing and refining a piece you already know very well)

Various levels of difficulty (short-term pieces that can be learned easily in one or two practice sessions as well as a long-term piece that may require work for longer than one month or one season)

Various contrasts of styles and moods (fast/slow, sad/happy, loud/soft, calm/energetic, intense/casual, smooth/jerky, or near/distant)

Various sounds and textures (melody with accompaniment, balanced voices, independent melodic line in each hand, rich resonance created by using the sostenuto and damper pedals, detached/connected, high register/low register, parallel movements/contrary motions, traditional/innovative)

Various styles of music (representative of musicians from different times and places)

Various types of pitch organization (including major, minor, modal, chromatic, whole tone, tonal, and atonal); rhythmic organization (including duple, triple, mixed, changing meters, and unmeasured); and structural organization (such as variations, ostinato pattern, ABA, ABBA, rondo, and sonatina)

Ensemble Music (Pieces to Play with Other Pianists or with Singers or Other Instrumentalists)

These include original compositions, arrangements of folk or popular music, and transcriptions of music for other combinations of musicians.

Exploring Sounds at the Piano
(Improvisational Activities)

Variations of specific material, expansion of musical boundaries ("How loud or soft can I play; how fast or slow can I play?"), dramatic characterizations ("Let it sound like a ferocious storm, a gentle breeze, a month-old child, an eighty-five-year-old great-great-grandparent, electric blue, faded green, a heavy boulder, or a cobweb"), and musical experiments ("What sounds do I get when I move this way, and that way, and this way, and that way?").

Technical Patterns (Material Selected to
Develop Technical Skills)

Technical patterns include sequential finger patterns and scales based on major, minor, modal, and chromatic patterns; solid or broken intervals (such as double thirds, sixths, and octaves); chords and inversions in solid and broken forms (using a more extended position of the hand); arpeggios (hands alone and hands together); cadence patterns (groups of chords transposed to various keys); and repetitive material (such as that found in *Exercises,* by Charles Hanon).

Etudes (Study Pieces)

Composed material that focuses on a specific technical challenge.

Sight-reading

Previewing a piece silently and then playing it carefully only one or two times. Developing ease in reading groups of pitches and rhythmic patterns.

Analyzing and Memorizing

Looking for patterns within a piece, identifying sets of notes by name or function, imprinting cues that will make it easier to retrieve the information. Studying the score away from the keyboard.

Listening

Hearing performances of pieces by various musicians (pianists and others). Listening without looking at the music and also while looking at it.

Activities "Off-the-Bench"

Standing and moving. To protect yourself from fatigue and injury, get off the piano bench for at least five minutes during every thirty minutes of practice. Use some of those breaks for large-muscle activities (such as conducting expressively, walking a rhythmic pattern, tapping a rhythm, or stretching) or verbalizing (singing and counting aloud). Spend time learning more about music theory.

Planning Your Practice Time

There are two approaches for planning how to use your practice time:

1. Decide what you want to accomplish at the piano and then determine how long it will take to meet those goals; or
2. Decide how much time you can devote to piano practice and then plan how you will use your time.

Either way, you will need to decide what to do and how to divide your time. You and your teacher can discuss ways to use your practice time efficiently. Table 7.1 shows four possible plans based on practice sessions of 30, 60, 90, or 120 minutes. If it is not feasible for you to spend time every day with every category, consider including certain activities on a daily basis (perhaps 1, 2, 4, 5, 7, and 10) and spend time with the other activities on alternate days (selecting 3 or 6, 8 or 9). Although the warm-up and cool-down portions would need to begin and end your session, all the other activities could be done in any order you preferred and could vary from day to day.

"An hour of practice?" you say. "How could I ever fill that much time? I'm just an early-level piano student. My longest piece is less than two minutes." The sample piano practice plan in Table 7.2 is not intended as a straitjacket that would constrict your pleasure in making music. Instead, it demonstrates how an hour of productive practice might be divided. Instead of staying with one activity until you become tired of it, do what you can in the time assigned to that activity and then move to another task.

Table 7.1 Four Plans for Piano Practice

Activity	Length of Practice Session			
	30 min.	60 min.	90 min.	120 min.
1. Warming up and cooling down	1	2	3	4
2. Repertoire	9	25	31	35
3. Ensemble music	2	3	4	10
4. Exploring sounds at the piano	4	5	10	12
5. Technical patterns	4	5	10	12
6. Etudes	1	2	4	5
7. Sight-reading	2	5	8	12
8. Analyzing and memorizing	2	3	4	10
9. Listening	3	5	8	10
10. Activities "Off-the-bench"	2	5	8	10

Table 7.2 A Sample Piano Practice Plan

Monday, 9:00–10:00 A.M.	
Activities	Timing (min.)
Stretching and body warm-ups	1
Major scales (from white-key tonics)	2
Parallel sixths (very slowly, with pedal)	3
Broken chords (hand-over-hand, major and minor)	2
Chord patterns (in various keys, major and minor)	2
Musical babbling (improvise; explore sounds)	5
Sight-reading	5
Memorizing new piece	3
Mozart: Conducting and counting aloud	3
Getting off the piano bench, getting a drink of water, and stretching a bit	1
Bartók: Playing straight through with score	3
Bartók: Studying score silently	3
Bartók: Playing straight through from memory	3
Clementi: Playing-through (with metronome set at M.M. $\quarternote = 60$)	5
Clementi: Playing-through (metronome set at M.M. $\quarternote = 120$)	3
Bach: Playing left hand part alone	3
Bach: Playing right hand part alone	3
Bach: Playing each motive as it appears	3
Ensemble piece: Tape-recording Primo part	1
Ensemble piece: Tape-recording Secondo part	2
Identifying and writing down your goals for next practice session	1
Writing down questions to ask your teacher	2
Stretching and cool-down	1

ACTIVITIES TO EXPLORE

ACTIVITY 7.1 *Using Your Time*

1. For one full week, maintain a journal that indicates how you spend all of your time. Notice what you do during each fifteen-minute segment of your day. Be quite specific.

2. Make a list of important things in your life—including piano practice, family activities, school and other work, meals, personal care and household chores, entertainment, exercise, religious activities, and other responsibilities. Decide how much time you want to devote to those various activities.

3. Establish a written schedule that includes time for everything you consider important.

4. For one week, follow your schedule very carefully. Throughout the week, annotate your schedule with a contrasting color of ink, indicating times when you did not follow your projected plans or when you needed a longer period of time to accomplish your goals. The purpose of this assessment is not to laud or chastise yourself for what did or did not happen but to gain information to use in planning future rehearsals.

5. At the end of the week, study your annotations and then create a revised schedule. Be realistic about what you can accomplish within a certain period of time. Determine the best times of day for various aspects of your piano practice. Notice what types of practice activities need different physical states. Incorporate that awareness in your revisions.

6. Once you have refined a workable schedule, stick to it. Make appointments with yourself. Block off those times and honor those commitments to your musical pleasure and personal growth.

ACTIVITY 7.2   *Choosing Your Verbs*

1. Notice how you and your friends respond to various choices of words. Describe your practice plans in different ways:

"I'm going to go *practice*."
"I need to *rehearse* now."
"Time to *start working*."
"I have to *prepare* for my lesson."
"Now I'm going to *play* my piano pieces."
"I suppose I'd better *review* those assignments before tomorrow."

2. Decide which phrases create the most positive feelings for you and elicit the most supportive reactions from your friends.

ACTIVITY 7.3   *Assessing Your Morale*

1. On a scale of 1–5 (1 = disagree strongly, 5 = agree strongly), indicate your responses to the following five statements:

_____   "I enjoyed this rehearsal."
_____   "I have more energy now than when I began practicing."
_____   "I accomplished a lot during this session."
_____   "I can identify specific things that I can do now with greater ease and security."
_____   "I am looking forward to my next practice session."

2. Total your five responses and keep track of your numerical assessments (the totals) over a period of several days.

_____   Mon.
_____   Tues.
_____   Wed.
_____   Thurs.
_____   Fri.
_____   Sat.
_____   Sun.

3. Be sensitive to your frustrations. Whenever your numbers drop below your own level of comfort (perhaps anything that totals

less than 15?), adjust your goals and explore new rehearsal strategies.

ACTIVITY 7.4 *Planning Your Practice Time*

This activity describes two different approaches (Plans A and B) to help you decide how to use your time. You can begin by selecting either specific activities or the timings of those activities. Both approaches can result in similar practice plans. Either can lead to very productive sessions. Both approaches depend on your knowing approximately how much time an activity will require and deciding how you will divide your time.

> *Plan A.* Decide what you want to accomplish and how much time you will allot to each activity. (For example, "I want to work on each of these twelve things, spending five minutes with each one. To do that, I will need to practice a total of sixty minutes.")
>
> *Plan B.* Decide how much time you will practice and how you will divide your time. (For example, "I can practice for sixty minutes. I want to spend that time working on these twelve things.")

1. On alternate days, explore different approaches to planning your practice time (Plans A and B). Take notes and make written observations about your reactions to those approaches.
2. Become aware of how much time you need to accomplish specific tasks. Incorporate that awareness in planning rehearsals.
3. Notice which approach is most useful at which times (such as late at night, the day before your lesson, when you feel energetic, on Monday morning, etc.). Consider factors such as length of session, time of day, concentration, health, other commitments, and deadlines.

ACTIVITY 7.5 *Listening to Another Person's Practice Session*

1. Listen to someone else's practice session (at the piano or any other instrument). Notice how that person uses time. Make written observations that concern effective rehearsal strategies you might borrow.
2. Ask that person to listen to one of your practice sessions. Notice how his or her presence affects your concentration and productivity. Invite your visitor to share observations that concern your rehearsal.
3. Compare notes on different approaches to practice. Periodically repeat the process.

THOUGHTS ABOUT WORDS

Always Do Your Very Best

When I was a child, my parents and teachers often challenged me to *always do my very best*. Decades later, as a teacher and parent, I realized that most successful adults do *not* approach every task with the goal of *always* doing their very best.

Two of my favorite activities, reading and weeding, provide some useful analogies. When reading, sometimes I glance at the headline of an article and sometimes I read with the goal of remembering significant facts. Occasionally I read a poem aloud, savoring the sounds of each separate syllable. Sometimes I read silently, slowly, with dictionary in hand, checking multiple meanings of unfamiliar words. In contrast, sometimes I dash through a short story, accepting unknown words in context while hurrying to discover who-done-it. The amount of time I invest in the activity of reading and the speed and care with which I read depend on the material I am reading and my goals in dealing with that material. There are times when browsing or scanning *is* the best use of my reading time.

When I'm weeding in the backyard, sometimes I can remove 80 percent of the weeds in thirty minutes. It might take me two more hours to pull 90 percent of the weeds and five hours in all to get 95 percent. If I stop weeding after only thirty minutes, I know that I have not done the most thorough job I could have done. But if I spend five or more hours attempting to remove every single weed, what is the price of that decision? So I ask myself, "Is it more important to pull 98 to 100 percent of the weeds or to settle for only 80 percent and then have time for other projects I value—visiting a friend in the hospital, mailing a birthday package, practicing the piano, reading a bedtime story to a grandchild, balancing my checkbook, or working on *Making Music at the Piano*?"

If we insist on doing everything at our highest level of competence, we probably will encounter two problems: frustration and avoidance. For competent adults, the reality of limited time and multiple tasks makes it impossible to accomplish every project at the best possible level. With almost any activity—including weeding, reading, exercising, editing, and practicing piano—we could reach a somewhat higher level of proficiency if we spent more time on it. Stopping before we reach our full potential may result in frustration and self-deprecation. That may lead us to the another problem, avoidance.

One way to avoid feeling frustrated about a project is to avoid getting involved with that project. Such a self-protective attitude, however, prevents us from sampling new activities and expanding our experiences. It limits us to doing only those things we expect to pursue to our highest level of competence. Several summers ago, I enrolled in a six-week pottery course. At the end of the term I chose not to invest further time and energy by enrolling for the next course. Although I stopped before I had fulfilled my potential as a potter, I took pleasure in having experienced the challenge of working with clay on a potter's wheel and glazing several bowls. I took pride that year in having crafted handmade holiday gifts for my two daughters and four new stepdaughters. Furthermore, because of my experiences in working with clay, my appreciation of pottery increased immensely. During those six weeks, I took the project seriously and did the best I could under the circumstances—although I knew I would not be achieving the greatest success of which I was capable. But that was OK with me and also with my pottery instructor.

Instead of trying to take everything to the highest level of quality of which we are capable—the level we might achieve if we stayed up later, pushed harder, invested more money, and neglected other commitments—I suggest that as responsible adults we need to seek *the best balance we can achieve.* In that context, what might seem like a compromise in the quality of our accomplishment may allow us to make responsible decisions that will enable us to create a better balance in our lives.

Watch the Clock

Novice cooks are cautioned that "a watched pot never boils," and children often are told not to keep looking at the clock during their practice time. Although it is important to concentrate on a task and not be distracted by the clock, my suggestion to you, an adult student, is that you *do* need to watch the clock. In order to plan effective rehearsals, you need to have a clear sense of how much time you need to accomplish specific tasks. When you have that information, then it will be easier to plan how to use your practice time efficiently.

If a recipe calls for baking a cake forty minutes at 350 degrees, you will not get the same results by putting the cake batter in the oven for half the time (twenty minutes) at twice the temperature (700 degrees). Hurrying the baking process will not lead to the same results. But by knowing your time constraints and working within them, you can select appropriate goals, accomplish them, and not feel squeezed. Cupcakes require less baking time than large pans of batter but can taste just as good as slices of a layer cake. Piano practicing involves many different activities. If you know how much time you will need to expend in order to accomplish a specific task, you can plug that activity into your scheduled goals and experience gratification rather than frustration.

Good Enough

Adult piano students already have learned to establish different standards for various projects. Different levels of precision in cutting are necessary when removing a brain tumor or clipping a magazine article. Different criteria are appropriate when measuring medications for a sick child and filling a swimming pool. Different timepieces are used for championship races at the Olympics and friendly games of volleyball after a picnic supper on the beach.

Successful adults have developed the ability to create appropriate standards of excellence, uphold goals that reflect an acceptable level of competence, and maintain a reputation for doing quality work. They have learned to complete projects within established deadlines and to meet at least minimal standards of quality in their jobs. Adults have learned that there are times when good enough *is* good enough.

ADDITIONAL RESOURCES

Books

Bruser, Madeline, *The Art of Practicing: A Guide to Making Music from the Heart* (New York: Bell Tower, 1997). "Combines physiological and meditative principles to help musicians of all levels release physical and mental tension and unleash their innate musical talent" (quote from book jacket).

Kaplan, Burton, *Musician's Practice Log* (New York: Perception Development Techniques, 1985). Includes charts as well as specific suggestions for developing effective practice procedures.

Provost, Richard, *The Art and Technique of Practice* (San Francisco: Guitar Solo, 1992). After writing a book for guitar players, Provost realized that his concepts were applicable to other musicians.

8 Using Musical Activities

CHAPTER OUTLINE

Concepts to Consider and Activities to Explore

Organizing Information
- Looking for Musical Patterns
- Writing in Your Musical Score

Working with Rhythms

Clapping	Using a Metronome
Tapping	Moving
Conducting	

Verbalizing
- Counting Musically
- Counting Subdivisions of the Pulse
- Systems of Counting

Sequential Counting of Pulse Units	Counting Note Values
Counting Numbers with	Naming Note Values
Subdivisions of Pulses	Substituting Ordinary Words
Counting Subdivisions of the Pulse	Counting with Rhythmic Syllables
Using Your Voice	Using *Solfège* Syllables
Singing with Neutral Syllables	Using Descriptive Phrases

Rehearsal Strategies

Practicing Hands Alone	Experimenting
Starting at the Very End	Improvising

Working with Pitch Patterns

Clustering Notes	Playing Impulse Units
Chunking	Spotting
Blocking	Isolating Pulse Notes

Refining Dynamics
- Spot-lighting
- Shaping
- Sectional Practice

Building Special Skills

Sight-reading	Performing	
Planning Choices of Fingering	Memorizing	
Trouble-shooting	*Aural*	*Kinesthetic*
Setting Goals	*Visual*	*Structural*
Selecting Appropriate Tempos	Developing Technical Skills	

Closing Thoughts

Additional Resource

In earlier chapters, I presented "Concepts to Consider" and "Activities to Explore" as separate categories, reflecting the usefulness of responding to two aspects of learning in two different ways. In this chapter, however, instead of clustering activities at the end, I incorporated them throughout. I have grouped musical activities into the following categories: Organizing Information, Working with Rhythms, Verbalizing, Rehearsal Strategies, Working with Pitch Patterns, Refining Dynamics, Building Special Skills, and Closing Thoughts.

As you read this material, I encourage you to experiment with different practice strategies. Identify activities you might utilize when approaching a new piece or working on a tricky passage. Try out different rehearsal strategies and discover which ones are most useful to you in your practice. When your Pianist's Practice Package includes a greater variety of rehearsal procedures, you will have more resources to utilize. Furthermore, when your practice time incorporates many musical activities, at the same time you are learning specific pieces you will be strengthening your complete musicianship. That will result in its being easier to transfer musical learning from one piece to another.

> *Each piece you encounter will present different challenges.*
> *At each stage of learning a piece, you will face different challenges.*

CONCEPTS TO CONSIDER AND ACTIVITIES TO EXPLORE

Organizing Information

Looking for Musical Patterns

When you are deciding how to practice a piano piece, it is important to be aware of the musical elements of contrast and repetition. Repetitions of musical patterns can involve rhythms, melodies, chords, textures, dynamics, and other expressive details. Some similarities are easy to hear, as when pitch patterns and rhythmic motives are repeated exactly or varied slightly. Other similarities may be perceived kinesthetically rather than aurally, such as passages in which the hands move in contrary motion, producing different pitches but mirroring muscular movements. Some passages may look very different on the page but feel similar in the body because of moving to a different register, transposing material to another key, or shifting between major and parallel minor. Some passages look alike on the page and sound similar but feel very different to the pianist as a result of moving material to the opposite hand, changing key signatures, using a different topographic plan, or shifting the placement of a rhythm within a measure.

Analysis—looking for patterns that are repeated or varied—is a process you can begin immediately. Notice what is the same and what is different. Search for patterns you can *hear* or *see* or *feel*. Your awareness of such patterns will help you decide how to practice them. In addition to playing a piece from start to finish, it is useful to locate similar passages and play them one after another. Learn to compare passages and skip around to different sections.

When we read words, we group letters into meaningful units. Consider the following string of letters divided into groups of ten:

onceuponat imetherewa sabeautifu lprincessw holovedaha ndsomeprin ce.

As those sixty-two letters are spaced, they have no meaning. They make no sense; they are nonsense. Once you start organizing the letters in relation to one another, however, they begin to acquire meaning. Years ago, when you were beginning to read words, you learned to recognize small details such as capital letters (*Once*), spaces (*upon a time*), and periods (after *prince*). Such details provided you with important organizational clues. Now look again at the same string of letters grouped into words:

Once upon a time there was a beautiful princess who loved a handsome prince.

If you continued the organizational process, you might observe that the sixty-two letters created fourteen words gathered in a single sentence. You could see that some words are longer than others: *a* has one syllable; *beau-ti-ful* has three syllables. Several of the words are verbs—action words like *was* and *loved*. Several of the words are nouns—*time, princess, prince*. Some describe other words (*beautiful, handsome*) and probably will be spoken with a bit more energy (*beau*-ti-ful, *hand*-some). Some of the words cluster into phrases, such as "Once upon a time . . . there was a beautiful princess . . . who loved a handsome prince." Usually when we talk, we do not analyze grammatical aspects of the English language, but our awareness of them adds to our understanding of language. That skill then makes it easier for us to sight-read bedtime stories, remember conversations, and talk with friends.

When you analyze music, you do something similar with notes. You notice musical patterns and make observations about what you see on the page. You do not need to take advanced music theory courses before you can begin approaching your music analytically. Analysis will make it easier for you to sight-read, memorize, perform, and—most important—

play musically. Musical analysis represents a worthwhile investment of your time and energy. If you are familiar with someone else's technical terms, use them. If not, create verbal or graphic descriptions that are meaningful to you.

When you notice details in your music and describe them, you are analyzing.

Writing in Your Musical Score

As you explore a piece, use your printed music to keep track of your discoveries. Do write in your music, using pencil, so you can change your mind. Let your score become a journal where you compile reminders of your musical observations and performance decisions such as those related to fingering, pedaling, articulation, dynamics, and gestures. Determine the key of the piece, or note the absence of a tonal center if the piece is not tonal. Identify basic chord patterns, especially those found at the ends of phrases and sections. Write in the definitions of words that are new to you. Select ordinary language to describe the expressive content of the piece. Indicate the counting system you plan to use. Decide on appropriate metronomic markings—target tempos for performance, as well as working speeds on different dates. Notice repeated sections. Use removable self-stick notes to jot down questions you want to ask your teacher and to frame tricky passages that will need special attention.

When I see a piano book that has totally clean pages with nothing written on them, I wonder whether the owner of that book has been approaching piano study as a form of typing. What has the student noticed about the expressive mood of the piece? What has been observed about the organization of the pitches? What fingerings are comfortable for that person? Writing in your own piano music is not a form of desecration. Your printed music is a very appropriate place to compile all sorts of observations and information.

Working with Rhythms

Clapping

There are two basic ways to clap music: fitting your clapping sounds with the rhythm or the pulse. Explore these distinctions with the folk song "Yankee Doodle" (see Example 8.1). When you clap with each word, you

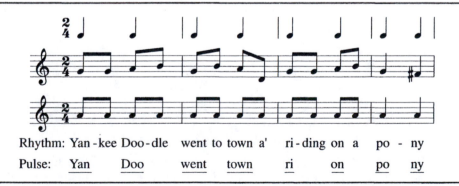

Example 8.1
Comparing Pulse and Rhythm ("Yankee Doodle")

are clapping the rhythm of this song. In contrast, when you clap only with the underlined syllables, you are clapping with the pulse of the music. Musicians need to become skilled in distinguishing between rhythm and pulse. They need to feel comfortable controlling both aspects of time and also using a wide range of speeds (very slow to very fast), dynamics (very soft to very loud), and gestures (very small and gentle to very large and energetic). When you clap, use a full, buoyant gesture so that one hand bounces off the palm of the other hand. Maintain flexibility at your joints (wrists, elbows, shoulders, and hips). Do not stiffen or immobilize your body while you clap.

Tapping

After clapping rhythmic patterns (with your elbows near the body and hands toward each other) but before playing them at the keyboard, often it is a useful transition to tap or pat the patterns on your lap or a tabletop (with palms down and elbows floating, away from the body). If you find it difficult to go directly from clapping to playing, insert some tapping activities.

For many piano students, the following is a helpful seven-step sequence of rhythmic activities:

Preview (look at the notation carefully; notice the expressive content as indicated by information related to tempo and dynamics)
Plan (decide what rhythmic words to assign to the passage; write yourself reminders)
Count (verbalize the rhythms at a steady pulse)
Conduct (experience the strong, steady pulses)
Clap (create the rhythm with both hands)
Tap (use loose wrists and a palm-down position) and then
Play

If you have experienced the energy level and mood of the piece when counting, conducting, clapping, and tapping, it will be much easier to incorporate that same expressive mood when you are ready to play the notes.

Conducting

Instead of clapping or tapping a steady pulse, some adult students find that they are more comfortable conducting a pulse pattern while holding a pencil or light baton, thus emulating their favorite musical maestro or mimicking Mickey Mouse—who shared the podium with the conductor Leopold Stokowski in Walt Disney's film *Fantasia.* The physical activity of conducting can help you understand and feel the rhythm of a passage. When you conduct a standard beat pattern and place the rhyth-

Down and Up and   Down and Up and   Down and Up and Down - Up -

Example 8.2
Describing a Conducting Pattern ("Yankee Doodle"). The arrows represent the direction the hand moves when conducting the song.

mic pulses in space, the sounds that occur between pulse points will deliver you to the next pulse. With the following patterns, use your right hand while you talk and describe where the conducting hand travels. Stand while you conduct. As you move your open hand, with the palm down, let it feel relaxed. Allow your wrist to bounce gently. Also allow your knees to bend slightly on first pulses (the downbeats).

Conducting Patterns

2:	**Down** and *Up* and **Down** . . .
3:	**Down** and *Right* and *Up* and **Down** . . .
4:	**Down** and *Left* and *Right* and *Up* and **Down** . . .
5 [2 + 3]:	**Down** and *Left* and *Right* and *Up* and *Up* and **Down** . . .
5 [3 + 2]:	**Down** and *Left* and *Left* and *Right* and *Up* and **Down** . . .
6 [3 + 3]:	**Down** and *Left* and *Left* and *Right* and *Right* and *Up* and **Down** . . .

Transfer this activity to a familiar song. As you sing "Yankee Doodle," move your hand down and up (conducting the song in $\frac{2}{4}$) and use descriptive lyrics (see Example 8.2).

Using a Metronome

Although the metronome can be a valuable rehearsal tool, I believe it should be sold with an attached label that says: "Warning! This device may be detrimental to the development of your musicianship. Use it with caution! The manufacturer does not assume responsibility for damages that result from misuse of this tool." The sound of mechanical ticks is predictable and punchy. When long chains of notes are absolutely even in dynamics and in time, the result is a mechanical effect.

With that warning in place, how can you utilize the metronome as a tool for developing musicality? Here are a few suggestions:

1. Use the metronome as a device for measuring time and monitoring sounds in time.
2. Notice metronomic markings selected by composers or editors. That information (such as (M.M. ♩ = 60) provides you with a definite, measurable suggestion of an appropriate tempo for the piece. Sometimes composers or editors provide a range of speeds (such as M.M. ♩ = 90–112), which can be very helpful to performers. Even when first working on a piece, imagine the music at the suggested performance tempo.

> *The greatest danger in using a metronome when you practice is that you may begin to sound like a metronome.*

Experience the piece in the tempo and mood that represent the musical goal. Long before you will be ready to play the piece at the target tempo, you can experience the music at that tempo (by conducting, singing, and moving). If you begin by imprinting a piece at a very slow tempo and later increase the speed, you actually are learning two completely different pieces, a slow one and a fast one. The gestures that work easily at a slow tempo probably will not be the gestures you will utilize at a faster speed. Divers do not practice doing flips in slow motion; baseball players do not practice hitting home runs in slow motion.

3. Use the metronome to determine the tempo that feels comfortable to you today, based on your understanding and technical control at that time. With a specific number as a reference point, a benchmark for future measurements, you can monitor your progress. "Today I played this passage securely at M.M. ♩ = 60. Last week my fastest accurate tempo was M.M. ♩ = 48. My goal is to become comfortable playing it at about M.M. ♩ = 110–120. Before my next lesson, I want to be able to play this passage at M.M. ♩ = 90."

4. Listen to various recorded performances and calculate the opening tempi of different pianists.

5. Set the metronome to tick various pulse units and divisions, checking yourself for steadiness and accuracy of rhythmic patterns.

[8] (M.M. ♪ = 208)	X	X	X	X	X	X	X	X
	1	2	3	4	5	6	7	8

[4] (M.M. ♩ = 104)	X	X	X	X	X	X	X	X
	1	and	2	and	3	and	4	and

[2] (M.M. ♩ = 52)	X	X	X	X	X	X	`X	X
	1	ee	and	uh	2	ee	and	uh

6. Without playing the notes at the keyboard, think through the piece. Let the metronome tick while you conduct the pulse pattern and count or clap the rhythms.

7. Expand your range of comfortable tempi. Begin with what feels like a very comfortable speed, then shift the metronome's speed by a few numbers higher or lower.

8. Set the tick for different note values. On the one hand, when you need to use a tempo that is slower than M.M. ♩ = 60, divide the pulse and set the metronome for a faster speed (such as M.M. ♪ = 120). By feeling smaller divisions of the pulse, it is easier to maintain a sense of momentum even when the larger pulse units are distant from each other.

```
60
    X         X         X         X
120
    X   X   X   X   X   X   X   X
```

On the other hand, when you need to use a tempo that is faster than M.M. $\quarternote$ = 240, group the pulses and set the metronome at a lower number (such as M.M. $\halfnote$ = 120).

```
240
    X   X   X   X   X   X   X   X
120
    X         X         X         X
```

Sometimes it is useful to increase the speed of a piece in very small increments, shifting the metronome by only one or two numbers each practice session. Sometimes, though, it is more helpful to make gigantic leaps, even skipping ahead forty or fifty digits. Some gestures actually are easier to do quickly than slowly, so be willing to take the risk. Sometimes a faster pulse speed actually will be easier to control.

Moving

In the tradition of the Swiss music educator Émile Jaques-Dalcroze (1865–1950) and his approach to training musicians, it can be helpful to use your body rhythmically. Move in different ways, especially making a distinction between pulse (the underlying, repetitive beat) and rhythm (a specific pattern that matches lyrics).

With a familiar, energetic song, such as "Yankee Doodle," put the beat unit into your feet by taking a step to fit each pulse. When farmers of Yankee Doodle's time were recruited and trained for the colonial army during the Revolutionary War, some of the young men literally did not know their left foot from their right. They did know, however, the differences between the crops they grew on their farms. So, to help recruits march in unison, the officers had them stuff some hay into their left boot and straw in the right. After that, marching together was as easy as One, Two, One, Two ("Hay Foot, Straw Foot, Hay Foot, Straw Foot").

Walk across an open space, moving at a comfortable but energetic tempo. Sing "Yankee Doodle" and step on the strong pulses.

Sing	Yan	Doo	went	town
Step	L	R	L	R

Sing	rid	on	po	ny
Step	L	R	L	R

After you feel comfortable stepping with the pulse, add another layer of sound (clapping the rhythm of the words). When this seems easy, tap the pulse with one hand and tap the rhythm with the other hand. Then change hands, reversing the combination. Put the rhythm in your feet and the pulse in your hands. Repeat this activity at several different speeds that reflect various moods such as weary, exuberant, determined, and angry).

Verbalizing

Counting Musically

To help develop a strong rhythmic sense, many piano teachers insist that students count aloud when learning pieces that are metric. It is possible to count accurately and still play unrhythmically. It also is possible to play musically without counting aloud. The activities of counting aloud and playing can interfere with each other, and sometimes it is useful to practice them separately. But when the activities of counting aloud and playing do not mesh easily, that usually identifies a weak link in the process of controlling pitch patterns in time. That difficulty has led countless piano teachers to a statement they have shared with generations of piano students: "If you can't count it, you don't really know it."

I encourage you to develop the skill of counting aloud as you practice. Since it is a physical skill, you will need to practice it, repeating your actions many times, not merely reading about the concepts. Remind yourself that the muscles needed to move your arms and hands (to clap patterns or depress keys) are different from the muscles needed to control your vocal mechanism (to verbalize). When you count aloud, let your voice sound buoyant and expressive, with slight gradations of pitch or intensity: "*One* Two and-uh *Three* let's go!!" If, instead, you speak slowly and like an automaton—"ONE TWO AND A THREE LET'S GO"—saying those words aloud will not help you play musically. The mechanical ticks of a metronome can lead to punchy, mechanical sounds from the piano. When you count aloud, keep track of groups of pulses and use your voice to create a vibrant, pulsating quality that reflects your pulsating heart.

> Do not let your voice sound like an unyielding metronome.

Counting Subdivisions of the Pulse

Read slowly the following numbers. First, let them be even in time; then intentionally make them sound abrupt, jerky, and mechanical:

One   Two   Three   Four

Now allow your voice to bounce lightly on each vowel sound, creating a duple division of the pulse:

-huhn	-oo	-ee	-or
WAN -	TOO -	THREE -	FOUR -
1	2	3	4

ONE - huhn   And-uh   TWO - oo - oo - oo   THREE-ee - ee - ee FOUR

Example 8.3
Counting Rhythmically

When you bounce twice on each vowel, you create a triple division of the pulse:

	-huhn-huhn	-oo-oo	-ee-ee	-or-or
WAN -		TOO -	THREE -	FOUR-
1		2	3	4

With three bounces, you establish a quadruple division of the pulse:

	-huh-huh-huhn	-oo-oo-oo	-ee-ee-ee	-or-or-or
WAN -		TOO -	THREE -	FOUR-
1		2	3	4

Study the rhythmic pattern in Example 8.3, then count it aloud, using an energetic, expressive voice. When you count, do not stop the sound of your voice abruptly, at each number. Instead, at whatever tempo you use, let the vowel sounds create a stream of energy that gently propels you toward the next pulse.

Systems of Counting

There are numerous systems of counting rhythmic material. All of them are helpful to some students, and I encourage you to explore several approaches. Become a specialist in one that seems comfortable to you, but return to other procedures periodically so that they can serve as alternative counting systems when you encounter rhythmic problems.

1. Sequential counting of pulse units

2. Counting sequential numbers with subdivisions of pulses

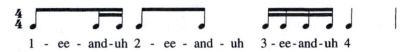

1 - ee - and-uh 2 - ee - and - uh   3 - ee-and-uh 4

3. Counting subdivisions of the pulse

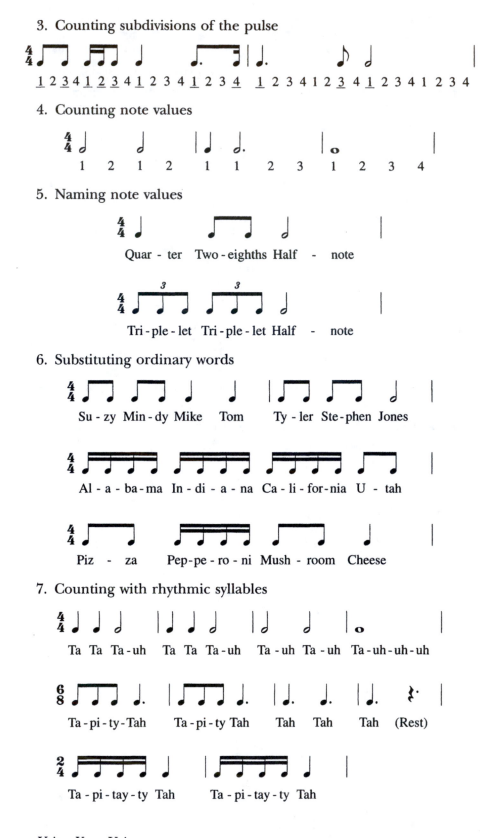

<u>1</u> 2 <u>3</u> 4 <u>1</u> <u>2</u> <u>3</u> 4 <u>1</u> 2 3 4 <u>1</u> 2 3 <u>4</u> <u>1</u> 2 3 4 1 2 <u>3</u> 4 <u>1</u> 2 3 4 1 2 3 4

4. Counting note values

1   2   1   2   1   1   2   3   1   2   3   4

5. Naming note values

Quar - ter   Two - eighths   Half - note

Tri - ple - let   Tri - ple - let   Half - note

6. Substituting ordinary words

Su - zy   Min - dy   Mike   Tom   Ty - ler   Ste - phen   Jones

Al - a - ba - ma   In - di - a - na   Ca - li - for - nia   U - tah

Piz - za   Pep - pe - ro - ni   Mush - room   Cheese

7. Counting with rhythmic syllables

Ta   Ta   Ta - uh   Ta   Ta   Ta - uh   Ta - uh   Ta - uh   Ta - uh - uh - uh

Ta - pi - ty - Tah   Ta - pi - ty   Tah   Tah   Tah   Tah   (Rest)

Ta - pi - tay - ty   Tah   Ta - pi - tay - ty   Tah

Using Your Voice

Your voice is one of your most valuable tools in developing musicianship.
By verbalizing during part of your piano practice time, you will develop

more melodic sounds and more expressive phrases. I am not referring to your vocal capacity as a solo singer or the natural quality of your voice, no matter how lovely it may be. I mean using your voice to demonstrate musical understanding and to internalize the expressive aspects of a piece. Some of the world's greatest orchestral conductors and instrumental soloists have terrible singing voices, yet they use their voices to demonstrate effectively the musical details they want to create instrumentally. There are many ways to use your voice when practicing piano music. Several systems of counting rhythmic patterns were described earlier.

> *Use your voice to emphasize rhythms, dynamic fluctuations, accents, and phrasing.*

Singing with Neutral Syllables

Instead of using one syllable repeatedly (*la la la* or *ta ta ta ta* or *duh duh duh duh duh*) it is more helpful musically—and more fun—to express yourself with a greater variety of vowels (*ah, oo, ee, oh*) and consonants (*d, t, b, sh, k, l, m, tsk*). The purpose of singing with neutral syllables is not to make sense linguistically but to reinforce expressive details related to grouping tones, articulating, and accentuating. Experiment with various vocal sounds and create your own lyrics to a familiar instrumental piece. Consider the examples in Example 8.4.

Using Solfège Syllables

Many adult early-level students already are familiar with the musical pitch syllables known as *solfege*. If you have seen the movie *The Sound of Music*, you know about *do, re, mi, fa, sol, la, ti, do* ("do, a deer, a female deer, re, a drop of golden sun," etc.).

The use of these musical syllables dates back at least to the thirteenth century. They were developed by European church musicians as a tool to help choirboys memorize scale patterns and relate each pitch to a specific sound. As *solfège* is used currently in music education, there are two different approaches: movable do and fixed do. Although both systems use the same terminology (that is, *do, re, mi, fa, sol, la, ti, do*), they reflect two distinct approaches to developing pitch control. With *fixed*

Example 8.4
Using neutral syllables. *Top*: Sh-boom; *Middle*: Theme from Mozart's Symphony in G/Minor, # 40; *Bottom*: Theme from Beethoven's Symphony in C Minor, # 5.

Example 8.5

Top: Examples of Solfège Syllables: 1 and 2 show movable do; 3 and 4 represent fixed do. *Bottom*: 1 = E-major (movable do; do-based major); 2 = e-minor (do-based minor); 3 = e-minor (la-based minor).

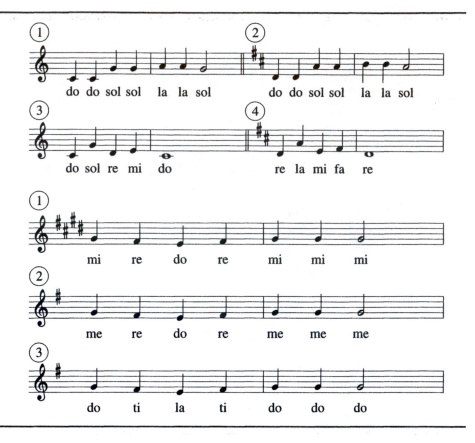

do, the syllable *do* always refers to the pitch known on the keyboard as C; syllable names are used in place of letter names. Proponents of the *fixed do* system, which is used extensively in parts of Europe and Asia, find that it helps students develop a strong sense of pitch memory. With *fixed do,* it is easier to remember what the pitch C sounds like and also what it feels like when the vocal cords vibrate to create a specific pitch.

With the *movable do* system, the syllable *do* always refers to the pitch that serves as the first note of a major scale. Advocates of this system find that it helps students develop a stronger awareness of tonal relationships and greater sensitivity to the function of pitches within the major and minor systems. That makes it easier to transpose melodies from C major to other keys. The *movable do* concept was central to the work of the Hungarian music educator Zoltán Kodály (1882–1967) and his approach to teaching children to read music. This system has been used extensively in the United States, and I find that it is very helpful when working with early-level piano students of any age.

Within the system of movable *do,* there are two approaches to using syllables with minor scales: *la*-based minor and *do*-based minor. With *la*-based minor, the sixth note of a major scale (*la*) serves as the tonal center for the related minor scale. With *do*-based minor, the home tone (tonic) of both major and parallel minor scales is called *do.*

Example 8.6
Opening melody of
Schumann's "Happy Farmer"

LH	5	3	2	1	5	3	2	1	2	3
A.	White	W	W	W	W	Black	W	W	W	W
B.	5	3 -	2	1 -	5	3	2	1	2	3 -
C.	Short	Long	Short	Long	Short	Short	Short	Short	Short	Long
D.	1	2	1	2	1	2	3	4	5	6
E.	C	F	A	C	F	B♭	D	F	D	C
F.	To	F	And	C	Then	go	right	back	to	C
G.	And	1 (2) and		3 (4) and		5	and	6	and	7 (8)
H.	Sol	do	mi	sol	do	fa	la	do	la	sol
I.	Do	fa	la	do	fa	ti	re	fa	re	do
J.	My	work	is	done	and	now	I'm	go - ing		home.

A	Color of the Keys (W = white key; B = black key)
B	Fingering Numbers
C	Proportions of Time
D	Counting the Number of Notes in a Fragment of the Melody
E	Letter Names
F	Naming Target Spots
G	Counting Pulses within a Longer Phrase Unit
H	*Solfege* Syllables (movable *do*)
I	*Solfege* Syllables (fixed *do*)
J	Expressive Lyrics

I encourage you to become comfortable singing some familiar melodies with movable *do* solfège. In conjunction with your keyboard study, explore the system of *do*-based minor. Let this vocabulary help you become more secure within a key and more comfortable transposing familiar patterns to other tonal centers (see Example 8.5).

Using Descriptive Phrases

By using words to describe a passage, you can verbalize information and remind yourself of different musical and technical aspects of a passage (see Example 8.6).

Rehearsal Strategies

Practicing Hands Alone

One of the most frequent practice activities for early-level students is playing a piece or a passage hands separately. This can be very helpful. With almost every piano piece, spending some time (at least in certain sections) practicing hands alone probably will be productive. Two-hand playing obscures all sorts of problems. When you listen to music played by a single hand, you can uncover many inaccuracies.

There are some disadvantages, however, to practicing hands separately. When you eventually put the piece together, as intended by the composer, each hand will provide the other with specific cues or signals. (Did you ever try to tie your shoelaces with only one hand?) By delaying the time when you start playing hands together, you actually are learning three separate pieces: one for right hand alone, one for left hand alone, and one for both hands. To avoid that inefficiency, there are several things you can do early in the learning process:

- Using both hands, tap the rhythm of both parts.
- Record one part and listen to it while you watch and become familiar with the other part.
- Put together very short sections that involve both hands.
- Play the melody in one hand and block the accompanying material in the other hand.
- Play only the notes that occur on a pulse (omitting the notes that deliver you to the next pulse).

Starting at the Very End

When working on a passage that seems difficult, sometimes it is useful to begin by playing the final note or chord. If you know where you are going, it is easier to reach your destination. Play the last note. Then play the last two notes. Continue to back up, adding one note at a time. Allow the rhythmic energy to propel you to the final goal. Instead of interrupting the musical flow by stopping in the middle of a piece or section, this strategy can help you become more aware of the pulse and keep it moving ahead. Descriptive words also can reinforce this activity:

1 note: "There."
2 notes: "To there" or "To [note name/A]."
3 notes: "Go to there" or "Go to A."
4 notes: "And to the end."
5 notes: "Go-ing to the end."
6 notes: "Keep go-ing to the end."

Experimenting

There is a difference between experimenting creatively (exploring musical options) and playing wrong notes or rhythms. If you intend to play an F♯ but carelessly depress the F key, that represents a mistake. But if you decide to substitute a G for the F♯, exploring the sound of a neighbor note, that alternative counts as an experiment. Use the assigned notes in the score as a starting point, but keep asking yourself: "What would it *sound* like if I . . . ?" and "What would it *feel* like if I . . . ?" Look again at Activity 1.3, "Experimenting with Sounds: Repeating and Varying Passages." Explore some of the options suggested in chapter 1. Those variants involve choices of tempo, dynamics, accentuation, duration, and articulation.

Composers place a few basic symbols on the page, trying to capture certain musical ideas. However, composers are dependent on other people to interpret symbols and produce sounds that convey the spirit of their music. Your interpretations, your insights, and your preferences are valid. Although accuracy in reading the basic score is expected, no two musicians will reach exactly the same decisions about what to do with the prescribed notes. You are free to explore what you and your piano can create on behalf of a composer. That is why *what ifs* are so important.

If you are pleased by the sounds created during an exploration, try to determine how you made those sounds: What did you do? How did it look and feel? Try to replicate the sounds you like. When you do not like the results, though, that is not a problem. The sounds you make will not hang around to haunt you the next time you play that piece. Unlike the experiments of visual artists (their sketches), your musical explorations will not clutter your practice room.

Improvising

In the eighteenth and nineteenth centuries, musicians were expected to improvise at their instrument. Improvising was considered an essential skill for all musicians. Although improvisation became a neglected art for many musicians in the twentieth century, it still is an important musical skill. I encourage you to explore this aspect of making music. As a result of improvising, you will develop greater technical control, harmonic awareness, rhythmic flexibility, understanding, performance security, and musical expressiveness. And, besides all of that, it is fun to improvise.

Unless everything you say is scripted, taken from a stage play or soap opera, you improvise whenever you speak. You arrange words in different ways to express your thoughts and feelings. Each time you tell people what you did last weekend, you probably vary your story slightly. You do not prepare a script, reporting on your "Saturday Night Live," and then simply repeat the words. You talk. You tell the story as you go along. Sometimes you will offer a twenty-second report, but at other times you might share an expanded version, perhaps even exaggerating some of the details (just a wee bit!). When you improvise, you play the notes you choose; you include what you want to share. When you improvise, there are no wrong notes. When you improvise, you have freedom to expand your usual range of dynamics and tempo. Play louder and faster, play softer and slower

> *Perhaps the most important thing for you to do during your practice time is* explore sounds and experiment *with gestures.*

than you would in the composed piano pieces you are learning. After you have experienced greater dramatic contrasts in your improvisations, you probably will find it easier to employ a wider range of expressive moods in piano pieces by other composers. After you create music to represent a dinosaur, create sounds to represent a dinosaur that is twice the size of the first one. After you improvise music to represent a scared child, create music to represent a terrified adult. After you choose music to represent a small cat, find sounds to represent a newborn kitten. Instead of telling yourself, "I need to play louder here," you might think, "Now I want to introduce an even more ferocious monster." Assume the role of the stage producer. Direct yourself to define characters. Project drama into the piano pieces you play.

Structure your piano practice sessions so that there is time to explore sounds. Improvisational activities need not replace your methodical preparation of composed pieces, but your experiments and musical improvisations comprise a valuable aspect of your musical development. In addition to using specific pitches, experiment with dynamics, registers, textures, pedaling, and articulation. Improvisations can be totally unstructured or they can be organized around a specific element such as a rhythm, melodic motive, technical pattern, series of chords, formal design, story, mood, or visual image.

Working with Pitch Patterns

The following activities relate to "Dreamscape" by George Peter Tingley (see Example 8.7).

Clustering Notes

Groups of notes in a piece can be clustered either with or without reference to pulse or rhythm.

1. Chunking. I use the term *chunking* for the process of finding notes (locating them on the keyboard), shaping the hand to prepare for those keys, and playing them in clusters (chunks) without regard to rhythm or tempo. It is especially helpful to chunk notes when practicing shifts to different sets of keys. Notice that in Example 8.8 both hands will cover five neighboring notes, using the same five pitches. Cover all ten keys, five in each hand (C-D-E-F-G). Then, as a chunk of sound, play all eight notes that appear in the first measure (LH: 51, RH: 253123). Continuing with each measure place the fingers over the keys needed and depress them as a single chunk. In going from one measure to the next, treat the two hands as a single unit and shift the entire set of ten fingers. Learn to trust that as you move your arms to a new location, your hands and all ten fingers will go along for the ride.

Example 8.7
"Dreamscape" by George
Peter Tingley. From the
collection *Dreamscapes*,
Book 1, © 1998 by Alfred
Publishing Co., Inc.
Reproduced with permission.

George Peter Tingley

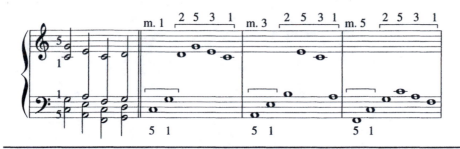

Example 8.8
Chunking Notes (Tingley "Dreamscape")

Example 8.9
Blocking Notes (Tingley "Dreamscape")

Example 8.10
Finger Pattern (Hanon, Exercise #1)

2. Blocking. I use the term *blocking* to represent sets of notes that are grouped and then played expressively and rhythmically (see Example 8.9). When blocking notes, select a speed and energy level that reinforces the expressive mood of the piece, thus previewing the performance goal. With Example 8.9 play each set of notes with a light, bouyant motion and create a gentle, dreamy, flowing sound. Experiment by using a relaxed tempo (M.M. ♩ = 84–120). Eventually the piece can be felt as duple meter ($\frac{2}{2}$), with two half note pulses per measure (M.M. ♩ = 60–72).

Playing Impulse Units

When working on a passage that has a long series of even note values, many pianists find it useful to distort the rhythm intentionally. As an example, use rhythmic variants with the right hand finger pattern of Hanon's Exercise #1 (see Example 8.10). As Hanon notated this pattern, it is to be played very evenly in time:

RH fingering: 1 2 3 4 5 4 3 2 1 2 3 4 5 4 3 2

But by creating places to stop and then surge forward, you will approach sets of notes with a single impulse, such as:

1   2 3 4 5   4 3 2 1   2 3 4 5 . . .

or:

1   2 3 4 5 4 3 2 1   2 3 4 5 4 3 2 1 . . .

or:

1 2 3   4 5 4 3   2 1 2 3   4 5 4 3...

or:

1   2 3   4 5   4 3   2 1...

or:

1 2   3 4   5 4   3 2   1 2...

For examples of impulse practice with a piece of music, see Example 8.11.

Spotting

When you practice and perform, it can be helpful to look away from the music placed on the piano rack and focus your attention on a specific key or finger. Before making a large skip, look ahead to the new location even before you begin moving toward it (see Example 8.12). Do look before you leap. Notice that within two measure groups, the hands center on the same pitch and simply shift hand over hand (LH–RH–LH–RH), crossing to new locations.

Sometimes it is useful to plan to shift your visual focus from one finger to another or one key to another. In Example 8.13, the right hand plays two intervals that involve a large skip, moving from C and A to B and G. Instead of watching the right hand's thumb travel over several keys (from C up to B), keep the hand shaped for the interval of the sixth. Then lift the entire arm and deliver the thumb to the key (B) directly

Example 8.11
Tingley "Dreamscape"

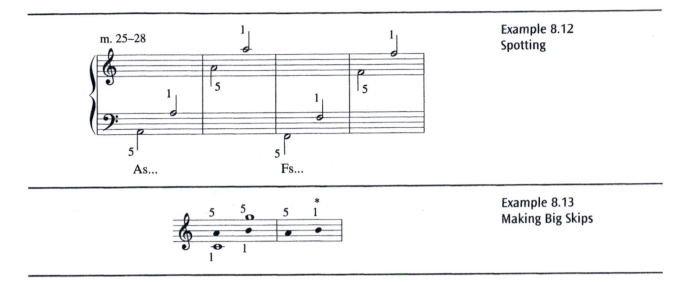

Example 8.12
Spotting

Example 8.13
Making Big Skips

above the key (A) that the fifth finger played a moment earlier. By focusing on the neighboring notes (5 on A and 1 on B) rather than the thumb's large skip (1 on C up to 1 on B), you will see a smaller distance. When you need to travel large skips, the astronautical approach (propelling the hand through the air to a new location) often will be more secure than the railroad engineer's route (staying right on the tracks).

Isolating Pulse Notes

With some pieces or passages, it is helpful to isolate the notes that occur on a pulse. This can be done on just the first note of a measure or with every pulse note. Before you are ready to play all the notes at a performance tempo, you can play selected pulse notes and imagine the missing notes that will deliver you to the next pulse. Look again at the entire three-page piece by George Peter Tingley (see Example 8.7). Then study Example 8.14. Select a comfortable tempo, but maintain a sense of the underlying rhythmic energy, imagining the intervening musical material that flows gently. In learning this piece, it is helpful to recognize that the pattern presented in the first measure actually provides the pitch material for the entire composition (thirty-six measures). The piece can be divided into five sections, as follows:

Measures 1–8	Each measure is played twice, repeated in the same location. C A F G
Measures 9–16	Each measure is played twice, repeated an octave higher. C A F G
Measures 17–24	Each measure is played twice, repeated an octave higher. A F C G

Measures 25–32   Each measure is played twice, repeated two octaves higher.

A F C G (only one octave higher)

Measures 33–36   Each measure repeats the same material in the same location.

C . . .

The entire piece can be summarized with the nine notes in Example 8.15. Play those pitches using the left hand's fifth finger. Then, while playing the same notes with the left hand, double them softly with the right hand's thumb (one octave higher).

Refining Dynamics

Spotlighting

Another strategy for developing proportional control of sound is to decide where on a stage you would place each character (note) and how bright a spotlight you would assign to each one. Sometimes it is helpful to be very specific in assigning levels of emphasis—for example, perhaps the melody in the right hand needs eight to ten units of sound, the countermelody in the left hand gets six to eight units, and the inner triplet figure has only two to four units. Musicians refer to this process as voicing layers of sound.

Example 8.14
Playing Pulse Notes (Tingley "Dreamscape")

Example 8.15
Isolating the Location of Left Hand Pitches (Tingley "Dreamscape")

Shaping

The horizontal aspect of dynamics is crucial to a sense of expressiveness and forward motion. When you experiment in shaping a line, internalize the sounds. Use your voice. Sing the melody. Try out various dynamic shapes; give more sound to certain tones. At this stage of making decisions, trust your musical instincts and choose the shaping you prefer. Later you will realize that the score itself provides clues related to harmony, texture, formal organization, pedaled resonance, and so on. Ultimately, though, it always will be your ears and your musical taste that determine your sound choices.

Sectional Practice

At any given moment, musicians need to be aware of two separate aspects of dynamics. Fine pianists constantly ask themselves, (1) "How does this one specific note relate to the notes before it and after it (horizontal shaping)?" and (2) "How does this note relate to other notes (higher or lower in pitch) that resonate at the same time (vertical shaping)?"

In dealing with layers of sounds (voicing), it is helpful to spend time with sectional practice. For pianists, *sectional practice* can refer to two different approaches:

1. Dividing a piece into distinct sections, described in terms such as *introduction, first phrase, second page, development section, measures 17–19, closing section, coda.*
2. Dividing a piece into layers of sounds, comparable to rehearsing the music assigned to a section of musicians within a performing group, such as all the brass players or violinists or tenors. With this sort of sectional practice, the goal is to clarify the proportion of sound you want to assign to each set of notes and then practice creating and controlling the balance of sound that you want. In this process, it is helpful to isolate layers. Using any comfortable fingering, play only the melody on top; then play only the inner voice; then play only the bass notes.

Building Special Skills

Sight-reading

Sight-reading is something you do with numbers and letters and words every day of your life. Long before children begin reading books, they observe traffic signs, notice messages on cereal boxes, learn to identify colors and shapes, and watch television ads. During the early stages of becoming readers of words, children play with letters, turn pages during story time, and watch big folks read. Children listen to adults talking and reading for years before they begin reading on their own.

To develop ease in reading music, provide yourself with many opportunities to read musical notation (see Appendix A, "Sight-Reading Checklist"). The skill of reading music at sight develops most easily when it is preceded by extensive readiness activities—listening and moving to music, singing, making music with rhythm instruments, watching and listening to others play music, observing musical scores, picking out familiar tunes (playing by ear), and improvising on chordal patterns. To become a good reader of music notation, you need to become familiar with elements that appear in pieces again and again, such as intervals, chords, rhythmic patterns, and expressive signs. When you read words or notes at sight, you are recognizing patterns you already have encountered.

As I mentioned in an earlier chapter, when you are developing music-reading skills it may be helpful to separate two aspects of notation: pitch (the *Where?* of reading music) and time (the *When?* of reading music). Ultimately the reading of pitch and rhythm need to fit together, but they can be practiced separately.

When working for continuity of pulse and accurate proportions of time relationships, it can be helpful to use a timekeeping device. Set the metronome at a tempo that allows you to feel unhurried and unharried. Provide sufficient subdivisions of the pulse to create a sense of momentum. Instead of being immobilized by the inertia of a very slow tempo, add a sense of movement by feeling more divisions of the pulse.

> *Facile readers of music do not decipher musical symbols one at a time.*

Facile readers of words do not process words one letter at a time. Adults who are fluent word readers usually were voracious readers of books when they were children. If you do a lot of music reading while building good keyboard habits, your ease in reading music notation also will grow.

One of the most enjoyable ways to strengthen sight-reading skills is to establish a working relationship with a piano ensemble partner. On a regular basis, play through stacks of piano duets. You probably will find that you and your partner are so busy keeping track of your own parts that you each take little notice of any flubs the other person makes. Many composers have created interesting duets that combine different levels of advancement, such as those to be played by a teacher (or more advanced student) and early-level student. Playing such duets will strengthen your reading and ensemble skills.

Planning Choices of Fingering

When you practice, you will need to decide how to assign ten fingers to many more keys. Fingering decisions are quite personal. They depend, at least in part, on the size, shape, and flexibility of the pianist's hand and body as well as the music itself. During your piano studies, you probably will encounter different editions of the same piece with contradictory fingering suggestions. Sometimes editors make a clear distinction between their own suggestions and the fingerings provided by the composer. At other times, you will have no way of knowing who provided a certain suggestion.

Begin by trying the fingerings printed in your music. If those suggestions do not solve the problem for you, explore other options. Whenever you decide to change the fingering, however, write on the music your alternate fingerings. Provide yourself with clear reminders of the fingering you plan to use in a passage. Later, if you change your mind again about a fingering pattern, erase those numbers and revise the fingering written in your score.

There are only a few basic options to choose from (see Example 8.16) when you decide how to finger a passage:

- Keep five fingers over five keys (A)
- Open the hand, spreading the fingers over a larger space (B)
- Contract the hand, squishing the fingers together (C)
- Move toward the middle of the keyboard, turning the fingers over the thumb (D)
- Move toward the outside registers, passing the thumb under the fingers (E)
- Deliver the hand to a new location, lifting the entire unit (F)

The most efficient fingerings are those that fit the natural shape of the hand, fit the topography of the piano keyboard, and coincide with

Example 8.16
Fingering options

natural accentuations of the music. Chopin's piano music often is described as being very pianistic. The notes fit the hand comfortably, the gestures feel natural, and the hand avoids fatigue because it constantly adjusts position. Chopin never forgot that the shapes of the right hand and left hand represent opposites. Chopin's music does not require all ten fingers to be equal in strength. Instead, it utilizes natural anatomical differences between stronger and weaker fingers. The notes in his pieces fit the pianist's hand as well as the piano keyboard. Often his music is technically challenging; but there always is an easy, efficient, natural way to depress the keys that he combines in a composition. The most successful composers of piano music incorporate sets of notes that correlate musical and kinesthetic aspects. When you hear such music, it sounds effective. When you play such music, the required movements feel comfortable. In the process of selecting finger patterns, listen to the sounds you create, but also notice the feeling involved in making those sounds. If feasible, let the right side and left side of the body mirror each other. In addition to choosing fingerings, try to select appropriate "armings" that allow both halves of the body to move in coordination.

Before you decide that a suggested fingering does not fit your hand, try it several times while making slight adjustments in the alignment of your hand and forearm. Check the placement of your fingers on the keys. Experiment with the height of your wrist and with various gestures. Many times the apparent awkwardness of a fingering does not result from the sequence of fingers assigned to those keys but from the placement of the hand on the keyboard. The size of your hand will affect fingerings, but when you plan fingerings for sets of notes be aware of the natural shape of your hand. Select fingerings that will allow for easy alignment and balance. Even if you have a large hand and can manage large stretches, it probably will be helpful usually to allow fingers 2, 3, 4, and 5 to remain over the space of four adjacent keys rather than spreading them over more keys.

Troubleshooting

Troubleshooting will be an important task during your practice sessions. If something is not going the way you would like, you need to figure out why. Is the problem related to:

Misreading pitches?

Misreading rhythms?

Misunderstanding a notational symbol?

Selecting an inappropriate tempo?

An error in the printed score?

Being unable to maintain a steady rhythmic pulse?

Awkward choice of fingering?

Choice of articulation?

Dynamics (horizontal, vertical, or sectional)?

Pedaling?

Fatigue (physical or mental)?

Inefficient use of the body?

Insufficient time invested in learning the piece?

What you do about the problem will depend on your diagnosis of the problem. Like a physician or mechanic, you cannot take appropriate action until you have diagnosed the situation accurately. "More practice" is rarely the best recommendation. Even if you do need to practice more, you also need to decide how to use your practice time effectively (for more on this topic, see Chapter 10, "Identifying and Diagnosing Problems.").

> *Technical and musical problems are not solved by endless repetitions.*

Setting Goals

Everyone is capable of achieving success. The greatest challenge in practicing is to create goals that you can meet with ease. When you do not meet a goal, the most significant aspect of that failure may be your selection of an inappropriate goal. At all stages of learning a piece or developing a skill, decide what strategies will enable you to strengthen skills needed on the way to your goal. Divide your work into smaller tasks.

> *Select goals that will result in success.*

During your practice sessions, you will need to set goals you can meet in varying lengths of time. What do you plan to accomplish in the next months, weeks, days, hours, half hours, quarter hours, minutes, or seconds? After setting goals and attempting to meet them, you need to decide whether or not you actually met those goals. If you did not, then you need to use that awareness as you continue the process of establishing your next set of goals.

Selecting Appropriate Tempos

Early in the process of learning a piece, it is useful to experience the music at a tempo appropriate to the expressive mood of the piece. Even before you can play all the notes up to tempo, allow yourself to imagine the piece at performance tempo.

> *Even when you practice a piece under tempo, it is important to maintain accurate proportions of time and appropriate contrasts of dynamics.*

The standard tempo indications provided by composers—such as *Allegro, Andante,* and *Presto*—describe not only the speed of pulses but also the expressive mood of the music.

Performing

When working on a piece, you need to make a distinction between times when you will stop and start and other times when—no matter what—you will keep going. Practice often involves a lot of stopping and restarting while you repair, improve, reinforce, experiment with options, and take care of problems. But actual performances should not involve stops and starts. Let a portion of your daily practice involve the activity of performing. The skill of not stopping needs to be practiced on a regular basis. You need to be able to turn off that little switch marked *Stop/Go* and, on command, keep the music going in spite of any disasters you experience or sounds you would like to replace. Because this sort of nonstop playing is a skill, you will have to practice it (see Chapter 11, "Preparing to Share Music," and Appendix C, "Performance Checklist [Last-minute Thoughts before Takeoff]").

> *You need to practice the act of performing.*

Memorizing

When children memorize a piano piece, they tend to play it over and over and over again until one day, almost like magic, they discover that they remember the piece and can play it by heart, without looking at the book. Whether or not you choose to perform your music without looking at the printed score, I encourage you to develop the skill of memorizing piano music. It is useful to approach memorization as a regular activity in your practice routine.

There are many benefits to the activity of memorizing. Performing from memory involves two distinct acts: imprinting and recalling. If you have imprinted information securely, it will be easier to recall the information. Whatever you imprint is in your brain, just as those car keys you have been looking for are somewhere in the house and that computer file was saved somewhere on your hard drive. It will be helpful to associate the process of memorization with the process of analysis and performance. Careful observation is the first step in memorizing. Do not wait until you can play through the entire piece without errors. If you begin by memorizing very short, easy pieces and short sections of more challenging pieces, your memorization skills will increase along with your technical and musical skills.

> *When you begin learning a piece of music, make meaningful observations right away.*

There are several distinct aspects of memory: aural, visual, kinesthetic, and structural. All of them are valuable. All of them can be strengthened. In varying proportions, most secure performers incorporate all four aspects of memory. As you practice, include a variety of activities that will reinforce your perceptions of how musical events sound and look and feel and are organized. In the process of memorizing, you will:

- Get to know the music more thoroughly
- Become more aware of patterns and variations
- Gain a better understanding of how the composer uses musical materials
- Strengthen your sense of the totality of the piece and how one musical element affects another
- Play with greater musicality

The following practice activities can be useful in memorizing a piece. Pay attention to several distinct aspects of the music, focusing on one category at a time.

1. *Aural.* Clap the rhythm of one hand's part. Sing the passage. Reinforce your imprinting of the material by labeling it in many different ways: letter names, scale numbers, finger numbers, syllables, counting patterns, or expressive words. Immerse yourself in the sounds of the piece, using the given notes as material for improvising. Talk to yourself, describing aloud what you need to do when you play the piece.

2. *Visual.* Observe information included in the printed music. Also observe what your hand and the keyboard look like when you play the notes. Notice various physical details such as the direction and duration of pitches, the keys moving down, fingerings, shape of the hand, movement of the wrist, pattern of the black and white keys, and so on.

3. *Kinesthetic.* Notice how it feels to play various sections. Notice what it feels like to remain with some keys longer than others. Be aware of the feeling you have when playing in different locations on the keyboard, at various speeds, and with various levels of dynamic intensity. Practice playing passages off the keyboard or on your lap. Walk to the pulse while singing the melody.

4. *Structural.* Be aware of basic organizational factors such as time signature, key signature, phrase lengths, repetitions, chord patterns, and variations.

As I mentioned earlier, the activity of memorization is a skill. In the process of memorizing, you will strengthen that skill. After working on a passage one day, the next time you return to it you may feel that you have forgotten everything you imprinted the day before. Even if that happens, your reinforcement of memory really is not lost. You simply need further reinforcement of the process in order to strengthen the memory paths. Each time you repeat the imprinting process, it becomes easier to imprint new information and recall other information. The next day, your review process will require less time. It is helpful to work with overlapping segments of a piece, reinforcing previous passages but also adding some new material each day.

Developing Technical Skills

Technique and musicianship are so closely related that they really cannot be separated (see chapter 9, "Developing Technical Skills"). At the same time you build your musical skills, you also strengthen technical skills that will enable you to create the musical effects you seek. Whenever you work on technical material, be aware of the expressive sounds you create. Play *music*, not just *notes*. In solving technical problems, you will resolve musical problems.

> *Every technical problem actually is a musical problem.*

Closing Thoughts

I do not intend to suggest that all of the activities described in this chapter should be used during every practice session or even with every piece. When you practice, pick and choose activities you find useful. Auto mechanics, when repairing a car, do not use every tool in the shop. They select specific tools to use with different cars. As a practicing pianist, you will not need to use every possible procedure with every piece. As you

> *Let your practicing be a time to investigate sounds and motions.*

gain experience in choosing helpful activities, notice which strategies are most useful to you. At what stage of your work are certain activities more helpful? How often do you need to repeat a certain activity? Which activities are worth repeating daily? What musical styles are helped most by which practice strategies? Which rehearsal strategies require longer periods of time or concentration? Which ones can be used when you have only a few minutes to work? Which activities can be done away from the piano?

Let your creativity and imagination turn practice sessions into explorations of musical puzzles.

Let your piano practice sessions become periods of time when you enjoy making music.

ADDITIONAL RESOURCE

Book

Shockley, Rebecca Payne, *Mapping Music: For Faster Learning and Secure Memory* (Madison, WI: A-R Editions, 1997). "A guide for piano teachers and students." Shockley presents her strategies for diagramming a piece and explains how a graphic description can serve as a map when learning a piano piece. Author includes more than fifty musical examples selected from piano repertoire (early to advanced levels). Her concepts can be applied to piano music at any level of difficulty.

9   Developing Technical Skills

CHAPTER OUTLINE

Concepts to Consider
  Technique and Musicianship
  Piano Technique as Ear-Training
  Gestures Used in Depressing Keys and Controlling Sounds
  Three Basic Categories of Technical Materials
    Scales
    Chords
    Arpeggios
  Parallel and Contrary Motion
  Working from the Middle
    Middle C
    Middle D
    Middle E
    Middle G-sharp/A-flat

Activities to Explore
  Chromatic Scales
  Chords
  Arpeggios

Thoughts about Words
  Repetitive Finger Patterns
  Etudes
  Peaks and Plateaus
  More or Less

Additional Resources

Technique is simply the development of a physical skill that enables you to accomplish something. As an adult, you have developed a wide variety of techniques and have become skillful in many areas. Some of these skills will transfer directly to the piano. Perhaps you already play another instrument and have become proficient in deciphering the standard system of rhythmic notation. Perhaps you are expert in managing resources and will use your practice time efficiently. Perhaps you play piano by ear and have developed a strong awareness of the correlation between pitches you hear and their location on the keyboard. Other skills you have developed may have less direct connection with your new activities at the keyboard, but I encourage you to look to them for valid analogies.

CONCEPTS TO CONSIDER

Technique and Musicianship

Technique is what enables you to make music, but piano technique is not just something done with the fingers or body. For musicians, technique can never be isolated from the music itself. Technique and musicianship are as closely interrelated as two sets of threads in a weaving, one set (the warp) going from top to bottom and the other set (the woof) going across and between those threads.

> *Technique must always be monitored by* listening *carefully to what happens.*

The most important reason to practice scales and other technical patterns is not what they will do for your fingers but how they will help your ears and your brain. By working daily with the pitch patterns upon which most piano music is based, you will develop greater aural awareness and kinesthetic comfort. As you learn to cluster information (encoding it in more compact sets of information), it will become easier to read and remember musical patterns. When you play scales and other technical routines, you can utilize those basic building materials to explore gradations of sound. In practicing technical material (musical patterns), you can strengthen your consistency and your confidence. You will gain more control of various rhythmic aspects of your playing, such as maintaining a steady pulse or making minute gradations of speed like those represented by *accelerandos* and *ritardandos*. You will increase your ability to concentrate, plan, and prepare for changes—in direction, register, fingering, dynamics, and touch. You will gain control in making gradual changes of dynamics—pacing long *crescendos* and *diminuendos*. You can strengthen your creativity by improvising with blocks of compositional material. When you spend time with technical material, you are investing in your total musical development.

Some athletes and musicians establish a set routine that they go through at every practice session, making sure that they repeat the same activities in the same order every day. Other people prefer to vary their activities but to incorporate daily something from each basic category of technical work. Some music students like to begin their practice with technical routines; others prefer to begin the day's work by memorizing a passage or playing through pieces without interruption. Then, later in the day, when they might feel tired, they will spend time with technical patterns. The crucial thing, though, is that whenever you practice technique, you *listen* astutely to the sounds you create, you *observe* carefully what it feels like to play those keys, and you *remind* yourself of the specific patterns the notes represent (such as intervals, scales, chords, and harmonic sequences).

> You need to experiment and find out which approach is most helpful to you.

Piano Technique as Ear-Training

Having a strong piano technique sometimes is equated with playing loud and fast. Velocity (speed) is a characteristic of many exciting piano pieces, and finger dexterity is an essential skill for pianists to develop. Finger wiggling and virtuosity, however, are not the only techniques needed when playing the piano. Virtuoso pianists do play loud and fast, but piano technique also necessitates the ability to play softly and to control minute variations of speed and duration of tones.

> Piano technique requires the ability to create and control a great variety of piano sounds.

To become comfortable playing technical material, in addition to knowing what specific notes belong in a pattern, you will need to feel at ease with three categories of information: visual, aural, and kinesthetic.

> *Visually,* pianists need to know where to go, what keys to use, which fingers to use, how to place the hand on the keyboard, the topographic appearance of patterns, and the appropriate alignment of the body at the instrument. When you play scales, you need to visualize the sequence of keys you will depress.
> *Aurally,* pianists need to know what specific patterns sound like (in terms of both pitches and dynamics). When you play a scale, you need to know what the next tone in the series will sound like before you depress the appropriate key.
> *Kinesthetically,* pianists need to know what patterns feel like and which gestures to employ in order to control them. When you play a scale, you need to anticipate the appropriate combination of muscular events before you create them.

For musicians, all technical training ultimately involves listening carefully and adjusting the body in response to sounds. Artistic pianists, at all levels, are able to create and control many piano sounds: a huge range of dynamics, effective use of the damper pedal to add resonance, and great diversity of speeds and expressive moods. Because of musicianship, pianists are able to imagine and select appropriate sounds. Because of technique, pianists are able to create and control the sounds they want to use.

When students have difficulty playing scales and other technical material, often there is a missing link related to one of the three categories described previously. Sometimes students do simply need to practice longer, reinforcing a new physical skill until it becomes an automatic response. At other times, however, it may be useful to reinforce a difference aspect of perception (visual, aural, or kinesthetic) in order to strengthen the broader understanding of concepts and the control of muscles. Students sometimes ask, "Why do I need to keep practicing scales and other technical patterns? I already know my scales. I learned them a long time ago." If you hear yourself asking that question, please return to chapter 2, "Learning about Learning." Reread the discussion of differences between content-related information (declarative memory) and skills (procedural memory).

> *To play artistically, pianists need to develop both musicianship and technique.*

Gestures Used in Depressing Keys and Controlling Sounds

When we walk and run, our natural movements include bending the knees and ankles. When we play the piano, our movements need to include flexibility of wrists and elbows. Lift your hands and then drop them gently onto your lap. Repeat that gesture while noticing the motion of your wrists. As you lift your hands (by lifting your arms), notice how your wrists move upward. As you drop your hands, watch your wrists drop to the surface of your legs. Inhale as you lift; exhale as you drop. Now, in contrast, lock your wrist and lift your hand without making any movement of the wrist. Sometimes that gesture is called the Iron Glove approach to piano playing. It involves moving the entire forearm from the elbow or the whole arm unit from the shoulder. Keeping your wrists locked, drop your hands onto your lap. Did you hear a thud? Did you see an abrupt movement when you landed? Do you feel a stiff jolt?

The coordinated keyboard movements of fine pianists incorporate a combination of downward and upward movements. Let your explorations at the piano include experiments with various gestures. Different motions will result in different (but very predictable) sounds. When you make a sound you like, notice how you moved. When you hear a tone quality you do not like, remember what gesture was involved in depressing the keys that time. Your awareness of the correlation between gestures and sounds will result in your playing with greater musical sensitivity.

> *Piano keys can be set in motion both by downward and by upward movements of the arm or hand.*

Both downward and upward movements can be used to create tones that are long or short, loud or soft, low or high.

Example 9.1
Gestures: ↓ = dropping;
↑ = thrusting;
〰↗ = walking.

- With downward motions, as soon as you reach the full depth of the key bed you need to stop the downward motion and allow the wrist to cushion the gesture, just as you would bend your knees when landing after jumping off a curb. At the piano, this motion sometimes is described as free fall, deadweight, dropping, sinking into a soft beanbag, or plopping onto a cushioned lounge chair.
- In using upward motions, you begin on the surface of the key and then push against that stable surface as you begin to move up, just as you might push against the arms of a chair when preparing to stand. This sometimes is described as plucking or twitching (for very soft, short sounds), thrusting (when creating very full sounds), getting off a hot stove, detached, or staccato.

Example 9.1 represents three distinct gestures that pianists use frequently. All of these gestures can be used in any register of the piano, at different speeds, with different duration of sounds, different amounts of energy, and different combinations of notes. All of these gestures incorporate subtle wrist movements in response to the expressive quality of the music.

- Beginning above the key surface and moving *down*. (Wrist drops below the level of the fingertips.) [Dropping: ↓]
- Beginning on the key surface and moving *up*. (Wrist moves up while the fingers float away from the keys.) [Thrusting: ↑]
- Moving into the key and then transferring weight to another fingertip before floating *up*. (Wrist rotates slightly as one fingertip pivots on the pad and the next finger prepares to depress another key.) [Walking: 〰↗]

When working on the technique of controlling sounds, it is useful to utilize basic tonal patterns such as scales, chords, and arpeggios in many different ways. Vary your gestures so that you can monitor the duration and loudness of sounds.

Three Basic Categories of Technical Materials

For pianists, three categories of pitch material provide the most basic building blocks of piano technique: scales, chords, and arpeggios. When you spend time on technical aspects of your musical development, the work should be mentally challenging, acoustically gratifying, and physi-

> *Let various pitch patterns provide frameworks for exploring sounds and motions.*

cally comfortable. Vary the patterns by using different speeds, dynamic levels, and expressive moods. Explore different registers, and experiment with different distances between hands.

Scales

When you play scales on the piano, you move from one finger to an adjoining finger, shifting the focused weight so that it will be centered on the next digit of the hand. For pianists, playing scales is like walking. That is very different from what woodwind players experience when they play scales. For woodwind players, each separate pitch requires a different configuration of the fingers. Two pitches that are neighbors on the music staff may be widely separated from each other in terms of the placement of fingers on the keys of a flute or clarinet. There are many ways to experience the feeling of fingers walking across the piano keyboard.

In working with scales and broken chords, I suggest that every day you experience them in two different ways:

- Listen to and work in every major and minor tonality. A five-note tonal pattern or a series of broken triads can be played in all twelve major and minor keys in less than two minutes. There is time during your practice to visit every tonality every day.
- Immerse yourself in a single tonality for several minutes. Experience what it feels like to be in the world of a specific key (such as C major or A♭ major or F♯ minor). Each tonality has a unique sound, look, and feel. Every day, explore a different tonal center. Improvise using the eight pitches that belong to a selected major or minor tonality.

The easiest scale pattern to experience at the keyboard every day is the chromatic scale, based only on neighboring keys (see Activity 9.1, "Chromatic Scales").

Chords

When playing solid chords, each finger within the hand needs to be balanced. Just as the three legs of a tripod adjust to uneven surfaces, when you play a chord your hand needs to adjust to the keyboard's topography. Before playing solid chords that have three or four notes, become comfortable playing single notes and pairs of notes, especially the intervals of fifths, sixths, and octaves played with your outside fingers, 1 and 5 (see Activity 9.2, "Chords"). Maintain the alignment of the hand and forearm, adjusting their relationship as the topography changes.

Arpeggios

Arpeggios are broken chords that extend beyond a single octave. However, I recommend that you begin arpeggio activities by playing three-note chords hand-over-hand, one tone at a time (see Activity 9.3, "Arpeggios"). After your ears, eyes, and hands become secure in finding the keys you need to depress and your ears are familiar with the sound of broken chords (creating a chain of chord tones), it will be much easier to develop the ability to play arpeggios with a single hand.

Parallel and Contrary Motion

On the music staff, when you see notes moving in parallel motion they appear to be similar. But in order to create those parallel pitches with two hands at the piano keyboard, the body actually controls opposing motions. In contrast, however, when you see notes moving in opposite directions (in contrary motion), they appear to be different but result from the right and left hands using similar, coordinated movements (see Example 9.2). When you swing your arms out and in (as if flapping your wings), the two halves of the body move the same way. But when you swing your arms across the body, moving them in the same direction (together to the right or left), the two halves of the body make motions that are in opposition to each other.

Working from the Middle

At the piano keyboard, often it is easier to move in contrary motion than in parallel motion. This concept is especially useful when developing technical control of pitch patterns.

Middle C

In terms of notated pitches on a music staff, *middle C is the center of the notational world.* Notice the mirroring in the sets of keys that create A minor chords (see Example 9.3). When developing reading skills, it is useful to relate pitch locations on the keyboard to pitch locations on the grand staff. When you can locate easily the seven ACE groups on the keyboard, you will be able to ace the challenge of locating any pitch at the keyboard. Once you establish control of seven sets of three white keys (ACE), those reference points will enable you to identify and locate all other neighboring pitches (G, B, D, and F as well as sharps and flats; see Example 9.4).

Middle D

In terms of the topography of the piano keyboard, *middle D is the center of the instrument.* Moving out from D, the black and white keys mirror each other. Your sense of kinesthetic comfort and coordination will be enhanced by using D as the central pitch (see Figure 9.1).

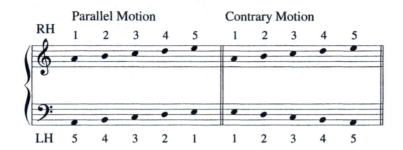

Example 9.2
Parallel and contrary motion

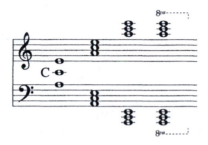

Example 9.3
ACE groups

Example 9.4
Neighbor tones

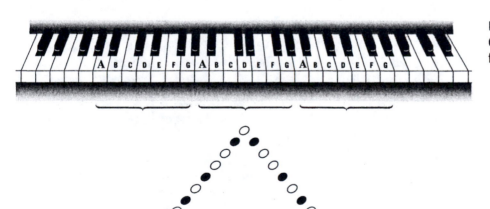

Figure 9.1
Color patterns moving out from D

Example 9.5
Contrary motion scales from E. Black note heads represent black keys; ○ = E; ● = F♯.

E Major Scale · E Minor Scale (Harmonic)

RH 1 2 3 1 2 3 4 5 · 1 2 3 1 2 3 4 5

LH 1 2 3 1 2 3 4 5 · 1 2 3 1 2 3 4 5

Example 9.6
Color patterns moving out from a central black key

G♯ A

A♭ G

Middle E

When you are working with major and minor scale patterns, E is a useful starting pitch. When you play an E major or E harmonic minor scale in contrary motion, the color patterns of the black and white keys mirror each other (see Example 9.5).

Middle G-sharp/A-flat

The middle of the set of three black keys also functions as a central mirroring point in terms of keyboard topography (see Example 9.6).

ACTIVITIES TO EXPLORE

ACTIVITY 9.1   *Chromatic Scales*

When one is playing a chromatic scale at the piano, no keys are omitted. In preparing to play chromatic scales, try the following sequence of activities:

1. With your right hand, using only the middle finger (3), begin on F♯ and play only black keys. Play F♯ and bounce lightly and quickly to the right, onto the neighboring black key (G♯). Continue ascending (going to the right, moving out to the very highest F♯), then change direction and descend, returning to the beginning key (see Example 9.7).
2. Play the same black keys (still using the right hand's middle finger on each black key), but add lightly the thumb (on the very next white key). This time, connect the sounds (walking rather than bouncing). When you come to a pair of white keys, play the first one and omit the second (see Example 9.8).
3. Play all of the keys in the chromatic scale. When you have two white keys together, use the thumb on the inside white key and 2 on the second white key (see Example 9.9).

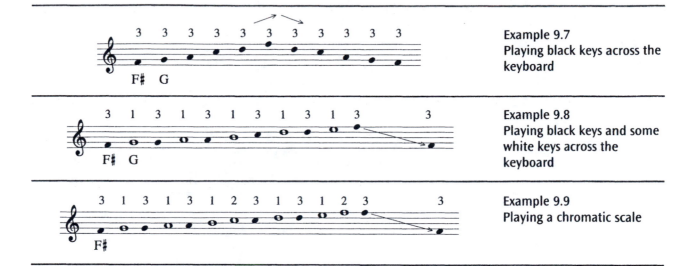

Example 9.7
Playing black keys across the keyboard

Example 9.8
Playing black keys and some white keys across the keyboard

Example 9.9
Playing a chromatic scale

4. Using the left hand, repeat Steps 1–3. Begin with the middle finger (3). Start on a B♭ and move out (down).

5. After you feel comfortable playing chromatic scales with either hand, combine the hands. Begin with the middle note of the set of three black keys (G♯/A♭), using the middle finger (3) of both hands. In contrary motion, the pitches played by the right and left hands will not be the same letter names, but the topography (pattern of white and black keys) will create a mirrored, coordinated fingering.

ACTIVITY 9.2 *Chords*

1. Drop the hand onto the keyboard and play single tones (use a middle finger; practice this both with a series of second fingers and with only third fingers). Maintain the sensation that the middle of the hand is centered securely, in direct alignment with the arm (see Example 9.10). Also experiment by initiating the motion with the finger *on* the key and moving upward.

2. Play a series of parallel sixths, always lifting and shifting the entire hand by half steps. Use your outside fingers (thumb and little finger). Develop a sense of what the interval of a sixth feels like and sounds like (see Example 9.11). As the keyboard topography changes, the hand and arm will need to adjust slightly to maintain a comfortable alignment of the muscles. With pairs of sixths, there are only four possible color combinations of keys (see Example 9.12): white and white, black and black (move hand closer to the fall board), black and white (move the thumb nearer the fall board, allowing the elbow to move nearer the torso), white and black (move the little finger nearer the fall board, allowing the elbow to float away from the body). *Note.* Instead of using sharps and flats to notate these patterns, ovals with black centers are used to represent black keys and ovals with white centers are used to represent white keys.

Example 9.10
Centering the hand on single tones

RH 3; 2

D D♯

Example 9.11
Balancing parallel sixths

5
1

Example 9.12
Possible color combinations of intervals

Example 9.13
Minor and major triads

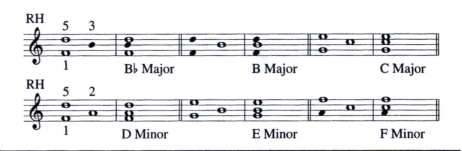

RH 5 3 — 1
Bb Major   B Major   C Major

RH 5 2 — 1
D Minor   E Minor   F Minor

3. Play a series of parallel triads. Play the outside notes alone; then add the inside note (see Example 9.13). Next, play the set of three notes simultaneously. *Note:* These triads are presented in inversions: the root of the chord is not the lowest note.

ACTIVITY 9.3 *Arpeggios*

1. Using both hands, play a series of triads one note at a time (see Example 9.14). For example:

	C E G	C E G	C E G	C
RH				3
LH			5 3 1	
RH		1 3 5		
LH	5 3 1			

2. Establish a tempo and rhythm that feels comfortable to you. Let the complete arpeggio sound and feel like a single swish of tones (similar to the strumming sound when a harpist or guitar player moves a hand across many strings).
3. Experiment by using various registers, dynamics, and articulations.

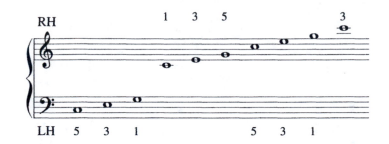

Example 9.14
Hand-over-hand arpeggios

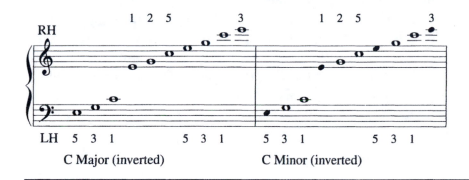

C Major (inverted)   C Minor (inverted)

Example 9.15
Major and minor broken
chord patterns

4. Use various combinations of pitch. Transpose the pattern to different tonalities. Invert the triad. Work with both major and minor patterns. (To create a minor chord, lower the third of the chord by a half step; see Example 9.15).

THOUGHTS ABOUT WORDS

Repetitive Finger Patterns

Repetitive finger patterns incorporate an alternation of movements that open and close the hand. With basic finger patterns such as those devised by Hanon, you can travel over the entire keyboard. As with finger exercises, it is essential that you avoid playing these patterns too loud, too fast, or too long. Always listen to your sounds, maintain a rhythmic pulse, and create a sense of buoyancy and musical vitality.

Etudes

Etudes (the French word for studies) are short compositions that usually focus on a single technical skill. Often etudes require great velocity. In the nineteenth century, two of the best-known composers of virtuoso piano etudes were Carl Czerny (1791–1857) and Frédéric Chopin. Many easier but gratifying piano etudes were composed in the nineteenth century by Muzio Clementi (1752–1832), Johann Baptist Cramer (1771–1858), Johann Friedrich Bürgmuller (1806–1874), and Stephen Heller (1813–1888).

Figure 9.2
Five-step plan (More or Less)

Less $\overset{5}{\longleftarrow}$ $\overset{3}{\longleftarrow}$ $\overset{1}{\bullet}$ $\overset{2}{\longrightarrow}$ $\overset{4}{\longrightarrow}$ More

Peaks and Plateaus

Technical growth does occur as a result of challenging yourself to reach new heights. But the consolidation and integration of technical skills takes place during those times when you remain on plateaus. Allow yourself to enjoy plateaus as well as peaks. Do not assume that staying put equates with sliding backward. If you always work on harder and harder pieces, it actually will be more difficult to develop a sense of comfort and facility. Note that the French word *facile* means "easy." Playing with ease and facility involves playing music that seems easy. Enjoy repeating what you can do well and using skills that have become secure and comfortable.

More or Less

As a strategy for increasing your zones of technical comfort—to increase your speed, expand your range of dynamics, extend your range of motion, and build your endurance—I suggest you try a five-step plan, "More or Less" (see Figure 9.2).

1. Begin by doing the task at a comfortable, moderate level.
2. Repeat the activity, doing it *a little more*: (a little faster, louder, higher, or longer).
3. Reinforce the activity by doing it *a little less*: (a little slower, softer, lower, or shorter).
4. Repeat the activity, doing it *even more*.
5. Reinforce the activity by doing it *even less*.

ADDITIONAL RESOURCES

Virtually every piano method series published today includes collections of exercises, patterns, and etudes. Your piano teacher can direct you to technical materials that are appropriate to your needs. When using such materials, remember that the development of technique always involves musicianship. Piano technique is a form of ear-training.

Books

Bernstein, Seymour, *Music-Physi-cality: Making a Physical Connection to Music Feeling for the Beginning Pianist* (Milwaukee: Hal Leonard, 1991). Guidebook with fourteen lessons to read and explore at the keyboard.

Fink, Seymour, *Mastering Piano Technique: A Guide for Students, Teachers, and Performers* (Portland, OR: Amadeus Press, 1992). Comprehensive study of coordinated movements (fundamental, applied, and synthesized). Systematic program for developing effective piano technique. Includes many drawings and musical examples. See also *Mastering Piano Technique: The Video* (Portland, OR: Amadeus Press, 1994), videotape, 86 minutes.

Sandor, Gyorgy, *On Piano Playing* (New York: Schirmer, 1981). Extensive discussion of basic technical patterns. Sandor, a distinguished concert pianist, always approaches piano technique in relation to the music.

YOUR NOTES

10 Identifying and Diagnosing Problems

CHAPTER OUTLINE

Concepts to Consider
   Musical and Technical Problems
   Describe Rather Than Judge
   How Did You Know There Was a Mistake?
   How Did You React To the Mistake?
   What Was Wrong?
   When Did the Mistake Occur?
   Where Did the Mistake Occur?
   Why Did the Mistake Occur?
   How Can You Avoid That Mistake in the Future?
   How Can You Minimize Making Mistakes in the First Place?

Activities to Explore
   Recording Your Practice
   Comparing Performances of the Same Work
   Locating Variants within a Piece

The process of identifying music performance problems is similar to what doctors do when they diagnose medical conditions. Before physicians can make appropriate recommendations for a sore toe, the cause of the discomfort must be identified accurately. There are many reasons that someone might experience a painful toe. It may be the result of dropping a brick on the foot, developing an ingrown toenail, walking on hot coals, stepping on a rusty wire, or being stung by a wasp. Or it may result from becoming dehydrated and getting a cramp, having gout or a diabetic condition, or wearing shoes that are too tight. Different causes of pain will lead physicians to different medical treatments. Different causes of mistakes will lead musicians to different responses to musical problems.

CONCEPTS TO CONSIDER

Musical and Technical Problems

To use your piano practice time productively, it is important to learn to assess your results and decide what would be an appropriate response. When you encounter a problem, you need to be able to identify and describe it before you can work to resolve it.

A very important aspect of your piano practice relates to troubleshooting—locating errors and determining the probable cause of the problem. This chapter focuses on procedures that can help you diagnose mistakes. Problems occur when some musical aspect is not understood and internalized appropriately or when the level of technical facility needed to resolve a musical problem has not yet been developed.

Describe Rather Than Judge

It is helpful to approach the process of diagnosing in a nonjudgmental fashion. Do not blame yourself for making a mistake. Simply notice the location of the error and try to determine what contributed to the mistake. In the spirit of an understanding physician who wants to alleviate the pain of a sore toe, make observations and collect information. Scolding, chastising, and blaming are useless responses to sore toes or musical problems. After you gather information, you can plan your responses.

How Did You Know There Was a Mistake?

When you become aware of a musical problem, ask yourself how you perceived the mistake. Did you become aware of a mistake because of something you

Heard? Felt?
Saw? Were told?

In the early stages of study, you may be unaware of your mistakes. Later, as you learn what goes into a musical performance, you will discover what can go wrong and will realize what makes something sound right.

How Did You React to the Mistake?

Some mistakes are mere inconveniences. Other mistakes may be considered disasters. Mistakes happen. Blemishes occur. Life goes on in spite of unwanted moments. When you are at the piano, there is a time to stop and a time to keep going. Stopping to work on every error is comparable to getting out of the car to repair each pothole when you encounter it. Potholes do need to be fixed. The moment you drive over a pothole, however (perhaps on your way to the airport?), is not the time to stop and repair it.

The most basic characteristic of music is that it keeps going. Like that drum-thumping pink bunny in the television advertisements, the beat goes on. If your heart stops beating, you die. When the musical pulse stops, the energy ceases and the music dies.

It is not helpful to respond to mistakes with either extreme distress ("I'm absolutely devastated!") or extreme nonchalance ("OK, so I goofed again. I made yet another mistake! Big deal!"). Either reaction will undermine your ability to deal effectively with mistakes. Mistakes indicate that you have misunderstood an important bit of information or need to strengthen certain technical skills. Mistakes may indicate that you are trying to do something too soon and would benefit from spending more time with music you could handle with greater ease. Mistakes may indicate that your practice time is insufficient or ineffective. Mistakes enable you to become aware of subtle musical differences incorporated by the composer. Mistakes help you realize that you did something too much or too little (such as duration, volume, shifting keyboard register, or depth of pedal).

Experienced pianists find it useful in their practice to make a distinction between performing (playing through a piece without halting to correct mistakes) and the process of woodshedding (stopping as necessary to work on problem spots). Both activities are important, and be-

> *Mistakes provide information that can be very helpful.*

fore you begin playing a piece you need to define your intended goal: "This time I will stop and start as needed. I will find and fix my mistakes," or, "On this play-through I will keep going no matter what bumps I encounter." If, when you practice, you always stop to make repairs, then you are training yourself to stop when you experience slips or mis-taken notes in performance situations. If you hesitate, stumble, and stutter during your practice performances, you probably will demonstrate those traits when other people listen to you play.

During a performance, it is counterproductive to think about a mistake that just occurred. Instead, you need to focus on the present or on what is about to happen. You cannot, at the same moment, regret the past, listen to the present, and prepare for the future. "But," you may ask, "if I don't stop as soon as I recognize a mistake, how will I remember where I had the problem and be able to work on it?" One useful rehearsal strategy is to record your performance and then listen carefully to the playback, stopping and starting the recording as frequently as necessary in order to locate and analyze mistakes. After you identify those specific problem spots and mark them on your musical score, you can focus on those passages and work to strengthen the weak links.

What Was Wrong?

Was the mistake the result of misreading the score or misplaying the passage? Before you can fix an error, you need to know what aspect caused the problem. Did the mistake relate to:

Pitch?	Dynamics?
Rhythm?	Articulation?
Pedaling?	Fingering?
Tempo?	Loss of concentration?

Errors in interpreting a composer's messages should be avoided as much as possible. The words *dog* and *dug, bog* and *beg, fog* and *fig* really do have different meanings. One little word in a story can make a big difference. A single note in a chord can make a big difference. Drivers learn to read international road signs. Musicians learn to interpret international music symbols.

Some misreadings result from ignorance—being unaware of a musical tradition, for example—or an oversight, such as ignoring a notational symbol. Sometimes different notational or stylistic customs will result in different interpretations. It is quite possible for different musicians to present different readings of a score. Sometimes those variances do not represent mistakes. Just as there are many translations of the Bible, some music compositions have been published in several editions. These reflect a variety of editorial decisions and interpretations by musical scholars. Often music editors really do not know what the composer intended, and so the published score presents the results of their research and their best guesses regarding performance decisions. Knowledgeable musicians learn to make their own decisions based on an understanding of musical traditions and stylistic customs. In fact, one characteristic of great performers is that they do not sound exactly like anyone else. Furthermore, each time they perform a composition, it will incorporate slight differences from their own earlier performances. Each performance represents a re-creation of the piece, not merely a rerun of notes presented in a certain order.

With notated music, mistakes refer to inaccuracies in reproducing the composer's specific instructions. With music that is not notated, such as improvisations or music passed on by oral tradition, the observation that something sounded wrong becomes a personal assessment rather than an absolute judgment: At what point can you say that the stew has been overseasoned? The response to that question depends on personal choices, intentions, and individual taste buds. Some people do like lots of garlic and paprika.

> *Sometimes students present passages that are not really wrong—they just are not very right.*

Playing a wrong note is not the worst of all possible errors when making music. It is possible to play all the correct notes and accurate rhythms and still not capture the essence of a musical composition. Notes are a necessary starting place, but artistic performances depend on musical decisions that require control of subtle gradations of sound.

When Did the Mistake Occur?

It is important to identify the location of a mistake. Be as specific as possible. On which page? In which section? Which phrase? Which measure? Which beat within the measure? When you want to remove the causes of a mistake, it is inefficient always to start working at the beginning of the piece. You need to zero in on the specific location of the mistake and focus your work on that particular passage.

Where Did the Mistake Occur?

Often the initial response to an automotive or musical problem is simply, "Yikes! Something is wrong! Now what do I do?" But until we determine where the problem is, we cannot correct the problem. Auto mechanics know that knocks in the engine, pops from the muffler, and squeaks in the brakes call for different responses. For pianists also, it is necessary to be specific when describing problems. Where did the error occur? keyboard or pedals? Did it involve hands or feet? right side or left side of the body? thumb or fifth finger? melody or inner voice?

Why Did the Mistake Occur?

An essential first step in avoiding future repetitions of an error is determining why that mistake occurred.

- Did the problem result from playing something wrong or because of a musical decision that went beyond an appropriate range of musical options?
- Did you misread some aspect of the notation, such as a clef sign, ledger line, tie or slur, change of signature, repeat sign?
- Did you misunderstand a musical tradition?
- Did the problem relate to timing—doing something too early or too late?
- Did the mistake happen because you had not yet developed control of a technical skill needed in a passage?
- Did the problem result from an inappropriate technical decision, such as an awkward fingering, insufficient time to change location, inappropriate expressive gesture, misjudgment in selecting a comfortable tempo?
- Did the mistake result from not assessing correctly the responsiveness of the piano or the acoustical qualities of the hall?
- Was the mistake unexpected, or was it a reappearance of an error made previously?
- Did the error result from fatigue, a loss of concentration, or a momentary distraction?
- Did the speed of the pulse fluctuate inappropriately, changing for nonmusical reasons because of technical problems?
- Did the mistake represent playing the right thing at the wrong time? Did you confuse two similar passages found in the same piece or even in another piece with similarities of key, rhythmic pattern, or chord sequence?
- Did the mistake occur because of an unexpected slip—your page turner turned two pages, you forgot to repeat a section, your eyes jumped to the wrong staff, you ignored a change of key signature?
- Was the choice of tempo too fast or too slow for this occasion? With most pieces of music, there is a considerable range of appropriate tempos. When we are excited, adrenaline flows through our body and we usually play faster. Often pianists find that there is a discrepancy between the tempo they would like to use and the tempo they actually can control with confidence. When you are selecting a performance tempo, your own technical comfort always must be the most important factor. Wanting to play something faster will not guarantee successful results.

How Can You Avoid That Mistake in the Future?

After you identify a mistake and assess the cause, you will be able to take steps to avoid duplicating that error. If you can understand why you made a mistake, you are less apt to repeat it. With notated music, consider why the composer's version seems more satisfying musically than your alternate version. If you understand the composer's musical intention, it will be easier to avoid introducing wrong notes or rhythms.

The avoidance of future mistakes calls for a combination of musical understanding and technical control. The two categories work together. Would a different fingering provide greater ease in a certain passage? Do you need to leave a key a bit sooner in order to have time to travel comfortably to a new location? Did you hold the pedal down too long and collect too much resonance? If you lingered a moment longer at the end of a phrase, imparting an expressive intensity, would that allow sufficient time to prepare comfortably for the next chord? Would it help to color-code your music, perhaps drawing blue pencil marks around flats and red reminders around sharps? For a passage with many high notes, do you need to lean in the direction of the upper register? Would it help to focus your visual attention on the keys that have the inner notes of the left hand's chords? In practicing and especially in working out problems, use your musical score as a place to write notes about what helps and what complicates. Use your score to accumulate written reminders of what you want to remember in the future.

How Can You Minimize Making Mistakes in the First Place?

To avoid making mistakes, it is important that the initial musical impressions and original physical gestures are appropriate to the music. Your experiences during the earliest stages of learning are extremely important. Take the time to understand the musical score before you begin playing the music. The specific practice strategies described in chapter 8, "Using Musical Activities," can clarify and reinforce the interrelated goals of musical understanding and technical fluency.

ACTIVITIES TO EXPLORE

ACTIVITY 10.1 *Recording Your Practice*

1. Using a tape recorder or digital sequencer, record a performance of a piece.
2. Play back your performance, listening carefully while watching the score. Take notes regarding problem spots or mistakes. Listen several times, focusing each time on a single aspect of the performance such as pitch, rhythm, pedaling, dynamics, or articulation. Create a list of problem spots, noting measure numbers, that need special attention.
3. The next time you practice this piece, begin by working on the problem spots.
4. Periodically rerecord the piece and reassess your performance.

ACTIVITY 10.2 *Comparing Performances
of the Same Work*

Locate two or more recordings of the same piece of music.

1. While watching a score, listen to the performances. Notice
   differences such as tempo, balance of sound, flexibility of pulse,
   pacing of dynamics, variants of notes, and articulation.
2. Consider whether those variations represent mistakes or
   different interpretations.
3. Decide which performance seems most convincing. What aspects
   of each performance do you want to emulate?
4. If you are listening to a piece you play, experiment with it, trying
   to duplicate performance details such as tempo, voicing, or
   dynamic contrasts created by different pianists.

ACTIVITY 10.3 *Locating Variants within a Piece*

1. Select a piece that has sections with slight variations of material.
   Compare the similar passages, noticing how the material is
   varied: differences of pitch, rhythm, dynamics, touch, texture,
   change of tempo, and so on.
2. Play the similar sections one after another, noticing how they are
   the same or different.
3. Establish a succinct way to identify and refer to each section:
   higher or lower register, major or minor mode, change of
   rhythm, change of pitch, change of dynamics, and so on.
4. Practice the different sections in various sequences, rearranging
   their order.

YOUR NOTES

11 Preparing to Share Music

CHAPTER OUTLINE

Aspects to Consider
 Defining *Performance*
 Practicing with Ease
 Creating A Performance Checklist
  Expressive Cues
  Rhythmic Cues
  Pitch Cues
  Physical Cues
 Developing Comfort in Performance
 Points to Ponder when Preparing to Perform
  Preparation (Before Your Performance)
  Concentration (During Your Performance)
  Affirmation (After Your Performance)
 Replacing Defective Tapes
 Creating Positive Images
 Selecting Helpful Messages
 Giving Yourself Permission to Feel Nervous
 Behaviors That Lead to Comfortable Performances
 With or without Score?
 Defining *Success*

Activities to Explore
  Creating a Performance Checklist (Last-Minute Thoughts)
  Noticing Reactions to Sharing Music
  Imagining a Successful Performance Experience

Additional Resources

What images occur to you when you see the word *perform?* For musicians, performance is simply the way we share music with one another. When we perform, we create or re-create music for ourselves or for others who are within hearing of the instrument. We change lifeless dots on a page to lively sounds that resonate in the present. We change a noun into a verb.

> *When we share music by performing it, we transform it.*

ASPECTS TO CONSIDER

Defining Performance

For some people, the word *perform* implies behaving in ways that are contrived and artificial rather than authentic and trustworthy. For them, *to perform* may suggest being untrue to themselves and being dishonest with other people. Some adults may equate performing with showing off and then struggle with uncomfortable childhood memories associated with criticism, embarrassment, or punishment. Others may relate successful public performance to lifestyles of certain opera singers, rock stars, or flamboyant athletes. In that case, unconsciously they may not even want to experience successful public performances. If you find that the images you associate with performance are unpleasant, then I suggest that you recognize those reactions. Perhaps you would be more comfortable using different vocabulary. If so, make plans to play a piece, share some music, or invite a friend to listen to you.

Your piano teacher probably will encourage you to learn some appropriate piano pieces and play them for other people. Those performances may take place at lessons, in class, or with a group of other students. Your first performances might happen in your own living room with just a few friends or on a stage with many listeners in the audience. Your debut as a pianist might occur at a mall with shoppers milling around or at a religious service with people sitting quietly. If the performance of a piece represents arrival at a destination, preparing to perform represents progress toward a destination. Periodic performances will enhance your ability to work effectively during the next segment of your musical journey. Most piano students notice a surge of growth after every performance, no matter how successful or unsuccessful it might have been. Perhaps the most compelling reason to perform for others is that, as a direct result of preparing and performing, you will grow as a pianist and musician.

Practicing with Ease

Getting ready for a successful performance actually begins when you start learning a piece. Everything that you do while learning and rehearsing a composition becomes a part of your preparation to perform that piece successfully (see Appendix B, "Beginning a New Piano Piece"). It is important for you to direct your practice in such a way that each phase of your learning is accomplished with ease. In order to accomplish that goal, you need to have a clear image of what you are going to do during your practice time and create goals you can accomplish. You need to use motions that are efficient and natural, free and flowing. You need to experience a sufficient number of repetitions in order to reinforce a particular skill. You need to know that you can achieve success on a regular basis. You need to select performance speeds that provide enough margin of safety so that you can meet your goals comfortably. If, on the one hand, at every stage of learning and rehearsing a piece you move with comfort and confidence, it is very likely that when you play for others your performances will have those same characteristics. If, on the other hand, the time you spend practicing is characterized by physical tension and emotional anxiety, those are the feelings you are apt to experience when you perform a piano piece for others. You cannot expect negative feelings to disappear just because you decide that you are going to perform.

Creating a Performance Checklist

Just as astronauts and race-car drivers run through final checklists before taking off, I find it useful to review silently some observations and reminders immediately before starting to perform a piece. I like to divide my own last-minute thoughts before takeoff into four categories of cues that actually are observations about the music. Those four sets of cues function as reminders of what I need to be prepared to do:

1. Expressive Cues
2. Rhythmic Cues
3. Pitch Cues
4. Physical Cues

Although the four categories include overlapping information, I recommend that you isolate the four categories and focus on them in the order listed here. Since no.4 (Physical Cues) will probably take you back to no.1 (Expressive Cues), the process becomes circular and strengthens your readiness (see Figure 11.1).

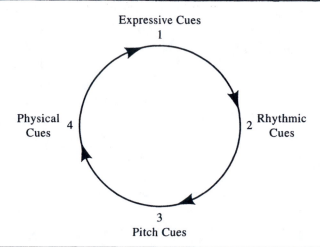

Figure 11.1
Performance cues

Expressive Cues
1

Physical
Cues 4

2 Rhythmic
Cues

3
Pitch Cues

These observations can take place throughout the process of learning a piece. However, about a month before you plan to perform a piece for the first time I suggest that you take time to write down your last-minute thoughts. Review your checklist during the final minutes before you play a piece. That process will help you focus on crucial musical details and also will provide specific reminders to strengthen your memory and reinforce your physical and mental readiness. The process of recalling last-minute thoughts also makes it easier to replace any negative last-minute thoughts that might be intruding. By reminding yourself of specific information and strengthening the imprint, it becomes easier to access the details you already had imprinted during practice (see Appendix C, "Performance Checklist [Last-Minute Thoughts before Takeoff]" for a form to use in compiling information related to a piano piece you plan to share).

> *Expressive Cues.* Include anything in the score that relates to musical mood, especially any words provided by the composer such as title, tempo indication, and expressive cues regarding mood or dynamics. Also include words that will remind you of the expressive mood you want to establish at the beginning of the piece. For the sake of this exercise, I suggest that you focus on what happens only at the very beginning of the piece. At this phase of the process, you are preparing for takeoff.
>
> *Rhythmic Cues.* Remind yourself of pertinent information related to rhythm. What is the time signature? What note value serves as the pulse unit? How is the pulse divided—into duple or triple divisions? What is the smallest rhythmic subdivision of the pulse? How would you describe graphically the organization of the rhythmic grid? Does the music begin on an upbeat or a downbeat? How would you count the opening measure? If you were conducting this, how would you cue the other musicians? As you think through a tempo-setting measure, where would you breathe? What are some of the rhythmic patterns that occur in the opening measures?

Pitch Cues. Remind yourself of pertinent information related to pitch. Use any vocabulary that feels comfortable to you at this stage of your development. Although technical terms can be helpful, they are not essential. What black keys will you need to use? If the piece is tonal, what sharps or flats are in the key signature? What is the tonality of the piece? What accidentals appear early in the piece? How do they relate to the basic key: Do they function as neighboring tones, borrowed chords, a preview of another tonal center, or other aspect? What scales and chord patterns appear? Identify the chords, in terms of both letter names and functions such as F major/tonic. How long is the first phrase? What is the harmonic language: Are there only major and minor triads or lots of dissonant intervals?

Physical Cues. Include any observations that will remind you of how you need to move. Where on the keyboard are the very first notes: on the far left, in the middle of the keyboard, to the far right? Where do you need to look? Which fingers will you use? Do you need to center yourself in the middle of the keyboard or to lean to the left or right? What do your feet need to be ready to do? Do you need to depress the damper pedal before making the first sounds? Will you be using the soft pedal? What energy level do you need to be ready to create? Even before you play the first notes, your body should feel different if you are going to begin *fortissimo* or *pianissimo*. What hand shape do you need to prepare? Will your left hand begin by playing two or more notes together or a scale or a broken chord pattern? Will your right hand need to play a single melodic line that unfolds one note at a time? Will you need to be ready to play legato or staccato? Will you be using only white keys or does your entire hand need to be placed closer to the back of the keyboard cover in order to reach some black keys? Do you need to be ready to play very calmly and slowly or to establish an immediate sense of virtuosity and speed?

If you have prepared a performance checklist and used it periodically as a part of rehearsing, then the last-minute review process—running down a checklist during the final moments before you play a piece—can be done in only a few seconds. Each detail will be associated with other bits of information, and when you recall one specific reminder you will gain access to a long chain of information. A single word or a short phrase for each of the four categories will elicit a tremendous amount of information.

Developing Comfort in Performance

Performing is a skill; therefore, it will be developed through structured repetition. Performance is a craft that also needs to be practiced and reinforced. At the earliest stages of your study, during lessons/classes or practice sessions you can start building performance security simply by defining occasional play-throughs as performances. For example, "The next time I play this piece, I will perform it. Even if I make a mistake, I will keep going. I will play the piece the best I can right then, from the beginning to the very end. Ready. Set. Go!"

As another strategy for developing comfort, play the same piece (perform it) for a supportive friend, classmate, or tape recorder. Later you will have opportunities to share a piece in a more structured setting such as a recital, repertoire class, or exam. The process, however, will remain the same. Sometimes golfers take a second try and do not count the first stroke. They take a mulligan. But for musicians there are no mulligans. The first take is the one that counts!

> *One time only. First shot counts.*

Points to Ponder When Preparing to Perform

"The feeling of being helpless," psychologists tell us, "is one of the most debilitating experiences we can have."[1] When we perceive ourselves as victims, momentarily we are stripped of all power to control and direct our own lives. That sense of powerlessness may result from natural disasters such as floods or volcanic eruptions. It can result from the end of a love relationship or the death of a loved one. It can also result from the loss of a job, rejection of an application, or physical assault.

> *Just as today's sunset is different from those of yesterday or tomorrow, each musical performance is unique.*

Ultimately, live performances are unpredictable events, and that is part of what adds to their excitement. In a live performance, no one will remove the flaws. Performers have the opportunity—nay, the responsibility—to share their insights, link the composer and the audience, and make each performance special.

A wise person once said, "There is a time to make things happen and there is a time to let things happen." Although life is unpredictable, there are many specific things you can do to enhance your comfort in sharing music with others. You can minimize the sense of helplessness that sometimes mars the joyous opportunity to share music.

> *Before, during, and after playing for other people there are actions you can take to increase the odds that the performance will be a satisfying experience for you and for your listeners.*

Preparation (*Before Your Performance*)

1. Ask yourself what you hope will happen because of the performance. Clarify for yourself why you are going to share your music.
2. Consider what you can do to maximize your own level of comfort and that of your audience.
3. Concentrate when practicing and practice concentrating.
4. Practice with imagination. Rather than playing the same passage a dozen times, play it in a dozen different ways: in rhythms, with different articulations, at various speeds, using various dynamic levels, using impulse units, blocking an accompaniment figure, and so on.

5. Provide yourself with many preview performances.
6. Think through the music away from the keyboard, looking at the score and without looking at the score.
7. Conduct the music, letting your gestures reflect the expressive content of the music.
8. Use the time just before performing to your own best advantage doing whatever adds to your sense of inner calm—such as concentrating, thinking through passages, fingering passages silently, meditating, reciting a mantra, humming, doing gentle stretching motions, praying, breathing, or focusing on last-minute thoughts.
9. Remind yourself of what you hope the audience will hear in your performance such as a particular mood, special balance of sound, unexpected harmonic progression, or expressive climax.
10. Become aware of preparation strategies that work for other people. Borrow ideas from athletes, public speakers, and performers of all sorts.

Concentration (During Your Performance)

1. Listen!
2. Focus on the music itself. Trust yourself and let the music flow naturally. It is imprinted in your cerebellum. Enjoy the results of your labors. Now is the time to relax and play. If you are in the habit of practicing with ease, your performance will reflect that.
3. Provide yourself (and your listener) with a guided tour as you travel through the composition. Serve as a tour guide through the musical landscape. Point out various features of special interest, such as a catchy rhythm, dynamic climax, expressive interval, or shift of register.
4. Breathe!
5. Acknowledge your listeners when you walk toward the piano: smile at them; let them know you appreciate their presence and emotional support. Let them anticipate with pleasure the music you plan to share.
6. In setting the tempo, think through a portion of the rhythm before you begin. Feel internally the speed of the rhythmic pulse before you begin playing.
7. Listen through the end of every sound. Remind yourself that notes represent sounds that continue through time, not simply the single moment when a sound is initiated.
8. Focus your attention on the music. Remind yourself of what you value in this music and why you wanted to share it.
9. Listen!

Affirmation (After Your Performance)

1. Accept all comments graciously. When you respond to a compliment by saying, "Oh, no, I messed up and made lots of mistakes!" are you really insulting that person's honesty and judgment by implying, "Oh, you dummy, you have no idea what you're talking about!"? When someone compliments you on a performance, the appropriate response is, "Thank you [period!]. I'm glad you enjoyed it."

2. Take time to assess what you learned during the process of preparing to perform the work. Consider what you could have done differently in approaching this performance.

3. Pat yourself on the back. Rejoice in your accomplishments. Enjoy the satisfaction of having followed through on a long-range project. Repeat to yourself the positive comments made by people who enjoyed your performance.

4. Look back—and look ahead!

Replacing Defective Tapes

Research indicates that when we imagine an experience, the brain imprints the image of that event as strongly as if we actually had experienced the event. Our memory system processes the imagined experience just as if it actually had happened. Athletes have learned to take advantage of this when preparing for athletic competitions. Musicians also can benefit from such mental exercises.

As a part of the process of preparing to play for others, imagine what you would like to have happen when you perform. This visualization activity is most effective when you incorporate vivid details, including colors, odors, sounds, emotions, and images of real people. For example:

- Imagine arriving at the performance site feeling rested, confident, and well prepared.
- Imagine what you will wear.
- Imagine where you will sit until it is your turn to play.
- Imagine concentrating during those final moments and what you will think about just before you play.
- Imagine doing a few windmills (arm swings across the body) and shoulder shrugs to loosen your large muscles.
- Imagine friends coming by to say, "Good Luck. We're looking forward to hearing you today. Hope everything goes well. You sure sounded good when we heard you play your piece yesterday. Enjoy yourself. We'll see you later. Let's have lunch together and celebrate."
- Imagine looking into the performance space and seeing people you love. In doing this mental exercise you can bring together all the people with whom you would like to be able to share this

experience—even if they cannot actually be there: Would your Great-Aunt Matilda—who loaned your parents her upright piano when you were six years old and died last winter—have enjoyed hearing the music you are going to play today? With this mental exercise, you also can prohibit the presence of anyone you do not want to have in the room. Or you can imagine that such people are there but have absolutely no power over your future: Try imagining that someone whose judgment you fear is eighteen months old, still wears diapers, cannot locate middle C, and is prone to temper tantrums. And you're worrying about what that individual will think about your musical performance?

- Imagine that your hands are warm, your arms feel light and flexible, and your breathing is deep and even.
- Imagine that your shoulders feel relaxed and that your head can turn easily in any direction.
- Imagine that you walk to the piano, smile at your friends, feel positive vibrations coming from them, seat yourself comfortably, adjust the bench, recall the opening sounds of your piece, prepare for the muscular actions needed in order to play the first phrase expressively, look at the keys you will depress and the specific fingers you will use, establish an expressive and comfortable tempo—and begin making music at the piano.
- Imagine that everything goes just the way you had hoped and the tricky spots you practiced extra hard in rehearsals go smoothly.
- Imagine that today the piano feels unusually responsive to your touch and the music sounds wonderful in this performance space.
- Imagine the wide variety of dynamic levels that you are able to control and the contrasts you are able to bring out clearly.
- Imagine that your muscles work efficiently and you enjoy sharing this music with friends.
- Imagine that when you finish, you listen through the end of the final sounds, let your hands return to your lap, wait a moment, stand up, turn to your audience, smile, and acknowledge the warm thanks of your listeners.
- Imagine that after your performance you hear words of congratulations from people you respect.
- Imagine that you celebrate with your friends, treating yourself to something special, such as a sweet, ripe pear—or a super-duper banana split with three kinds of ice cream (jamocha almond fudge, black walnut, and pink peppermint with big chunks of candy), four sauces (hot fudge, marshmallow, caramel, and strawberry), and five bright red maraschino cherries, garnished with whipped cream and chopped walnuts.

- Imagine that you feel proud of your accomplishments, energized by the experience, and affirmed by your friends and teachers.

Creating Positive Images

But what if you have never had such a positive performance experience? What if your previous public performance experiences (musical or otherwise) seemed more like nightmares? In that case, I believe it will be even more important, before your next performance, that you take yourself through a detailed scenario that imprints on your brain some of the images and feelings that would have been associated with highly positive performance experiences. The more fearful you are of experiencing an unsuccessful performance, the more important it is for you to provide yourself with many images of successful performances.

When we listen to a radio station on a long-distance trip and begin to hear static interfering with the reception, usually we can shift the dial and select another station that comes in more clearly. Similarly, when your mind sends negative thoughts that undermine your self-confidence, treat your mind as you would that radio station. *Do* touch that dial! Shift to a different set of messages, coming from another source of energy.

Think of your mind as a sort of tape recorder. When the tape is defective and the messages are garbled, remove that twisted tape. Replace it with another cassette tape that will convey clearly affirmative messages. When you feel demoralized by worrisome voices, you do not have to sit there passively. You have the option of selecting other messages. You are not a victim. You can act in behalf of your own best interests.

Selecting Helpful Messages

Instead of telling yourself, "I know I'm gonna mess up," substitute another message such as, "I have prepared carefully. It is reasonable for me to expect to be successful."

Instead of hearing yourself say, "I'm going to be so embarrassed," try reminding yourself, "My friends already know that I am not perfect, and they like me for myself."

Instead of predicting that the world will end if you make a mistake, acknowledge that "No matter what I do on that stage, the sun will come up tomorrow and the people I love will still love me. Nothing that happens in my performance will affect the flow of tides, changes of weather, or votes in Congress."

Instead of reminding yourself, "The passage on that second page is really difficult," reflect on the fact that "Yesterday, on the first page, where the left hand has a lovely melodic line, I was able to create a wonderful balance between melody and accompaniment."

Instead of "I sure hope I don't vomit onstage," remind yourself that "In the last hours before the performance I will select healthy foods that are easy to digest."

Instead of "I hope the keys don't get slippery," recall that "I plan to bring a handkerchief." If your hands often perspire a lot, remember, "While I am waiting to play, I will wear absorbent cotton gloves."

Instead of, "Everyone is used to hearing Vladimir Horowitz play this piece at a breakneck tempo and will expect me to play it just that fast," remember, "I did my research and listened to several different recordings. Each pianist chose a different tempo and, for a variety of reasons, all of the performances made musical sense. In practice sessions, I experimented with several tempi but selected one that enables me to emphasize significant musical details that would be lost to the listener if I played the piece at a faster speed. I'm technically and musically comfortable with the tempo I have chosen. It works for me."

Instead of "Last week someone on the committee glared at me in the hall," remember that "Teachers are happy when students play well, and they will recognize the progress I have made this semester."

Instead of "I'm scared," substitute, "I'm excited."

Instead of "I wish I didn't have to do this," try, "This occasion will provide me with an excellent opportunity to strengthen my musical skills. Because of my performance experience this week, six months from now I will be an even better musician."

Instead of "If I feel nervous that must mean I am going to fail," remember that "When the adrenaline is working, my body is preparing to help me fight a tiger. Although I do not expect to find any tigers lurking around the piano during my performance, it is OK if my heart beats faster or my small muscles do not work quite as efficiently. My body is simply doing what it is designed to do. My body is preparing to take good care of me, to protect me. It is OK for me to feel nervous. I care about this music and I care about my listeners. I would like for things to go well. I can expect to feel different, but feeling nervous will not prevent me from playing well. In fact, experienced performers report that their nervousness often results in performances that are more exciting to hear. If I am not revved up, if I am not excited, I cannot expect that my listeners will feel excited about the music I have prepared to share with them."

Giving Yourself Permission to Feel Nervous

I have found that it actually is helpful for students to expect to feel nervous. Give yourself permission to have a queasy stomach or shaky knees or sweaty palms. The simple act of observing your reactions will help you deal with those involuntary physical responses: "Oh, I notice that my right leg is moving all by itself. That's weird! On a scale of 1–10, my leg is moving at about a 7. Oops, it just increased to an 8. I wonder if my leg would drop off completely if the shaking ever reached a 10 on the Involuntary Motion Scale?"

You probably will discover that as soon as you acknowledge and calmly describe your involuntary responses to stress, as soon as you allow yourself to feel those responses without assigning moral values to them (that is, equating nervous with bad and not nervous with good), and as soon as you stop trying to prevent responses that are automatic and healthy, your troubling responses to stress will diminish. They might even disappear before you start playing.

At the 1994 Winter Olympics in Norway, a television interviewer naively asked a skater, "Were you nervous when you performed yesterday?" The experienced, prizewinning skater responded quickly, with a voice full of disdain and perhaps even disbelief at the question, "Why, of course, I was nervous!" As you approach a performance, you can remind yourself that when you feel nervous you are in great company, along with Olympic skaters, Barbra Streisand, Rudolph Serkin, Vladimir Horowitz, and virtually all other successful performers.

As a performer, you do not need to stop feeling nervous before you play. Instead, you need to learn how your own body responds to the feelings associated with a performance situation. Accept those automatic physiological responses, prepare for them to the best of your ability, focus on the music itself, and seek ways to put your excitement to use in order to make your performance more exciting to those who are listening. You can be successful even if you feel nervous.

Nervousness is not a predictor of a disastrous performance.

One of my favorite cartoons features a wide-eyed elephant seated at a grand piano in the middle of the stage of a big concert hall. The hall is filled with elegantly dressed people who have come to hear a piano recital. Before the elephant begins to play his first piece, he (or is it she?) looks out at the posh audience and asks nervously, "What am *I* doing here? I can't play this thing! I'm a *flutist* for crying-out-loud!"

Dan Jansen, the Olympic champion skater, had participated in several Winter Olympics before he won a Gold Medal in 1994 in the 1,000-meter event. In two previous Olympics, including the year his sister died of leukemia just a few days before his race, he missed winning the Gold Medal by a very small margin. In 1994, however, when Jansen was interviewed after achieving his longtime goal, he described the feelings he had experienced just before that race in Norway: "I felt calm. I felt if I had prepared my best and I did my best, I would not be disappointed in where I finished."[2]

When you play for others, you do not have to be perfect. You do have some responsibilities—to demonstrate that you care about the music, to respect the audience, and to prepare for the performance to the best of your ability. When you have approached the task with your best efforts, then—like an Olympic champion—you deserve to feel proud of your accomplishments even if, during the performance, something happens to remind you that you are human.

You have a right to share your love of music even though you might make a mistake while playing.

Behaviors That Lead to Comfortable Performances

To the extent that you can do so, try to incorporate the following behaviors in preparing for performances:

- Select a piece you expect to be able to play with comfort. There is no advantage in choosing a harder, more impressive piece unless you can enjoy making it sound easy.

- Select a speed you can control with comfort. With all pieces, there is a range of acceptable tempi. Provide yourself with a reasonable comfort zone so that you will have time to think and to control your gestures. Experienced drivers, on icy roads, know that choosing a speed that is just slightly slower can result in a huge increase in safety (as well as greater comfort for passengers). Remember that when the adrenaline gets going, you are apt to play faster than you intended. Plan accordingly.

- Create for yourself a moat of safety and comfort. Surround yourself with a protective bubble. Allow plenty of time to arrive and get settled. Just before you play, ten more minutes of practicing will not be helpful. Instead, allow yourself ten more minutes of knowing you are in the right place at the right time.

- Employ familiar actions that counteract muscular tension. Wiggle your lower jaw; shake your wrists; stretch your arms; roll your head; shrug your shoulders; bounce up and down; tighten and release your muscles. Rather than trying to keep yourself from experiencing nervousness, acknowledge your symptoms without imposing judgments.

- Focus on what you are going to do. Think about the performance. Think about the music. Prepare yourself mentally. Do not try to distract yourself by getting into trivial conversations with other people and trying to take your mind off of things. That is exactly what you do not need to do. Instead, focus on the music you are going to share.

- Act as though you are where you want to be, doing what you want to do. When you perform for others, you are an entertainer. The archaic use of the verb *entertain* carries with it the meaning "to show hospitality to." Allow your listeners to be glad to see you. Let them believe that you are glad to see them. Remind yourself of what Mrs. Anna, in *The King and I,* promised her son would happen if he would "just whistle a happy tune": "You can be as brave as you make believe you are!"[3] Research by performance psychologists actually shows that positive attitudes do influence our behavior and lead us to greater success. So, go ahead and whistle a happy tune. Look at your audience. Hold your head erect, smile, and walk to the piano with a confident stride.

- Take time before you start. Check the bench. If necessary, adjust its height, placement, angle, and distance from the piano. Think through your performance checklist. With your hands still in your lap, imagine your opening tempo. Before your first gesture, take a breath, providing yourself with an upbeat.

- When performing, ignore any mistakes that occur. When you respond to your mistakes by saying something unprintable, looking angry, shaking your head in disgust, or apologizing after the concert, you create a situation more uncomfortable for your listeners than any initial discomfort they might have felt. Imposing your own disappointment or discomfort on others is not a very hospitable thing to do. Some mistakes you notice will not even be heard by listeners. Other mistakes may be perceived by others but for only a fraction of a second. Do you really expect your freinds to beleive that you have never spilled a drinke or missspelled a word? You are human, aren't you?

- Maintain the rhythmic flow of the music. If you play a wrong note and then take time to correct that particular pitch, you interrupt the heartbeat of the music and create a more troubling rhythmic problem.

- Continue listening throughout the final sounds of the final phrase. Don't stop the music before it ends. Silence also is a powerful element of music. Films and theater productions do not end with the final word but with the final image: "It's not over until it is over."

- Let your listeners know that you appreciate their presence and support. Don't ignore them or insult them. Allow them to believe that you did the best you could under the circumstance. In fact, that is exactly what you did!

With Score or without Score?

When actors perform a play in a theater, they leave their script offstage. They immerse themselves in their roles and re-create a story, even if they improvise certain lines. Sometimes preachers, politicians, and television announcers speak without using visual reminders. At other times, however, they use a printed speech, cue cards, or the TelePrompTer. The impact of their words does not depend on the presence or absence of notes.

When you make music at the piano, I encourage you to consider your own responses to the question "With score or without score?" There are separate aspects of the memorization issue: (1) whether to *memorize* a musical score and (2) whether to *perform* the music without using the score. I find it useful for all students to memorize some of the material they study, including basic technical patterns and some piano pieces. The process of memorizing strengthens the understanding of the music as well as the control of musical concepts. Being freed of the script creates greater ease for many pianists. I predict that there will be times when you want to be able to play something from memory—just as you might want to recall a favorite joke to share with friends rather than reading it from a joke book. Within structured academic settings, the skill of playing from memory often is considered a requirement in training students who plan to become professional musicians. In contrast, for early-level adults who are studying piano only for their own pleasure, the goal of performing without a musical score should not prevent them from sharing music.

There are times when you read words and times when you speak extemporaneously. Even if you read printed material, those messages can sound expressive. So I challenge you always to let the music come from your heart—whether or not you play the music by heart.

Defining Success

At the beginning of this chapter, I talked about defining performance. Now I want to talk about *success*. I predict that you will not become rich and famous as a result of your piano performances. There is a very good chance, however, that through your involvement with music you will be enriched and you will have opportunities to enrich the lives of others.

The performance of notated compositions requires the involvement by at least three individuals: the composer, the performer, and one or more listeners. Without you (or another person), a composer's music remains on the page, as a set of dead dots. With you, the music can become alive, and your insights can make every performance a unique experience. When that happens, you have become an integral part of the creative process.

It is not your job as a musician simply to repeat a series of preprogrammed events. Robots and other machines can produce that more consistently than you can. However, it does become your responsibility as a pianist to interpret the composer's musical ideas and to share yourself with others who listen to the music. That can be a risky process for everyone involved. The composer trusts that you will study, understand, and communicate the expressive ideas that went into the composition. The listener trusts that you will present an honest, accurate reading of the composer's intentions. You, as the performer, trust that your best efforts in preparing have led you to a clear understanding of the composer's intentions. You also trust that your best efforts will be acceptable to your listeners. The process will not result in perfection, but it can result in gratifying musical experiences that are valued by everyone involved.

So, when you share music with others, ask yourself whether you are willing to settle for appreciation rather than adulation, competence rather than perfection, and enrichment rather than riches. One pianist's successful performance is never undermined by another pianist's successful performance. And no other person can present your unique musical insights as successfully as you can.

ACTIVITIES TO EXPLORE

ACTIVITY 11.1   *Creating a Performance Checklist*
(Last-Minute Thoughts)

Review the material in this chapter regarding four categories of re-minders—expressive, rhythmic, pitch, and physical. Select a piece of music you are studying.

1. Using the form in Appendix C, "Performance Checklist (Last-Minute Thoughts before Takeoff)," create for yourself reminders of various aspects of your piece.
2. From each of the four categories, select one thought that will trigger useful last-minute reminders just before takeoff.

ACTIVITY 11.2   *Noticing Reactions to Sharing Music*

1. Prior to performing a piece, create for yourself a series of preview situations. Compile observations about those play-throughs and your reactions. Create a summary chart or journal that includes the following information:

Place	Listeners and their responses
Time of day	How you prepared for the
Piano and its physical condition	performance
Pianist (you) and your physical and emotional states	

2. Assign a number between 1 and 10 that represents your emotional reactions to each performance: 1 = "I never want to do that again." 10 = "That was a wonderful experience! I can't wait to share that music again!" For this activity, do not assess the accuracy or quality of your musical performance, only your reactions to sharing the music.
3. Notice the factors over which you had some control, such as wearing comfortable shoes, focusing on the music, choosing the tempo, keeping your hands warm before playing, adjusting the bench, selecting the range of dynamics, using the damper pedal, smiling at your listeners, keeping your shoulders down, maintaining a flexible wrist, looking before leaping to a new keyboard position, aligning the hand and forearm, and so on.
4. Observe specific ways in which your body responds to the act of performance.
5. What reactions did you have to different situations and repeated performances?
6. On the basis of your previews, decide how many preview performances you will want to experience before your first official performance of a piece.

ACTIVITY 11.3 *Imagining a Successful Performance*

Review the section in this chapter "Replacing Defective Tapes." Create an imaginary videotape recording of sharing your piano music with good friends. Incorporate vivid details, including the place, audience, and reactions to the music.

ADDITIONAL RESOURCES

Books

Bernstein, Seymour, *With Your Own Two Hands: Self-Discovery through Music* (New York: Schirmer, 1981). Presents ideas about practicing and performing. Bernstein notes that all of life's experiences affect practice. He also reminds readers that the skills gained from practicing piano will influence other aspects of their lives, and he equates practice with self-mastery.

Bruser, Madeline, *The Art of Practicing: A Guide to Making Music from the Heart* (New York: Bell Tower, 1997). For amateur and professional musicians, pianists and others. Practical suggestions for developing free and natural movements. Encourages tuning into natural coordination and musicality.

Dunne, Phyllis, *The Scared Bug: A Guide to Overcoming Stage Fright.* (Omaha: Special Dunne Music, 1995). An experienced teacher considers aspects related to building students' self-esteem. Humorous illustrations, in cartoon format, present commonsense ideas for debugging performances.

Freymouth, Malva, *Mental Practice and Imagery for Musicians* (Bouder, CO: Integrated Musicians Press, 1999). Written by a violinist, but applicable to piano study. "Practice guide for optimizing practice time, enhancing performance, and preventing injury."

Nathan, Amy, *The Young Musician's Survival Guide: Tips from Teens and Pros* (New York: Oxford University Press, 2000). Young musicians share insights and experiences related to music study, performance and life.

Salmon, Paul G., and Robert G. Meyer, *Notes from the Green Room: Coping with Stress and Anxiety in Musical Performance* (San Francisco: Jossey-Bass, 1992). Authors describe some performance experiences of professional musicians.

Provost, Richard, *The Art and Technique of Performance* (San Francisco: Guitar Solo, 1994). Provost deals with various aspects of preconcert preparation and performance anxiety. Written for guitarists but applicable to all musicians.

Videotapes

Concerto (Kansas City, MO: SH Productions), videotapes #301–303. Series of three videotapes that share the final preparations of three concert artists rehearsing and performing with conductor and orchestra. Features Mozart concertos for piano (K. 453 and 467) and for violin (K. 216), performed by pianists Claude Frank and Lilian Kallir and violinist Pamela Frank, respectively.

Dudley Moore Introduces Concerto!, vol. 2 (New York: BMG Classics, 1993), RCA Victor Red Seal videotape #09026-61782-3, 51 minutes. Rehearsals and discussions of Beethoven's Piano Concerto No. 1, in C Major, Op. 15. Musicians at work include host Dudley Moore, conductor Michael Tilton Thomas with the London Symphony Orchestra, and pianist Alicia de Larrocha.

Memorization in Piano Performance (Van Nuys, CA: Alfred Publishing, 1995), videotape #14673, 64 minutes. Stewart Gordon describes various strategies—motor, visual, aural, analytical, and spatial—that can enhance the process of memorizing. Gordon also deals with fears of memory loss during performance and relates memorization procedures to each of the five senses. For teachers and students.

The Trout (Christopher Nupen Film), videotape #2292-46239-3. Documents the final preparations for a historic 1969 performance in London of Schubert's Quintet in A Major for Piano and Strings, D. 667 ("The Trout"). Conveys vividly the joy of sharing music with friends. Five young musicians (pianist Daniel Barenboim, cellist Jacqueline Du Pré, double bassist Zubin Mehta, violinist Itzhak Perlman, and violist Pinchas Zukerman), early in their careers, rehearse and perform a work that was composed when Franz Schubert was twenty-two years old.

YOUR NOTES

12 Avoiding Common Pitfalls

CHAPTER OUTLINE

I don't have time to practice.

I only have a few minutes, so it isn't even worth getting started.

I'm too tired to practice efficiently.

I *have* to get this project finished!

I feel claustrophobic in that practice room.

It's too hot/cold in my practice room.

I'm bored.

People keep interrupting me.

I'm distracted when someone turns on the television.

My back/arm/hand hurt when I practice.

I feel isolated when I practice.

I don't want to cut my beautiful long, fashionable fingernails.

I don't like the music my teacher assigned.

My family needs me.

I piano I have to practice on is in terrible condition. The bench is too low.

I really do practice regularly, but I never get any better.

I can't see the musical score easily.

I sound so awful I don't like to hear myself play.

I sounded great when I practiced, but everything falls apart when I play for someone else.

My teacher insists that the music I want to play is much too difficult for me.

The music stores in my town only carry early-level piano music intended for children.

My neighbors object to the sounds of my practicing.

I understand what I need to do, but I just can't do it.

I never expect to become a great pianist.

I don't understand the assignment.

This is a stupid course!

I'm only a beginner.

I can't do this!

Many difficulties can interfere with effective piano practice. In this chapter, I will respond to some of the frustrations I often have heard expressed by adult early-level piano students. If you ever encounter any of these frustrations, take heart. You are not alone.

I don't have time to practice.

Every person has exactly the same number of minutes in every week. You make time for the things that are most important to you. You set priorities. If you have decided that you want piano study to be part of your life now, you will need to schedule regular piano practice time just as you make time to eat, sleep, spend time with family and friends, take care of household chores, maintain personal hygiene, and go to work or attend classes. Many pianists find it helpful to make regular appointments with the piano and then honor those commitments just as they would keep an appointment with a doctor or hairdresser or tax accountant. Although the piano will not bill you for a missed appointment, you will pay a price for missing your practice sessions.

At times you need to reassess your expectations and even consider making some drastic adjustments in your commitments. How often do you really need to knead bread? How many times will you watch a rerun of a favorite TV program? Should some projects be postponed or reassigned? Full-time college students often accept heavy work loads at their jobs, ignoring the reality that a full load of academic courses is itself a full-time job. It is unrealistic to try to combine full-time study and heavy work loads. Like everyone else, even you have limited amounts of energy. When you push beyond those limits, "something's gotta give, something's gotta give, something's gotta give." If you do not devote sufficient time to your piano study and practice, you undermine your chances of achieving satisfaction and success at the piano.

Many early-level adult students have told me that their piano time is essential to their sense of balance. They find that their practice time is a time to nurture themselves and explore the creative process. For them, time spent at the piano is neither a burden nor a luxury; it is a personal necessity.

Rosie, who was almost four years old, wanted to go into the backyard and play. On this occasion, Rosie's mother wanted the little girl to stay inside: "You can go out later, Rosie. This isn't a good time for me to take you outside. I need to finish fixing supper." "But I *need* to go outside, Mommy!" Rosie insisted. "Why do you need to go out now?" "I need to talk to a worm and smell a flower." As an adult piano student you will have to decide what gets priority in your life. You will have to decide when you need to talk to a worm or smell a flower. You will need to decide how to distribute your time and energy.

In observing successful piano students, I have noticed that often the most successful ones are those who have developed a keen sense of guessing right. How fast can they play the most difficult passage? How many preview performances will they need before expecting to have a strong final exam hearing? How much in advance will they need to have a piece ready before sharing it comfortably with listeners? How much (or little) sleep will they need? How long will that chord resonate?

Learning to pace oneself and one's resources appropriately is an essential factor in performing comfortably. The ability to guess accurately has little to do with talent, education, brains, musical potential, commitment, hard work, or dedication. It has a lot to do with common sense and knowing yourself and your environment. As you learn to guess accurately, however, you will gain confidence in being able to achieve the goals you establish for yourself. When you do achieve success, notice what you did in preparing for that event. When you experience disappointments or setbacks, analyze what you did or did not do to prepare for the activity. Notice what makes you feel comfortable or insecure. As you accumulate insights, let them influence your future decisions about how to prepare.

I only have a few minutes, so it isn't even worth getting started.

It is appropriate to have different types of goals for different practice sessions. Long, uninterrupted sessions are useful, but short sessions can be effective in dealing with smaller projects (see chapter 7, "Planning Effective Rehearsals").

I'm too tired to practice efficiently.

Everyone has an optimum time for productive work, and it is helpful to determine your best time for working effectively. At any given time, however, you can vary what you will choose to focus on during a practice session. By building a collection of diverse practice activities, you will be able to select projects you can handle efficiently even when you are physically or mentally fatigued (see chapter 8, "Using Musical Activities").

I *have* to get this project finished! I *have* to get it completed by a certain time!! I *have* to get this passage learned perfectly!!!

When you feel stressed by deadlines, there are three appropriate responses to the dilemma: (1) adjust the task; (2) adjust the timetable; and (3) adjust the level of acceptable achievement. Some projects cannot be rushed or compressed without creating serious problems for yourself or others.

I feel claustrophobic in that practice room.

Architects often recommend that music practice rooms be built with a window that provides a beautiful view. In reality, though, many music students find that they have to practice in dreary, windowless cubicles. Even at home, many students work at a piano placed against a blank wall. If you will be practicing in a room without a view, I suggest that you explore your environment and find out where you can go to see a pleasant sight. Make regular visits to a window or courtyard before you feel trapped. Within your practice space, provide yourself with visually gratifying images. Surround yourself with a collection of small pictures or favorite postcards with beautiful scenes. Place a mind-stretching travel poster near your piano. Leave the room periodically and stretch your body in all directions (left/right, down/up). Close your eyes and visualize a beautiful scene.

It's too hot/cold in my practice room.

Be prepared to dress for a variety of temperatures, with layers of clothing that can be added or removed. Your body can adjust to a wide range of temperatures. Keep a bottle of drinking water available.

I'm bored.

Oops! You *do* have a problem! Creative practice involves noticing things about the music and about yourself. I suggest that you approach practice as a series of puzzles broken into small challenges you can solve with ease. Adjust your goals and practice procedures. Involve yourself with meaningful repetition, and avoid mindless repetitions. Challenge yourself to remain alert and productive.

People keep interrupting me.

You will need to train yourself and others to honor your practice times. Try creating and displaying a sign that shows your family and friends that you mean business (such as "Caution! Musician at Play—Do Not Disturb"). Post your rehearsal schedule and expect that it will be honored. If you have young children, set a digital timer before you start practicing so they can see how many minutes are left in your practice session. They can learn to watch the countdown and wait for the buzzer to signal the end of your rehearsal. Let them know that you plan to do something special with them after you complete your piano practice. If you want to be unavailable to others except for very serious emergencies, signal your intentions by wearing a certain hat or scarf when you go to the piano to practice. If phone calls are a source of interruption, switch on the answering machine or unplug the phone. If forgotten tasks creep into your thoughts during practice, jot yourself reminders, but don't stop working at the piano. Those unfinished tasks will be there later.

I'm distracted when someone turns on the television.

In many homes and dormitories, the piano is placed next to a television set in the living room, den, or commons area shared by many people. For practicing pianists, that is not an optimum placement of the instrument. Try to make some changes in the use of shared space. If that is not possible, negotiate time schedules so that your piano-practicing times and someone else's favorite television programs won't conflict. In order to practice productively, you will need peace and quiet.

My back/arm/hand hurts when I practice.

Pain is a useful signal that should not be ignored. When we experience pain, it usually means our body is telling us that we have been playing too long or too loud or too fast or using our mechanism inappropriately. Practicing should not hurt. When we experience pain, we need to stop what we are doing, change our activity, stretch, shake out our muscles, rest, move to different repertoire, and then resume practice with great care.

If pain occurs frequently, you need to analyze what precipitates the pain. When does the pain occur? What specific pieces or technical passages cause pain? Are you slumping or sitting stiffly? Are you practicing too long? Are you sitting too long, too high, too low, too close to the keyboard? Are you misaligning the hand and forearm? Are you using awkward fingerings? Are you key-bedding (pressing against the bottom of the key)? If you experience pain, it is appropriate to discuss the condition with your piano teacher. If the pain persists, you may need to seek a medical evaluation.

I feel isolated when I practice.

A certain amount of private time is essential to musicians. Musicians need opportunities to listen to themselves alone and to experiment in producing and controlling a variety of sounds. Singers and instrumentalists usually rehearse and perform with at least one other person, and often they participate in ensembles and rehearsals that involve other musicians. Pianists and organists, however, tend to be the most isolated of all musicians. Most of their repertoire was composed for a single person, and most of their practice time is spent by themselves.

If you feel isolated and want to be around others, it may be helpful to incorporate into part of your practice routine some specific activities that involve other people. As a part of your regular plan, arrange to play something for someone else: "Just before noon, can I come over for five minutes and play my new piece for you?" Instead of a racquetball partner, identify a piano practice partner with whom you can work on certain skills, such as technique, harmonization, and sight-reading. Play scales and cadence patterns for each other, taking turns selecting keys and establishing various tempi. Divide practicing projects. Trade roles in transposing melodies and providing accompaniment patterns. Play four-hand pieces at one piano. Sight-read choral scores, dividing soprano/alto and tenor/bass parts between four hands. During some of your practice sessions, plan to take short (!) social breaks. Share stretching activities with a neighbor. Acknowledge your need to feel connected with others. Incorporate into your practice routine interactions that can be useful musically.

I don't want to cut my beautiful long, fashionable fingernails.

Would you really expect to set a new world record in a track-and-field event while wearing riding boots or water skis? Every sport and physical activity has equipment that helps participants perform more effectively. Pianists can have their nails shaped, manicured, and even painted with fancy designs. But pianists need to keep their nails short enough to prevent clicking against the keys. They need to be able to feel the keys with the fleshy pads of their fingers and maintain a firm arch at the knuckles.

I don't like the music my teacher assigned.

Here is where you can use your negotiating skills as an adult who has learned to interact with other adults. At times it might be appropriate to ask your teacher to substitute other repertoire to which you might feel more connected. Most technical and musical skills can be developed through many different pieces of music.

Sometimes, though, you may be stuck with curricular expectations that your instructor is required to uphold or with approaches your teacher previously used successfully and simply does not want to relinquish. Then it is time to remind yourself that a few bites of carrots or spinach or broccoli have never been fatal. Many adults expanded their taste buds when they attended a summer camp and were required to sample all the food on their plate. Musicians also can experience healthy growth as a result of exploring unfamiliar musical tastes.

You do not have to love every person you chat with. There is much to be gained from interactions with strangers. Some casual acquaintances eventually will become good friends—once upon a time, you had not yet met the person who is now your best friend. Other strangers, however, will continue to be people to whom you merely nod and smile when you pass them in the hall.

My family needs me.

For many adult students, both amateur and professional, spending time at the piano is a necessity, not a luxury. When you assess the needs of your family, do not ignore your own emotional and intellectual needs. When your personal needs are being met, you will be better able to respond to the physical and emotional needs of those around you.

Sometimes professional and personal crises do need to take priority. The reevaluation of your goals and projected timetable is always an appropriate response to adult realities. Postponing a task for a day or two need not doom your project. Long-term crises, however, need to be acknowledged. Putting a project on hold for a while will not prevent you from returning to it later, after the crisis has been resolved. Reframing your expectations is a mature and valid response to unpredictable events.

The piano I have to practice on is in terrible condition.
The bench is too low.

If you practice on institutional instruments, you need to find out who is responsible for maintaining the pianos and get acquainted with the technician who works on those pianos. If you own the instrument on which you practice, you need to establish a strong working relationship with a dependable tuner or technician. Find out the most efficient way to report problems that need professional attention. In caring for all the pianos within a school, piano technicians must establish priorities in terms of servicing instruments designated for performing, teaching, or practicing. Acoustic pianos often are out-of-tune. This reality is especially frustrating to students who play another instrument that they tune before and during every practice session. Piano technicians cannot check every piano every day—and probably not even every week. As problems develop, students who use those instruments regularly need to convey timely information to the technician. Learn how to describe the problems you encounter and put your requests in writing. The maintenance of acoustic pianos involves three aspects of work: tuning, regulating, and voicing. Technicians can do something about sticking keys, broken strings, noisy dampers, and squeaky pedals. You can do something about sticky keys and dusty piano cases.

When you practice, your body needs to be supported by a firm, flat bench of an appropriate height. A shaky folding chair is not a satisfactory substitute for a piano bench. If piano benches keep walking away from practice rooms, you may need to discuss the problem with members of the piano faculty or administration so that priorities can be established for replacing equipment that disappears or is broken. As a mature adult, you already have learned the difference between squeaking (informing responsible coordinators) and squawking (complaining or whining). Utilize that knowledge.

I really do practice regularly, but I never get any better.

If you practice frequently and efficiently, you should be able to notice your growth and feel a sense of accomplishment every time you practice. If you do not perceive results, you probably need to reassess how you practice and what you are attempting to accomplish. Effective practice is not the same as playing through a piece once or twice—or even a dozen times. It might be useful to ask your teacher to listen to you practice, observe how you use your practice time, and recommend adjustments in your approaches to practicing.

In the process of learning to play piano, many adults have uncovered learning disabilities or vision problems that had been camouflaged for years. Be aware that help is available to students who are diagnosed as having specific difficulties in processing information or in seeing musical scores.

I can't see the musical score easily.

If you use bifocal or trifocal glasses, you may want to follow the lead of many professional musicians who must read music accurately in rehearsals. Have your optician create a pair of reading glasses that allows you to look through any portion of the frame for reading a score placed on your music rack. If the corrective lens in your trifocals controls only a small portion of the glass, you are apt to drop your chin or distort your position at the instrument.

If you use large-print magazines and books, it would be worthwhile locating large-print piano books as well. Although some of these materials are designed for pre–school age children, many large-print materials are appropriate for early-level adult students as well as children.

I sound so awful I don't like to hear myself play.

Musicality and artistry can be characteristic of the piano sounds you create from the very first week of study. You do not have to endure months of bleats and blats before the piano will respond with beautiful sounds. You can create musically satisfying results immediately.

I have nothing but the greatest respect for musicians who learn to play another instrument. If you already have developed musicianship in playing another instrument, that skill will transfer to the piano. The care with which you monitor sounds on a violin or trumpet will transfer to the sounds you create on a piano. The rhythmic vitality of a flute melody can be duplicated on the piano. The expressive flexibility of a beautiful cello line can be created on the piano. The dynamic shaping of a haunting French horn melody can be performed on the piano as well. The sensitive phrasing of singers has a direct correlation to piano music.

If you do not like the piano sounds you are creating, reassess how fast you are playing the notes and how you are making sounds. Especially watch for tension at your wrist. Even beginning piano students can find ways to shape musical phrases and balance foreground and background material. If you are able to hold a can of soup in your right hand and simultaneously pick up a feather with your left hand, you will be able to have your right hand's melody notes project more than the left hand's accompanying material.

I sounded great when I practiced, but everything falls apart when I play for someone else. I get nervous when I play for my teacher.

Every music teacher has heard students say, "I played it perfectly at home, just before my lesson." And when we hear that, we do believe you. Learning to deal with the extra challenges of a lesson or public performance is a predictable aspect of learning to share music with others. Playing for others is a different experience, but there are strategies for becoming more comfortable in performance situations. Performance is a skill that can be developed, but the process involves repetition and requires time (see chapter 11, "Preparing to Share Music").

My teacher insists that the music I want to play is much too difficult for me.

Although it usually is advisable for students to spend most of their time working with music that will sound good very soon (rather than several months from now), perhaps it is time to clarify your priorities and to negotiate a bit. Is it important to you to play certain pieces yourself or simply to spend time with that music? What about purchasing recordings of your favorite virtuoso piano works? What about listening to recordings while following along with the score, using that piece as a music-reading or theory project? Is there a particular melody you want to be able to play? Can you locate simplified or duet arrangements of a theme? Did your favorite composer write easier piano compositions that would be more accessible to you? Are there pieces by composers of the same stylistic period that are similar in mood but more appropriate for you technically? Can you locate two or three easier pieces to learn as stepping-stones on the pathway toward your heartfelt favorite? Are there certain aspects of a piece that appeal to you, such as a particular tempo, expressive mood, harmonic language, or rhythmic trait? Can those traits be found in easier works by other composers? Are there certain passages of a piece that could be turned into technical challenges or exercises? What if you agreed to limit yourself to spending only 10 percent of your total practice time with music your teacher considers "too difficult"?

There is little advantage to you in massacring musical masterpieces. Furthermore, it is inadvisable to invest hours of practice in repertoire that might result in physical damage to your playing mechanism. This is a concern that needs to be discussed. Perhaps there are compromises or options that you have not considered. The tremendous diversity of piano repertoire surely includes music that you would enjoy learning and that your teacher would enjoy teaching. Keep searching!

The music stores in my town only carry early-level piano music intended for children.

Most music stores will order music they do not have in stock. Across the country, there are many music stores that maintain a toll-free number and send out music the same day they receive an order. With the growth of Internet sites, there are even more sources for ordering music. When you discover an item you might want to obtain someday, make a note of it—composer, title, publisher, catalog number, current cost, brief description of the work. Add it to your Want List, and order it for yourself. When you locate favorites you would recommend to other early-level adults, let your local music merchant know about them so that those items can be added to the material kept in stock.

My neighbors object to the sounds of my practicing.

If you ever hear your neighbors' radio, television, recordings, computer programs, dishwasher, conversations, or parties, you should be entitled to play the piano at reasonable times of day. Most residential neighborhoods and apartment buildings maintain quiet hours (such as 10:00 P.M. to 9:00 A.M.), but those neighborly courtesies should not prevent you from being able to spend time at your musical instrument in the privacy of your own home.

Get to know your neighbors. Be aware of their special needs (work schedules, new baby, serious illness or other crisis, etc.). Place the piano against a wall that is not shared, put a rug under your instrument, keep the windows and doors closed when you play, and negotiate a regular schedule that includes predictable times for your practice.

If it seems absolutely impossible to find reasonable compromises in schedules, shop for a mute that can be installed inside an acoustic upright piano by placing a sound silencer against the strings or for a piano designed with a muting device controlled by a pedal. Investigate the technology that makes it possible to install player systems in an acoustic piano. Consider investing in one of the higher quality digital pianos designed with a touch-sensitive keyboard and headset that will enable you to listen to yourself in complete privacy.

I understand what I need to do, but I just can't do it.

Please go back and reread chapter 2, "Learning about Learning." Children spend most of their time learning new skills. For them, the process of repeating and consolidating a new skill is challenging and gratifying. They consider it play. In contrast, successful adults spend most of their time doing things they already know how to do well. For them, certain phases of developing new competencies can be very frustrating. But repetition need not be drudgery. Before your frustration level overwhelms you, remind yourself of the difference between cognitive and kinesthetic knowing. Your understanding of a concept can be achieved in a flash of recognition. Your ability to utilize that concept consistently depends on extensive reinforcement of muscular responses. Time and repetition are essential to the process. Your acknowledgment of that reality will go a long way toward controlling the level of your frustrations.

I never expect to become a great pianist.

Implicit in that statement is the tag question, "so why should I bother?" Perhaps you are taking piano classes or lessons under duress, because of curricular requirements for your music degree program. Perhaps you are overwhelmed by the virtuosity of professional pianists. If that is the case, I suggest that you substitute a different question: "How can I utilize my piano study to help me become a better musician?"

Singers and instrumentalists spend most of their time controlling a single melodic line. Conductors and pianists need to be aware constantly of the interrelatedness of every note. Pianists deal with the same musical problems that conductors confront when directing a performance by a chorus or band or orchestra. What is an appropriate tempo that will work for all sections? What sounds need to be spotlighted (placed in the fore-ground)? What notes serve as background material? How do the subdivisions of the pulse determine an appropriate tempo? How can the rhythmic syncopation be emphasized? Which tone in that chord needs to get the most sound? How much separation between sounds is needed in order to create vitality? How can the sequence of chords make sense over a period of several measures?

At the piano (and organ), keyboard players deal with all three aspects of music: melody, rhythm, and harmony. No other single instrument accomplishes that. Thus, when singers and instrumentalists learn to control multiple sounds at the piano, they develop a stronger sense of how their own parts fit into a complete composition. The result is that they will become more knowledgeable, more sensitive, and more musical when dealing with their primary instrument.

I don't understand the assignment.

Ask questions. Review previous assignments. Take notes. Study your score. Consult reference materials. Get the necessary clarifications. Remind yourself that "there are no stupid questions." Help your teacher figure out the missing links.

This is a stupid course.

Sorry about that. But your time is valuable, so the appropriate question becomes: "What are you going to do to turn your piano studies into a worthwhile experience and not simply a waste of your time?"

I'm only a beginner. What do you expect from me?

I expect you to sound musical at the piano. I expect you to approach your study with commitment, to practice regularly, to set appropriate goals, and to reread chapter 5, "Developing Musicality."

I can't do this!

Oh, yes, you can! Be kind to yourself, be creative in your practice, and take things in small steps. The pathway you are exploring can be enjoyed even as you stroll along at your own pace. You *can* make music at the piano.

YOUR NOTES

13 Looking Ahead

CHAPTER OUTLINE

Concepts to Consider
  Preparing for Independence
  Suggestions for Highly Successful Students

Great Expectations	Using Questions
Standards of Artistic Excellence	Counting
Attention to Detail	Teaching Sight-reading
Involvement	Good Practice Habits
Attention to Technique	Include Theory

  Creating Healthy Closure to Your Piano Lessons
  Staying Involved with Music
  and . . .

Activities to Explore
  Goals for Now and Later
  Want List

Thoughts about Words
  Stopped, Quit, Ended, Put Aside, Gave Up On, Terminated

Additional Resources

At the beginning of this book, I shared my assumptions that you are capable of working independently but currently are studying with a piano teacher. Although I did not say so in that introductory section, throughout this book I also have assumed that eventually your formal piano classes or lessons will come to closure. Seasons and semesters and centuries do end. Even if you are taking lessons outside a school situation, it will be appropriate periodically to reassess your priorities. If you decide to stop directed piano study, for whatever reasons, your continued participation in musical activities will depend on the habits you have developed—including your ability to work independently.

CONCEPTS TO CONSIDER

Preparing for Independence

Many times I have met strangers who, when they learn that I am a piano teacher, begin recalling their experiences as a piano student. Frequently I hear them say, "I had some lessons as a child, and I didn't take it very seriously. I stopped lessons right after I messed up on a recital, but I wish my parents hadn't let me quit." In those confessional-sounding messages to a stranger, I often perceive (in either the words or the tone of voice) residual layers of frustration, sorrow, and sometimes even disgrace.

If you decide someday not to continue your formal study of piano, I hope that you will not equate closure with failure. A long time ago, when I was a little girl, my father took some pottery classes through an adult education program. The pottery objects he created more than half a century ago brought great pleasure to our family. My favorite piece, a blue vase, has been cracked slightly for many years. It no longer holds water and fresh flowers, but it sits on a bookcase in my office and holds beautiful dried flowers as well as strong memories of a loving parent.

My father took part in pottery classes for only a few months, but the good feelings from those creative experiences lasted beyond his lifetime. I believe that piano students should be able to take piano lessons for a while, shift focus to other activities, and still retain positive memories of their musical experiences. If your formal piano instruction stops, you still will be able to participate in music-making activities. You will, however, need to function more and more as your own teacher.

Suggestions for Highly Successful Piano Students

Steve Roberson, a professor of music at Butler University in Indiana, has done extensive research on highly successful piano teachers.[1] Roberson identified ten common habits that characterized their teaching. I believe variants of those same ten habits can increase your success as a piano student as you supervise your own learning.

1. *Great Expectations.* Roberson noted that all of the teachers he studied set extremely high standards for their students. They asked a lot from their students, and the students met those expectations.

Although I encourage you to set great expectations for yourself, I also remind you that you need to set expectations that represent realizable goals. It is important that you acknowledge realistically the difficulty of a piece you want to learn, the level of your current technical skills, and the amount of time available for working on a piece. Even if a particular goal could be realized eventually, your level of frustration will remain more manageable if the time set for reaching the goal is not too distant. Furthermore, if you make inappropriate technical demands on yourself, forcing yourself to play music that you are not ready to learn with ease, you risk bodily injury as well as emotional distress.

Money management counselors advise clients that one of the best ways to feel prosperous is to adjust needs and wants in order to fit the reality of available resources. If you have $5.00 to spend on a meal but order an entrée priced at $17.50, you probably will experience some distress. Although you might savor the flavors of the food, you probably will not enjoy the total experience because of the wide discrepancy between your wants and your wallet. However, if you chose to order something priced at $4.10, you could be nourished, leave a tip for your server, and still have some coins left to jingle in your pocket.

Before you actually end lessons or classes, I recommend that you talk with your teacher about repertoire and materials that would be appropriate for you to work on independently. Obtain suggestions about sources of information (see Appendix D, "Annotated List of Resources"). Talk with your teacher about musical styles, collections, or specific piano pieces you want to add to your repertoire. If your teacher believes that the challenges of those pieces are drastically beyond your current level of technical comfort, find out what easier compositions or collections might provide you with similar musical satisfaction.

I recommend that you continue to work simultaneously on a variety of materials that represent various levels of technical difficulty. Include:

Music for today: pieces that will sound good the second or third
time you play them

Music for next week: pieces that can be learned during a few days of practice

Music for next month: challenging materials that will need a longer time to prepare well

Music for next season: more difficult pieces that represent long-term projects

It may be helpful for you to translate Great Expectations into the goal of upholding a great and honorable expectation that you will work efficiently, will respect yourself and your abilities, and will uphold a high level of musicianship in all of your piano practice and play.

2. *Standards of Artistic Excellence.* Artistic excellence involves paying careful attention to nuances and subtle details: dynamics, articulation, pedaling, and both tempo stability and tempo flexibility. Artistry certainly calls for all the right notes, but artistry never ends with the notes. The composer's notes provide a basic script (just as a playwright's words provide a text), but the real challenge to musicians (and actors) is to make the original material come alive, invest insights and feelings in the performance, and share emotions with an audience.

3. *Attention to Detail.* Early in your study, I hope you learned the importance of using the musical score as a source of basic information. I assume you understand that every detail on a page of music is pertinent to the performance decisions you will make about fingerings, dynamics, articulation, phrasing, pedaling, and tempo.

4. *Involvement.* Roberson found that the piano teachers in his study were highly energetic, intense, active, focused, respectful, and enthusiastic. Energy, intensity, activity (physical and mental), focus, self-respect, and enthusiasm are valuable traits for successful piano students, as well.

5. *Attention to Technique.* The teachers in Roberson's study "were vitally concerned about careful and appropriate technical preparation for their students." "Firm fingers and a loose wrist" were important characteristics of the students' technical approach to the instrument.

Even if you stop having regular lessons or classes, you may find it useful periodically to have technique tune-ups with your teacher. Ask your teacher to listen to your repertoire and technical skills and then alert you to any potential bad habits before they become deeply ingrained in your playing. Request that your teacher recommend revisions to your daily technical workout and also suggest ideas for maintaining and strengthening your technical skills.

6. *Using Questions.* The questions that the highly successful teachers asked their students encouraged students to think for themselves:

"How do *you* want it inflected?"

"How do *you* want it to sound?"

"What do *you* consider the climax of that phrase?"

"Where do *you* want to start getting slower?"

"How do *you* plan to practice that passage?"

"What do *you* want your listeners to hear?"

"Why do *you* think the composer used that variation?"

During your own piano practice, ask yourself specific questions that will help you clarify your goals and help you assess your accomplishments:

"Why is this a problem?"

"How can I make the passage seem easy?"

"Do I need more or less of this variable?"

7. *Counting.* According to Roberson, "Counting was deemed to be absolutely essential by all eleven teachers" (see chapter 8, "Using Musical Activities," for several different approaches to counting).

8. *Teaching Sight-reading.* In order to strengthen your music-reading skills, you need to sight-read regularly (see Appendix A: "Sight-Reading Checklist"). Schedule some time every day to explore new materials. Read a wide variety of published music. (Just as not every word you read comes from great novels, not every note you sight-read has to be part of a musical masterpiece that you intend to polish and perform publicly. For sight-reading practice, select music that builds on your current level of technical skill, interests you, and challenges your musicianship. Choose music of an appropriate and comfortable level of difficulty. Choose tempi that allow you to maintain a steady pulse while playing notes and rhythms accurately. Incorporate expressive details. Pay attention to dynamics, articulation, and pedaling.

Many musicians have developed strong sight-reading skills as a result of playing piano duets and other ensemble music with friends. As an alternative to watching a television program or renting a videotape, spend time exploring duets with a piano partner. In prephonograph eras, the recreational activity of duet playing enabled nineteenth-century musicians to become intimately familiar with symphonies, string quartets, operas, and other music not composed for two-handed pianists.

9. *Good Practice Habits.* As we have discussed throughout this book, your development of effective practice habits will enhance your success as a piano student. Senseless repetition is a waste of time. Know what you want to accomplish. Understand what tools will help you reach your goals. Listen intently and make discriminating judgments about your playing. Keep asking yourself:

- How did it sound?
- How did it look?
- How did it feel?

10. *Include Theory.* Music theory is not an isolated intellectual study but a tool for describing musical events and for understanding ways composers organize musical materials. Your ease in learning is enhanced when

you can cluster information. Train yourself to think as a composer. Analyze your music and create shortcuts in your learning process. When you perceive groups of notes rather than isolated notes, you will encode the information much more easily and recall it with greater confidence.

Creating Healthy Closure to Your Piano Lessons

During the time you study piano, I encourage you to create something that represents your piano work. That thing might be a recording (on audiotape or videotape or sequencer disk) of your playing, the score of a piano piece you composed (and notated by hand or on computer), a list of piano pieces you have played for friends, a collection of programs from musical events you attended, information about your favorite pieces or composers, a collage of snapshots of you (alone and with friends) making music, or a personal journal of your musical experiences.

Compile for yourself some sort of remembrance (souvenir) or documentation of your musical involvement.

At least six weeks before you plan to stop your lessons or classes, acknowledge that decision and be sure your teacher is aware of it. During the time of transition, let your teacher become a resource person who can help you identify and obtain materials to use after your period of formal instruction ends.

Staying Involved with Music

Consider some specific strategies for remaining involved with music. These might include some of the following activities:

1. Explore Appendix D, "Annotated List of Resources," which includes progressive sight-reading materials, reference books and anthologies that identify solo and ensemble repertoire (early-level to advanced), information about developing skills as an accompanist and chamber musician, and music periodicals related to piano study and performance.
2. Work independently on solo piano music, selected by you and your teacher, representing a variety of styles and levels of difficulty.
3. Sight-read music from collections of easy piano pieces.
4. Make music with other people: play piano duets; in multikeyboard ensembles; with solo singers or a choral group; keyboard with a folk group, rock band, or country and western band; or chamber music with string or woodwind players.
5. Make music occasionally—for special events, parties, or holiday celebrations.
6. Participate in a music group, such as community chorus or choir, handbell choir, band, or orchestra.
7. Attend concerts and music presentations at various venues in your community: libraries, schools, museums, community centers, retirement homes, music stores, churches, and so on.

8. Become involved in music advocacy projects—supporting music in the schools, arts opportunities for all citizens, bond issues for performing arts centers, projects for public radio, and zoning decisions that affect independent music teachers in residential areas.

9. Recommend music-related materials to add to your community's public library: books, magazines, music, videos, and recordings.

10. Support children's participation in music. Help them practice, take them to concerts, play duets with them, and provide other enrichment activities.

11. Enroll in other music instructional activities. Take courses in music appreciation or music theory, attend seminars focused on music of other cultures, and participate in workshops to develop special skills such as improvising or playing hammered dulcimer.

12. Purchase music, recordings, and videos.

13. Listen to music and support local radio and television stations that broadcast music you enjoy.

14. Interview friends or relatives (older or younger) about their musical experiences and preferences.

15. Schedule periodic piano lessons, using creative scheduling such as shared or overlapping lessons with a piano partner, biweekly private lessons, or occasional coaching sessions with chamber music partners in preparation for a specific performance.

16. Investigate special topics that interest you, such as music from your local region, music composed by a certain category of musicians, music of certain periods or countries, or specific instruments or performers.

17. Participate in short-term opportunities such as music retreats, chamber music weekends for amateur musicians of all levels, a reunion with fellow music students, and travel tours to attend special musical events.

And . . .

Robert Moore Trotter (1922–1994), professor of music at the University of Oregon and a past president of The College Music Society, was one of many people who had an early influence on my development as a musician and teacher. Professor Trotter insisted that every course is an introductory course. At the close of each academic term, he would celebrate "the end of a beginning." Acknowledging that students' growth continues beyond a specific grading period, he established the tradition of ending his final lecture of a semester with an unfinished thought, an incomplete sentence, an open-ended challenge. Thus, his last word to students was the word: "And . . ."

I want to close this book in a similar way, encouraging you to continue your musical growth. I wish for you a gratifying musical future that includes productive practice, pianistic development, increased sensitivity to sound, communication with other musicians, artistic explorations, **and** . . .

ACTIVITIES TO EXPLORE

ACTIVITY 13.1 *Goals for Now and Later*

Identify three piano-related goals for each of the following categories:

1. Within the next week I want to:
   A. _____
   B. _____
   C. _____

2. Within the next month I want to:
   A. _____
   B. _____
   C. _____

3. Within the next year I want to:
   A. _____
   B. _____
   C. _____

4. Within the next five years I want to:
   A. _____
   B. _____
   C. _____

ACTIVITY 13.2 *Want List*

Create a Want List of materials you would like to obtain (purchase, borrow, or receive as a gift) in the next year.

1. *Books*

   _____
   _____
   _____
   _____

2. *Musical Scores*

   _____
   _____
   _____
   _____

3. *Recordings*

_____

_____

_____

_____

4. *Videotapes*

_____

_____

_____

_____

5. *Musical Experiences (Travel, Concerts, Conferences, etc.)*

_____

_____

_____

_____

THOUGHTS ABOUT WORDS

Stopped, Quit, Ended, Put Aside, Gave Up On, Terminated

If and when you decide to stop studying music with a piano teacher, I believe it will be appropriate for you to create healthy closure to that activity. When the ending of an instructional experience represents a positive decision (rather than termination by default), you are much more likely to pursue involvement in other meaningful musical activities. Making music at the piano can continue to be a gratifying activity even if your piano lessons do not continue forever and ever and ever. Your participation with music can go beyond learning to play a few easy pieces in a recital. The gratification you receive from being involved with music can extend far beyond the time of your formal relationship with a piano teacher. Even if you decide to reframe your goals, reassess your interests, and redefine your priorities, you can continue to grow as a musical person. As you continue making music at the piano, Good Luck,

and . . .

ADDITIONAL RESOURCES

Books

Clark, Frances, *Questions and Answers: Practical Advice for Piano Teachers* (Northfield, IL: Instrumentalist, 1992). This collection of wise words is drawn from more than a quarter of a century of Clark's columns for *Clavier* magazine. Although the material originally was intended to answer questions from piano teachers, most of the questions and answers relate to appropriate concerns of early-level adult piano students. Frances Clark's respect for students of all ages and her commitment to the creative process of studying music at the piano are evident in every answer she provided.

Machover, Wilma, and Marienne Uszler, *Sound Choices: Guiding Your Child's Musical Experiences* (New York: Oxford University Press, 1996). Directed to parents and grandparents who want guidance in making sound choices about their children's involvement with music. Many of the discussions and resources relate to musical learning and are pertinent to adult early-level piano students who want to make sound choices about their own involvement with music.

Sacks, Oliver, *A Leg to Stand On* (New York: Summit/Simon and Schuster, 1984). Neurologist and poet Oliver Sacks explores the power of music to heal and restore.

YOUR NOTES

APPENDIX A
Sight-Reading Checklist

Before you begin to "sight-read" a piece (that is, play it for the first time), spend a few moments preparing for that first reading. Preview the piece, looking for the following information:

- *Title*—Clues to performance style and mood?
- *Composer*—Clues to stylistic period?
- *Clef signs*—Same throughout or changing?
- *Key signatures*—Major or minor or something else? Constant or changing?
- *Time signature*—Same throughout or changing? What note value is defined as the pulse unit? How are the pulses grouped and divided?
- *Dynamics*—Specified and implied, horizontal and vertical aspects?
- *Expressive indications*—Words and symbols, descriptions from composer or editor?
- *Texture*—Interactions between hands, melody/accompaniment, equal parts, relation to other instrumental or vocal parts?)

Also consider the following aspects:

- *Fingering and finger patterns*—Placement of hands, changes?
- *Tempo indications*—Same throughout or changing?
- *Rhythmic patterns*—Shifts in rhythmic material, changes in pulse divisions?
- *Counting procedure*—Using sequential pulses, note values, rhythmic syllables, other?
- *Mood indications*—Same throughout or changing?
- *Traffic signs*—Repeat signs, first/second endings, da capo, octave signs, direction of stems, beaming of notes, accidentals, ties, fermatas?
- *Phrasing*
- *Articulation*—Slurs, staccato, touch directives
- *Pedaling*

- *Formal organization*—Repeated and contrasting sections, cadential patterns of chords
- *Accidentals*—What do they represent? Change of key, intensification of tone, shifts between parallel major and minor?
- *Harmonic implications*—Tonal center?
- *Special problem spots*—Changes of location, rhythm, etc.

APPENDIX B
Beginning a New Piano Piece

During the process of learning a piece, it can be helpful to incorporate the following activities (in whatever order you prefer) at some stage of your work:

- Collect observations about the piece:
    Title
    Composer
    Tempo and mood indications
    Descriptive and expressive words in the piece
- Construct a geographic template (aspects of pitch):
    Tonal organization (major, minor, other)
    Melodic motives
    Chords that are used frequently
    Texture
    Dynamics and accents
    Range of pitch
    Sectional changes
- Create a temporal template (aspects of rhythm):
    Time signature
    Pulse unit, subdivisions of the pulse
    Rhythmic motives
- Scan the entire piece visually, looking for patterns.
- Locate on the keyboard the sets of pitches that are needed. Chunk them in sets of keys that fit easily under the fingers. Practice moving easily to those locations.
- Identify the basic rhythmic material. Establish a comfortable approach to counting the material. Practice counting and tapping the rhythms.
- Preview the piece at a moderate tempo, experiencing the rhythms at the energy level and expressive mood of the piece. Count; clap; tap; play.
- Play the entire piece (hands together, under tempo) at a speed you can control consistently. Confirm all rhythms for accurate proportions and consistency of pulse. Verbalize musically the rhythmic material.

- Look for repetitions (sections that are repeated or varied, changes of register, shifts to other keys). Divide piece into practicing sections.
- Preview the dynamics of the entire piece (range of dynamics, abrupt or gradual changes of dynamics, layers of dynamics, accents, rests).
- Notice any pedal indications. Plan to incorporate pedal at an early stage of learning the piece.
- Play through the entire piece hands separately at a tempo you can handle with ease while maintaining a steady pulse.
- Identify tricky passages that will need extra work. Create technical patterns or exercises based on special problems in the piece.
- Use a metronome occasionally to determine your current comfortable tempo for playing the entire piece and also to solidify certain passages. Set the metronome on different note values, representing the pulse unit or divisions or groupings of the pulse.
- Use various practice strategies to work out technical challenges and strengthen difficult passages: conducting, tapping, chunking, blocking, playing pulse notes, verbalizing, moving, improvising, and so on.
- In working on the piece, alternate between sectional practice (working on spots at various speeds) and play-throughs at a comfortable tempo (with no stops for potholes).
- In your musical score, write yourself reminders regarding performance discoveries: fingerings, gestures, dynamics, counting patterns, naming chords, and so on.
- Periodically review some of the previous steps to reinforce aspects of the piece.
- Prepare a performance checklist (see Appendix C, "Performance Checklist [Last-Minute Thoughts before Takeoff])" and create for yourself positive images of performing music for supportive friends (see Chapter 11, "Preparing to Share Music").
- Share the piece with someone.
- Record your performance and study it, noticing successful characteristics as well as problem spots. Decide how you will work on those places.
- Find out something about the composer and composition.
- Try to locate and listen to recorded performances of the piece. Notice how different pianists control variable elements such as duration, dynamics, and resonance.

APPENDIX C
Performance Checklist (Last-Minute Thoughts before Takeoff)

_____

Composition

_____

Composer

1. *Expressive Cues*

_____
_____
_____
_____

2. *Rhythmic Cues*

_____
_____
_____
_____

3. *Pitch Cues*

_____
_____
_____
_____

4. *Physical Cues*

_____
_____
_____
_____

APPENDIX D
Annotated List of Resources

PIANO REPERTOIRE INFORMATION

The following resources list piano repertoire, describe the levels of difficulty of specific works, and provide publication information in order to obtain the music. Many publishers have issued graded anthologies of intermediate-level piano repertoire (by a single composer as well as collections that represent many different composers). Some of these collections also provide sound materials (recorded piano performances on audiotape, compact discs, or MIDI discs).

Albergo, Cathy, and Reid Alexander, *Intermediate Piano Repertoire: A Guide for Teaching*, 4th ed. (Oakville, Ontario, Canada: Frederick Harris Music, 1999). A reference book that lists solo piano repertoire grouped by four style periods (Baroque to twentieth century). Identifies specific works, with composer, title, level of difficulty within intermediate category, and publisher. Also includes holiday music and ensemble literature (for one piano/four hands, two pianos/four hands, two pianos/eight hands). Authors identify some of their personal favorites.

Albergo, Cathy, Reid Alexander, and Marvin Blickenstaff, *Handbook for Teachers: Celebration Series* (Oakville, Ontario, Canada: Frederick Harris Music). Presents progressive study modules based on repertoire from the *Centennial Celebration Series* (see "Graded Materials").

Beattie, Donald, *Guide to the Masters: A Plan for Piano Studies from the Easiest to Advanced Collections of the Great Composers* (St. Louis, MO: G. Henle USA, 1994). Lists piano repertoire published by Henle, grouped by levels of difficulty.

Magrath, Jane, *The Pianist's Guide to Standard Teaching and Performance Literature* (Van Nuys, CA: Alfred 1995). 568-page reference book that lists early intermediate to early advanced piano music. Organized alphabetically within four stylistic periods. Magrath provides publication information and brief descriptions, identifying works by level of difficulty.

GRADED MATERIALS

Most beginning piano methods are part of a progressive series designed to provide music for several years of study. Often the early method books lead students directly into anthologies of piano pieces, grouped according to level of difficulty.

Centennial Celebration Series, 10 levels (Oakville, Ontario, Canada: Frederick Harris Music, 1989). Materials include repertoire albums, study albums, student guides, and recordings that correspond with ten examination grade levels of the Royal Conservatory of Music in Toronto, Canada. Pieces are grouped by four stylistic periods. *Syllabus* for the Course of Study describes specific technical requirements at each of ten levels and suggests appropriate repertoire for each level.

Clarfield, Ingrid Jacobson, and Suzanne West Guy, *Mystery to Mastery*, Books 1–2 (Van Nuys, CA: Alfred, 1996). Each book includes only four pieces of piano repertoire. The Music Insert, however, presents three separate versions of each composition: Urtext (unedited score, providing an uncluttered view of the composer's manuscript), Workout Score (with practice suggestions from Clarfield and Guy), and Artistic Version (with very specific performance suggestions regarding motions and expressive goals). With each piece the authors also include background information, preparatory exercises, and specific technical tips.

Dietzer, M'lou, *First Impressions: An Intermediate Piano Method*, Music and Study Guide Series in 9 vols. (Van Nuys, CA: Alfred, 1995). Intended for students who have completed a beginning piano method. Early Intermediate includes Levels A–C; Mid-Intermediate is vols. 1–3; Late Intermediate is vols. 4–6. Each book includes pieces from four stylistic periods. The preview suggestions ("Tips for Teachers") would be useful for adult piano students. Each volume presents a Study Guide as a pull-out booklet. Compact disk available for levels A–C. Dietzer also has nine correlated theory volumes, *First Impressions: Music Theory*, published in 1997.

Emonts, Fritz, *The European Piano Method*, 3 progressive levels. Trilingual: text in English, French, and German. Incorporates innovative sounds and delightful color illustrations by Andrea Hoyer (Mainz, Germany: Schott Musik, 1992).

Faber, Nancy and Randall, *For the Older Beginner—Accelerated Piano Adventures* (Fort Lauderdale, FL: FJH Music, 1998). Piano method "based on discovery, creativity, and adventure through music making." For beginners (ages eleven and up). At each level the series includes four books (*Lesson, Theory, Performance,* and *Technique and Artistry*).

Hall, Pauline, and Paul Harris, *The Oxford Piano Method* (Oxford and New York: Oxford University Press, 1994). Method series includes *Piano Time* (repertoire), *Practice Makes Perfect* (technique), duets, and other supplementary volumes. *Classics* has early-level arrangements of themes from orchestral and operatic works.

PIANO ACCOMPANYING AND CHAMBER MUSIC

The books listed here discuss the art of accompanying and provide specific suggestions for developing skills as a collaborative musician. Early-level instructional materials for string and wind instruments often provide early-level piano accompaniments (for example, Suzuki repertoire for violin, cello, and flute; graded materials of the Associated Board of Royal Schools of Music in England; and sequential books of the Royal Conservatory of Music in Toronto, Canada).

Grill, Joyce, *Accompanying Basics* (San Diego: Kjos, 1987). Guide for piano students in developing basic accompanying skills. Grill discusses a wide variety of topics and includes piano duets, as well as accompaniments with voice or instruments.

Haroutounian, Joanne, *Chamber Music Sampler*, Books 1–3 (San Diego: Kjos). Intermediate trios for piano with violin and cello. Includes parts for all three players. Haroutounian provides useful rehearsal suggestions for novice chamber musicians. These collections present easier complete movements selected from longer compositions by eighteenth- and nineteenth-century composers.

Johnson, Katherine D., *Accompanying the Violin* (San Diego: Kjos, 1984). Includes two versions of the text, one written for children and one for adults. Provides both the piano and violin parts for twenty-six early-level pieces. Johnson discusses a wide variety of issues for pianists to consider when collaborating with string players.

Weekley, Dallas, and Nancy Arganbright, *The Piano Duet: A Learning Guide* (San Diego: Kjos). Twenty-five pages of text precede complete pieces (intermediate-level duets for one piano/four hands).

SIGHT-READING MATERIALS

Bastien, Jane Smiser, *A Line a Day Sight Reading*, Levels 1–4 (San Diego: Kjos).

Covello, Stephen, *Step, Skip & Repeat*, Books 1–2 (Fort Lauderdale: FJH Music, 1997).

Guhl, Louise, *The Magic Reader*, Books 1–5 (San Diego: Kjos, vol. 1–3, 1989; vol. 4, 1990; vol. 5., 1991).

Haroutounian, Joanne, *Rhythm Antics* (San Diego: Kjos, 1988).

Massoud, Kathleen, *Let's Sightplay! Creative Exercises to Develop Sightplaying*, Books 1–4 (Fort Lauderdale: FJH Music, vol. 1, 1995; vols. 2–3, 1996; vol. 4, 1997).

Sheftel, Paul, *A Tune a Week* (New York: Carl Fischer, 1998). "Ear tunes" explore the full range of the keyboard. "Eye tunes" present a limited set of notes on the staff. MIDI accompaniments are available.

MUSIC PERIODICALS

American Music Teacher (Cincinnati, OH). Six issues a year. The professional magazine of the Music Teachers National Association (MTNA). Founded in 1876, MTNA represents more than 26,000 teachers of music performance at all levels. Magazine includes peer-reviewed feature articles, reviews of books and music, advertisements, Annual Directory of Recent Publications, information on music technology, and professional news.

Clavier (Northfield, IL: Instrumentalist). Ten issues a year. Includes articles about pianists and piano teaching, reviews of new publications, and advertisements.

Keyboard Companion (Los Angeles). Four issues a year. Focuses on early-level piano study. Regular departments include "Adult Piano Study," "Home Practice," "Motivation," "Technique," "Rhythm, "Repertoire," and "Technology." Although the periodical is directed to piano teachers of early-level students, each issue includes information useful for early-level adult piano students. Musical sound examples are posted on a Web page.

Piano and Keyboard (San Anselmo, CA). Six issues a year. Articles about pianists, pianos, piano repertoire, and piano technology. Directed to amateur and professional pianists.

Piano Today (Bedford Hills, NY). Four issues a year. Each issue prints several short piano pieces of various styles along with articles about piano styles, piano technique, and suggestions for performing classical and jazz/popular keyboard music.

Notes

Chapter 1

1. Frances Clark, Louise Goss, and Sam Holland, *Musical Fingers*, Book 1 (Princeton, NJ: New School for Music Study Press, 1983), p. 2. In the introductory material directed to students, the authors explain: "A study of technic is a study of the way to produce any sound you want to make at the piano. Learning this 'way' includes developing skills in three areas:—developing the ability to create in your imagination the *sound* you want to make;—developing an awareness of the way your hands and body *look* to make that sound;—developing an awareness of how your hands and body *feel* to make that sound." Clark, in her music books and other writings, often reminds piano students of the importance of being aware of how they *sound*, *look*, and *feel*.

Chapter 2

1. Barry Green with W. Timothy Gallwey, *The Inner Game of Music* (Garden City, NY: Anchor/ Doubleday, 1986).

Chapter 3

1. Arthur Loesser, *Men, Women and Pianos: A Social History of the Piano* (New York: Simon and Schuster, 1954), p. 603.
2. Ferruccio Busoni, *Sketch of a New Aesthetic of Music* (New York: Schirmer, 1911; reprint ed. New York: Dover, 1962), pp. 43–44.
3. Reimar Riefling, *Piano Pedalling* (New York: Oxford University Press, 1962), p. 1.

Chapter 4

1. John Thompson, *Modern Piano Course for the Piano: Teaching Little Fingers to Play* (Florence, KY: Willis Music, 1936).
2. John Cage, *Notation* (New York: Something Else Press, 1969). The pages in this book are unnumbered. The quotation from Toru Takemitsu appears on the same pages as excerpts of scores by Wilfred Mellers and Arne Mellnäs.
3. Ibid., across from excerpt of score by Arthur Bliss.
4. Gyorgy Sandor, *On Piano Playing: Motion, Sound, and Expression* (New York: Schirmer Books, 1981), p. 55.

Chapter 5

1. Conversation overheard following a solo piano recital by Thomas Mastroianni at Ward Recital Hall of the Benjamin T. Rome School of Music on the campus of The Catholic University of America in Washington, D.C.

Chapter 6

1. Conversation with James Makubuya, music educator from Uganda, Africa, during his graduate studies at The Catholic University of America in Washington, D.C.

2. The concept of creating maps of a piano piece is explored in depth by Rebecca Payne Shockley in her book *Mapping Music: For Faster Learning and Secure Memory* (Madison, WI: A-R Editions, 1997).

Chapter 11

1. Barbara English Maris, "Points to Ponder When Preparing to Perform," *American Music Teacher*, April/May 1987, pp. 30–31. The strategies related to preparation, concentration, and affirmation were selected from an article that identified more than seventy specific things musicians can do before, during, and after a performance. This adaptation is used with permission.

2. Interview of Dan Jansen, *Daily Item*, Sunbury, PA, April 15, 1994.

3. In *The King and I*, the Broadway musical by Richard Rodgers and Oscar Hammerstein 2nd. Libretto published by Random House in 1951.

Chapter 13

1. Steve Roberson, "Ten Habits of Highly Successful Piano Teachers," *American Music Teacher*, August/September 1993, pp. 10–13. This adaptation of Roberson's article, "Suggestions for Highly Successful Piano Students," is used with permission.

Index